Career by Design

COMMUNICATING YOUR WAY TO SUCCESS

THIRD EDITION

Sharon L. Hanna

SOUTHEAST COMMUNITY COLLEGE

Upper Saddle River, New Jersey

Columbus, Ohio

Library of Congress Cataloging-in-Publication Data

Hanna, Sharon L.
Career by design : communicating your way to success / Sharon L. Hanna.— 3rd ed.
p. cm.
ISBN 0-13-114960-1
1. Career development. I. Title.

HF5381.H135 2005
650.14—dc22

2004008441

Vice President and Publisher: Jeffery W. Johnston
Senior Acquisitions Editor: Sande Johnson
Assistant Editor: Erin Anderson
Production Editor: Holcomb Hathaway
Design Coordinator: Diane C. Lorenzo
Cover Designer: Jeff Vanik
Cover Art: Susan Brosh
Cartoon Illustrations: Ben Thomas
Production Manager: Susan Hannahs
Director of Marketing: Ann Castel Davis
Marketing Manager: Eric Murray
Marketing Coordinator: Tyra Poole

Photographers acknowledged in the Preface.

This book was set in Goudy by Integra. It was printed and bound by R.R. Donnelley & Sons Company. The cover was printed by Coral Graphic Services, Inc.

Pearson Education Ltd.
Pearson Education Singapore Pte. Ltd.
Pearson Education Canada, Ltd.
Pearson Education—Japan

Pearson Education Australia Pty. Limited
Pearson Education North Asia Ltd.
Pearson Educación de Mexico, S.A. de C.V.
Pearson Education Malaysia Pte. Ltd.

10 9 8 7 6 5
ISBN 0-13-114960-1

Contents

CHAPTER 2

Interacting Positively with Others 45

CHAPTER 3

Getting What You Want 85

CHAPTER 5

Interviewing with Confidence 185

CHAPTER 6

Developing Your Career 227

Preface

Why do people work? The first answer that often comes to mind is money. Yet, is that all there is to it? If so, thousands of educators, including myself, would have pursued other careers. As you design your career, you are wise to ponder the question of why you want to work and consider the reasons you have chosen a particular path. If your career involves what you consider to be meaningful work, the rewards are innumerable. These include:

- To gain a significant purpose in life
- To use talents and abilities
- To broaden knowledge
- To enlarge one's social sphere
- To become more interesting and interested
- To experience enjoyment and have fun
- To increase self-esteem
- To develop better physical and mental health
- To make a meaningful contribution

The list is a long one. To avoid or shortchange this vital part of life would be a major mistake, and to work only for money invites dissatisfaction and disappointment.

Think of the most personally rewarding reasons for pursuing a career. Then, consider what would be the most satisfying career for you—just the first of several important decisions. After a selection, the active design of your career takes center stage. Without deliberate planning and action, it's possible that you will achieve satisfaction—but not likely. This book leads you through an entire career life.

Beginning with the *self*, you will gain insight and understanding of all the elements of a successful career. Learning to interact positively with others, including ways to improve interpersonal skills, follows. The actual career design includes research and choices, then culminates with a successful job search. The final chapters invite you to examine the entire career path, develop positive work relationships, and learn how to handle challenges.

As you either have discovered or will discover, one point is clear. No one way is 100 percent best for everyone's career development. This book contains many opinions, ideas, research findings, and recommendations. Even though general consensus exists, much is debatable, and critical thinking can help you choose what will work best for you.

As the subtitle of the book suggests, the ability to communicate and interpersonal skills will lead individuals to success—or to failure. A Rider University survey of 428 companies named interpersonal relations as one of the top five entry-level requirements and listed it as the top barrier to promotion. In looking at the new workplace of the future, publications in the United States (Carrig, 1999) and Canada (*Canadian Manager*, 1999) rate interpersonal and communication abilities as essential. In fact, the assertion is made that interpersonal and communication skills will either make or break a person's career success (Carrig, 1999). Recognizing that this is true, this book does what most career books do not: it interweaves communication and other interpersonal skills throughout the chapters. You can benefit greatly both professionally and personally from learning and practicing the interpersonal skills that are not a "given" for anyone.

The most challenging task for this edition was to explore and understand all aspects of online technology in terms of career development. Use of the Internet for career and job research and for job seeking has virtually exploded. This book will assist you in being an active participant in the electronic revolution of career development. Changes in this area occur so quickly that any book runs the risk of being outdated, and the personal responsibility of job seekers is to stay abreast of new developments.

What will not change are the basics of presenting yourself honestly and confidently in writing and in person. As you design your own career, this book can be a useful companion and valuable guide. I agree with Larry Hubka, Ph.D., Chief Academic Officer, Quest Education, who says, "There is an old adage in the business world that says, 'You never have a second chance to make a good first impression.' Unfortunately, colleges have not done a very good job preparing students to apply in writing and to interview for career positions. I believe all college-level curricula should address these critical areas."

By reading this book and completing the Key Steps activities at the end of each chapter, along with taking courses that enhance your career skills, you will have an advantage that will set you apart from the competition. I would like to know how the process goes for you. I invite comments, suggestions, and questions from you—the reader!

Is a career that important? My response is an enthusiastic "Yes!" Even though being a wife and mother has been greatly rewarding, my life would not be fulfilled without the rewards of an extremely satisfying career. My hope is that through this book you will catch my enthusiasm and then learn and apply the material to ensure your own career success. Above all, enjoy the process and the rewards of career development by your own design!

Sharon L. Hanna
SharonLHanna@yahoo.com

Acknowledgments

Praise is good for both the receiver and the giver. One of the most gratifying parts of completing a book is to thank those who were so helpful.

My husband and best friend Bob assisted with almost every task, offered encouragement and support, and was always there for me. Our shared marriage, so full of love and affirmation, has allowed us to live very satisfying professional and personal lives. I'm deeply grateful to him.

Lyn and Lisa Patterson, my daughters, were willing to share their experiences in this book. They are tremendous individuals.

Pat Peterson, Southeast Community College Learning Resource Center, was a constant source of help in the research. She is a valued colleague who demonstrates a high degree of expertise in her own career.

I wish to thank the talented Ben Thomas, who contributed several cartoons for this book. I also want to thank Karen Baxter, Jerry Baxter, Jon Bresnahan, and Bang Tran, who took photographs for the book. I appreciate all of their talents.

In sharing their experiences and advice, employers throughout the country and the faculty, staff, and students at Southeast Community College contributed immeasurably to the credibility and practicality of the book.

I appreciate the time and expertise of reviewers who have offered helpful feedback regarding this book and I would like to thank (for this edition) Carolyn Boulger, University of Notre Dame; Ramona Stephens, Northeast State Technical Community College; and Corey Vigdor, DeVry University and (for the previous editions) Nellie Boyd, Norfolk State University; Rita Delude, New Hampshire Community Technical College; Charissa Dunn, Bartlesville Wesleyan College; Lane Johnson, N. Harris College; and Rosann Rookey, Middle Georgia College.

The absolutely fantastic, positive group of people at Prentice Hall were always available and helpful in a positive and professional manner, including Sande Johnson, Editor; Erin Anderson, Editorial Assistant; and Eric Murray, Marketing Manager. I'm very appreciative of Gay Pauley, Holcomb Hathaway, who was outstanding in all ways as she directed the book's production. I also want to commend the Prentice Hall book representatives who introduce this book to those who teach.

As these acknowledgments come to an end, my recommendation is that you generously recognize the contributions of people as you pursue a career. Acknowledge their well-meant advice, praise, constructive criticism, help, and services. Those who are appreciative are invariably appreciated and are more likely to enjoy a successful professional life.

To everyone who helped in the design of this career development book, my deepest appreciation.

Dedication

To Bob Dinkel, my husband and very best friend, who has contributed so much of his time, effort, and support to my career while being successful in his own;

To Jerre Casselman Garcia, my beloved aunt, who served as my career role model;

To Lisa and Lyn Patterson, my daughters, who are achieving success after success in their own careers and of whom I'm extremely proud;

and

To all of my students, from whom I've learned and grown.

About the Author

Sharon L. Hanna is Chair of Social Sciences, Academic Education, at Southeast Community College in Lincoln, Nebraska. She has developed courses in both career development and interpersonal relations. Her enthusiasm for teaching has been demonstrated to a variety of students in New Jersey, Illinois, and Nebraska, and she has earned awards for faculty achievement and outstanding teaching. Her research on the strengths of stepfamilies has been published in academic journals, and she served as national president of Stepfamily Association of America. She is also the author of *Person to Person: Positive Relationships Don't Just Happen*, 4th Edition, published by Prentice Hall in 2003. Married to Bob Dinkel for 25 years, she has two daughters, two stepsons, a granddaughter, and a grandson.

Self-understanding is the gateway to career success.

Beginning with the Self

Picture yourself happily involved in a career. You love your job and, most of the time, are eager to go to work. Does this sound impossible? Close your eyes and visualize an ideal job. This dream can become a reality with successful career design and development. Finding satisfaction can be challenging. Even though a 1999 Gallup poll found a degree of contentment among 86 percent of respondents, only 39 percent were completely satisfied with their jobs.

The beginning of a fulfilling career is the self. According to Harvard Business School Professor Linda A. Hill (1994), individuals who effectively manage their careers are prepared to learn about themselves, are willing to make necessary changes, and can cope with associated stress and emotions. Self-knowledge is consistently found to be a key characteristic in success. Self-discovery is an evolving process; we are ever changing so our quest is ongoing. A starting point is the self-appraisal at the end of this chapter. Answer the ten questions honestly, and you're on your way.

Your Developmental Areas

A useful framework of self-understanding explores four developmental areas of self: physical, mental, emotional, and social. Together, these comprise a whole self.

PHYSICAL SELF

Appearance and condition of the body make up the physical self. Characteristics such as race, age, bone structure, and certain physical disabilities are outside our control. Yet, we can influence several aspects of appearance and health.

How would you describe your physical self?

In their self-descriptions, especially related to appearance, individuals tend to overemphasize perceived flaws and be overly critical. "I'm too fat," "I'm too thin," "I have such thin hair," "I have such thick hair," "I'm too short," "I'm too tall" are commonly heard. We might wonder if anyone is satisfied!

The best possible appearance is a worthy goal. Most employers are impressed with individuals who are clean and neat and who make an effort to present their best appearance. "I like an inviting smile and a professional appearance," says Sue Collins, director of a day-care center. Unfortunately, attractiveness is often a factor. Research has found that physical attractiveness is associated with work success (Mehrabian, 2000). As long as attractiveness continues to be a factor, the best you can do is maximize appearance as much as possible. Specific suggestions related to interviewing appearance are covered in Chapter 5.

Making positive changes is exciting and will benefit you both personally and professionally. Think of any changes you can begin to make now that will improve your physical appearance and move you toward **wellness,** which is a high degree of physical and mental well-being.

Increasing the level of physical activity has amazing benefits, and it's well within your reach. You can easily incorporate activity into your regular day. "Instead of parking in the closest spot, I find one that requires me to walk at least a block each way," reported a young man. When you have a "break" in your day, use it to walk, or do what one woman does. "Instead of just listening to music at home, I dance and really exert myself while having fun." The body was meant to move, and when it does, both health and appearance are enhanced.

Health is obviously a significant factor in career success. Even though we often think of health only as the absence of illness, a more realistic picture places it on a continuum.

VERY ILL — ILL — FEELING OK — WELL — VERY HEALTHY

Place a mark on the health continuum that describes you and then indicate how healthy you'd like to be.

If you have experienced being very healthy or can describe yourself that way now, you know there is a great difference between that level and just feeling OK. Feeling energetic, vigorous, rarely tired, alert, and at peace with yourself will reap major rewards as you design your career. One interviewer remarked, "The fact that she radiated good health was a major asset."

Achieving wellness includes physical and mental activity, healthy nutrition, adequate rest, effective stress-coping strategies, and the elimination of destructive health habits such as excessive use of alcohol or other drugs. A particularly deadly habit that can directly affect your career is cigarette smoking. Adult male and female smokers lose an average of 13.2 and 14.5 years of life, respectively (Centers for Disease Control, 2002). Because of the proven health risks and for other reasons, many employers either hesitate or refuse to hire them. Said one, "If I detect the smell of smoke on an applicant, I don't even consider him or her. It's a real turn-off." There are health concerns for nonsmokers, too. Several studies show the danger of secondhand smoke (Aschwanden, 2000), and because of this, private and government offices are increasingly smoke-free. Think of all aspects of your physical self and elect to do all you can to achieve the best you can be!

Being actively involved in an enjoyable activity enhances physical health and psychological well-being.

MENTAL SELF

Especially applicable to the career field are your learning abilities, thought-processing patterns, problem-solving skills, beliefs, and attitudes that are all included in this part of the self. Cognitive (thought) development continues throughout one's life and is integral to career development.

How mentally capable are you? **Intelligence** can be thought of as mental ability and is usually assessed on tests of language, mathematical, and reasoning abilities. The concept of multiple intelligences (Gardner, 1993, 1999) broadens the scope and includes a variety of competencies useful in the employment field, such as interpersonal skills. You may have a high IQ, which reflects a score on a certain test; however, this probably won't matter as much as your eagerness to learn and your ability to solve problems.

How well you have performed academically will be of definite interest to many employers. Lisa Patterson, CPA and senior manager at Ernst and Young LLP in Los Angeles, reports that a high GPA is mandatory in many fields, including accounting. A study supports her idea by showing that college grade point average is often used in personnel selection (Roth & Bobko, 2000).

Academic achievement is usually the result of a high degree of motivation. Those who truly want to do well frequently do. Employers tend to believe that if you were motivated to achieve educational success, you will behave similarly on the job. A common interview question has to do with what motivates you. Hopefully, you have developed a high level of self-motivation.

Are you curious? Name at least four subjects of curiosity.

Curiosity about a number of subjects can make you a well-rounded person who is both interested and interesting. Being curious or confused and then asking meaningful questions set the stage for learning. Asking questions on the job is expected. "At some point I know an employee won't know what's going on, and I want questions," said a partner in an accounting firm. Bob Dinkel, a business owner, remarked, "I don't mind mistakes now and then. What is frustrating is when the person doesn't ask a question that could have avoided the error." If you're hesitant about asking questions, begin to look upon them as ways to learn and then overcome your reluctance.

Are you willing to ask questions? If not, what is the reason?

How much have you ever thought about thinking? Where did you learn to think? Most of us take our thinking abilities for granted, and few people have been taught specifically how to think. **Thinking,** the ability to activate and then pursue mental activity, is necessary in any job. Certain occupations demand **creative thinking,** the ability to generate new ideas; others require **critical thinking,** an aptitude for probing deeper and examining the logic of differing points.

Alertness, flexibility, and a keen desire to exercise your brain are critical elements in career development. They also affect life satisfaction. As Carolyn, an older student who had just returned to college, said, "My mind has been resting on a shelf for too long. Now I'm applying my brain power, and it's an exhilarating feeling!"

Undoubtedly, a profoundly influential aspect of the mental self is **attitude,** a state of mind that is reflected in how we approach life. Even if the word has possibly been overused, its impact is too powerful to ignore. Creating and keeping a positive attitude toward your work, your employer, and life in general has the most profound impact on career success (O'Neil & Chapman, 2002).

A positive attitude is not equivalent to a "Pollyanna" way of looking at life. That is, you can still have a positive attitude and realize that life is not absolutely wonderful all of the time. Being positive means that you look on the brighter side of events, that you are more "up" than "down," and that you usually feel responsible and in control of yourself. You are a person who emphasizes solutions, not just problems. Positive people are generally energetic, motivated, and alert, with a marvelous zest for life. The opposite is true of those with a negative attitude who are typically perceived as gloomy, lazy, complaining, fault-finding, blaming, and impossible to be around. Even though misery may love company, people tend to avoid miserable and negative people.

Employers want people with positive attitudes because they personally contribute a great deal and also serve as invaluable role models. "I feel energized being around her" and "It's hard to stay 'down' around him" are typical reactions. A person with a negative attitude can infect other employees, as well. "Working around him is like carrying a heavy pack around all day" was how one employee was described.

"Even if a person doesn't have all the necessary skills and knowledge, a positive attitude can make a big difference. It's crucial."

JODY HORWITZ, Vice President of Human Resources, The WB Television Network, Warner Bros., Los Angeles

Also important is your belief about the future, which can be described as either optimistic or pessimistic. Research supports the value of optimism in all aspects of life including career. Attitude is definitely noticed by employers and those whom you service. Bob Resz, a retired college dean, asserts, "What distinguishes the good teachers from the mediocre ones is not method, style, or personality; it's attitude."

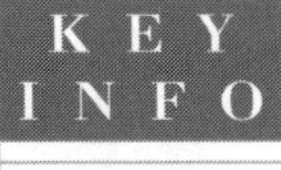

Optimists vs. Pessimists (Harju & Bolen, 1998)

Among college students, high optimists enjoyed the highest overall quality of life satisfaction. Low optimists were dissatisfied and used more alcohol and other avoidance behaviors in order to cope.

How can you improve your attitude? A powerful ally is the mental self, which creates much of our reality. Thoughts and subsequent actions construct what is "real" in life. The next time you find yourself thinking dreary thoughts, choose uplifting ones instead. Besides changing thoughts, what else can people do? Can you teach attitude? Sheryl Piening, instructor of management and human relations courses at a community college, believes that it's certainly possible to teach attitude-altering tools. "After identifying positive and negative behaviors, nearly 50 percent of my students see that they have some attitude work to do," Sheryl says. Eliminating behaviors associated with a negative attitude and developing positive ones can change mental outlook. Other suggestions follow.

- Read books such as *Learned Optimism: How to Change Your Mind and Your Life* (Seligman, 1998) and *Person to Person: Positive Relationships Don't Just Happen* (Hanna, 2003).
- Associate with positive people and model their behaviors.
- Take courses related to personal development and understanding. Your experience may be akin to a student who exclaimed, "After only two interpersonal relations classes, I have a better attitude about life!"

Assess your attitude. Name personal behaviors that demonstrate either positiveness or negativity, or both. Think of ways to change your behavior so that you project even more positiveness. What else can you do to develop or maintain a positive attitude?

If asked about attitude in a job interview, hopefully, you can honestly describe yours as positive and optimistic. A potential employer may not ask; however, attitude has a way of revealing itself in your verbal and nonverbal communication.

Beliefs about the self have a tremendous impact. **Self-fulfilling prophecies** are beliefs that are acted out and, thus, confirmed. For example, Craig believed he was persuasive. He convinced his supervisor to try an idea that could save money for the company. This success confirmed his original belief, and he continued to use these "selling" skills. If he had believed he couldn't persuade others, what do you think the likely result would have been? Examine your self-fulfilling prophecies. Keep the ones that are useful and change those that are not.

Thoughts also influence your emotions. Have you ever felt mildly depressed? What were you thinking at that time? It is likely that your thoughts were either causing or at least contributing to the feeling. Ashley interviewed for a job she really wanted and was told that someone else was selected. She immediately thought, "Either I didn't interview well, or they just didn't like me. This is probably the way my job search is going to go." As a result of her thoughts, she feels dejected and hopeless. She could use an effective technique called **cognitive restructuring,** or thought changing. "Just because I wasn't selected doesn't necessarily mean I didn't interview well or that they didn't like me. I'll think of this as a learning experience and keep looking." Obviously, her feelings of dejection and hopelessness would disappear.

Think of a recent less-than-positive thought, then change it to a positive one. How could your emotions have been different?

EMOTIONAL SELF

Human beings are emotional, and our feelings both enrich and disturb our lives. Emotions such as happiness, sadness, concern, pride, anger, and excitement bring texture and color to human existence. Life without emotion would indeed be drab.

"Complex" is a common way of describing the emotional self. Many people find it difficult to get in touch with their feelings, and they may not know what can occur in the presence of emotion. Three components are possible when emotion is experienced. One is physiological arousal or response. Our nervous system, various glands, and organs within the body are active during an emotional state. Have you ever blushed in an embarrassing situation? The redness of your face was caused by what was going on inside your body. What physiological arousal is likely when you're frustrated or angry?

A second component of emotion is subjective cognitive state—awareness and appraisal of the feeling. When you are happy, you may not be aware of physiological arousal; yet, you just know you are experiencing happiness. Emotion's third component is expression—observable verbal or nonverbal behaviors. Expression of emotion can help or hinder people in their careers. For example, facial expressions can reveal what you're feeling. If you look friendly, interested, and enthusiastic, you are much more likely to get and keep a job. Conversely, going through an entire interview with a "poker face" will probably lead to rejection.

Check your own emotional expression. What do you actually do when you are happy or sad? Angry or afraid?

Expressing your feelings can lead to emotional well-being and enhanced relationships. Emotional suppression, not showing feelings, isn't healthy; yet, too often, inexpressiveness is equated with self-control. People who keep their feelings to themselves are often described as "strong." Instead, a healthier belief is that expressing feelings appropriately and constructively requires strength. Emotional control could be defined as deciding whether, when, and how to express. Andrew, a person not used to expressing his feelings, heard a rumor at work that he had been passed over for promotion. He seethed all morning, then announced loudly to his supervisor that he was quitting, and walked out. He stopped to pick up his mail and found a memo congratulating him on his promotion. His display of emotion was not only inappropriate; it was disastrous! A well-adjusted person can choose whether to express or not to show a feeling and, in a given situation, can select from any number of responses.

People who do not have appropriate outlets for emotions such as frustration, anger, and disappointment may have emotional outbursts that destroy career opportunities and relationships. Assertiveness, discussed later in this chapter, can provide a satisfying outlet for most emotions. Additionally, there are ways to release emotion privately that provide relief. When you become annoyed or upset, try any of the following:

- Deep breathing (see end of chapter)
- Taking a brisk walk or engaging in any physical activity
- Hitting a soft (stuffed) object (privately!)

- Writing down your thoughts and feelings
- Crushing pieces of paper, then throwing them into the wastebasket (this might clean your work space at the same time)

A favorite is what I call a "primal sigh." It includes taking a deep breath and then making a sighing sound while exhaling. This is preferable to a primal scream, which is not recommended in the workplace!

Changing what you feel is possible by altering your thoughts, behaviors, or both. Control theory (Glasser, 1984) emphasizes the importance of what we do. Have you ever whistled or hummed cheerily and then recognized a slight mood elevation? If so, you were using basic control theory.

What are you feeling right now? Change the emotion. First, alter your thoughts. Then, do something that is different from your present activity or behavior.

In regard to success, in recent years the emotional self has taken center stage. **Emotional intelligence** is a potential to learn practical skills based on five elements: self-awareness, motivation, self-regulation, empathy, and adeptness in relationships (Goleman, 1995, 1998). Being able to recognize the meaning of emotions and to think and problem-solve on the basis of them is the cornerstone of emotional intelligence (Mayer, Caruso, & Salovey, 1999). Emotions affect performance as well as relationships. Having intelligence in this area means that we acknowledge and value emotions and then apply their energy in our daily work (Reed-Woodard & Clarke, 2000).

How important is emotional intelligence? In a measure of excellence in 121 companies and organizations, emotional competencies were at the top of the list of abilities that are necessary for effective performance. Compared to IQ and technical expertise, emotional competence was viewed as twice as important (Bates, 1999). Emotional success is fundamental if you want to achieve work and life success (Mehrabian, 2000) and essential to a productive workplace (Smigla & Pastoria, 2000). For both professional and personal reasons, doesn't it make sense to do all you can to increase your level of emotional intelligence? Take advantage of coursework, books, and other sources that offer emotional insight.

The more we learn about our emotional self, the more we can use our feelings to enhance our lives. Everyone can benefit from the full experience and constructive expression of true feelings.

SOCIAL SELF

Who you are in relation to others and how you interact are vital to your well-being and will significantly affect career development. Teamwork is required in today's work world, so the ability to get along with others is essential.

You and other individuals create what can be called a social climate. Its influence is either positive or negative. Conflicts occur; yet, congenial people who genuinely like others can manage disagreements effectively. Ways to do so are discussed in Chapter 7.

A social self with an appropriate sense of humor, a cooperative attitude, sensitivity, and fairness is a plus. How well do you get along with people? This is a common interview question. The importance of the social self was underscored by young professionals who were asked, "What do you know now after being in the work world for a few years that you wish you had known in the beginning?" How to develop camaraderie or fellowship with clients and co-workers was identified as most important by Lee Lamirault, benefits coordinator, Princess Cruises, Los Angeles, California. "If you can't communicate, you're nowhere," he said. Mary Tesselaar, an executive assistant at Ernst and Young LLP, concurred that it's necessary to know how to make a client or customer happy and how to provide positive service.

"Interpersonal skills are needed as much as technical expertise. Coursework in this vital area would be extremely beneficial."

MARY TESSELAAR, Executive Assistant, Ernst and Young LLP, Los Angeles

Agreeing with the young professionals, Donald O. Clifton, CEO of the Gallup Organization, said:

> A Gallup survey indicated how the quality of human relationships in the workplace impacts workers' satisfaction, retention of employees, and how well employees do their work. I believe the human relations skills people bring to the workplace are the most important skills they bring.

Personality, the cornerstone of the social self, is covered in this chapter, whereas Chapter 2 discusses interactive skills. Polishing the social self lays the groundwork for career success.

The Whole Self

Fortunately, we aren't like Humpty Dumpty who couldn't be put back together again! The four developmental areas comprise a whole, and examining the integrated self is fascinating.

Can you remember a time when you didn't feel well physically? What were you like mentally, emotionally, and socially?

Having problems in one area of self usually diminishes one or more of the other three. The good news is that a positive spillover effect also occurs. When one area is improved, generally, the others are, too. Sara, who was depressed and shy, showed little promise of career success. Then she lost weight and had her hair cut and styled. As a result of physical improvements, she felt happier and became more sociable. The connections among the four areas are powerful.

Striving for a whole integrated self is a worthy goal. Additionally, seeking balance deserves attention. Some people devote a great deal of time and energy to their mental self yet exclude their social development and are strangers to their feelings. Others have vigorous social lives to the detriment of their physical and mental well-being. Check yourself periodically and aim for a healthy balance. You don't want to learn the hard way that you are an integrated being!

Personality: The Unique You

Begin to describe yourself. If you are like many people, you begin with physical descriptors and may have difficulty going further. **Personality** is the "unique you," a distinctive pattern of behaving, thinking, and feeling. A combination of characteristics is possessed only by you and is how others know you. Personality gives an individual a separate identity. Have you ever heard someone say, "He has no personality"? While the person may be extremely reserved or dull, there is still a personality!

Personality awareness and understanding can be challenging; yet, as you design your career, knowing who you are and why you behave as you do is instrumental. Consider these cases.

- Jason is miserable at work. He enjoys being around people, yet his job demands that he analyze data in a back office.
- Abby is frustrated because her supervisor often interrupts what she is doing and tells her to work on something else. She wants to complete one task before beginning another one. Also, her job duties are often changed, which annoys her.
- Ming perceives her employer as one who makes illogical decisions and who lets his emotions direct his interactions. Bryan's impression of the same employer is that he is caring and sensitive.
- Emily and Jeff have become impatient with their supervisor because she has not made a major decision about their positions at work. Additionally, they consider her to be unorganized.

An understanding of personality types would help these people. Carl Jung (1923, 1968), a pioneer in psychological types, believed that behavioral differences are based on the ways people approach life. Based on his typology with some of their own refinements, Isabel Myers and her mother, Katharine C. Briggs, developed the Myers–Briggs Type Indicator® (MBTI). Its applications in education, business, the artistic world, and decision making have been extensive.

Intended to be used for people who are "well," the indicator focuses on positive aspects and preferences for thinking, feeling, and acting. You can use it to make wise decisions about all aspects of life including career choices. An added benefit is that it increases understanding of different behaviors (Myers, 1995), which can help us cope with people and their differences constructively.

PERSONALITY PREFERENCES AND TYPES

The MBTI has four categories with two preferences in each. These pairs of preferences are identified in Figure 1.1 and described later in this section. People have degrees of both preferences in a category; most of us have a partiality toward one. For example, you may have a desire for frequent social activities indicating an extraverted preference, yet also enjoy and actually seek solitude and quiet activities because of some introversion.

All eight preferences have advantages and disadvantages. An understanding of each can help you maximize the strengths of the preference and minimize the drawbacks. Important to realize is that the meanings of the preference words are somewhat different from their dictionary definitions and popular usage. For example, "judgment" in the MBTI does not mean judgmental. Also, often

FIGURE

1.1 Preferences: Myers–Briggs Type Indicator®.

Extraversion–Introversion (E or I)

External or internal orientation to the world and source of life energy

Note: The spelling *extraversion* is used in this book; extroversion is equally correct.

Sensing–Intuition (S or N)

Ways of taking in and processing information

Thinking–Feeling (T or F)

Use of thought or feelings in decision making

Judgment–Perception (J or P)

Modes of dealing with and living in the outer world

misunderstood are "extraversion" and "introversion"; unfortunately, the confusion has led to the assumption that it's better to be more extraverted.

Extraversion/Introversion. What is meant by extraversion and introversion? Think in terms of life energy or force. What charges your battery? If your preference is **extraversion (E),** energy is drawn from external sources including other people, and you probably project energy outward. Extraverted and outgoing people prefer to operate in the outer world of people and things. If there were such a word as "ingoing," it would describe an introverted preference. **Introversion (I)** means having an interest in the inner world of concepts and ideas. The source of life energy is within and comes from solitary experiences. Those with an introverted preference reenergize themselves and don't rely on external stimuli. In fact, interaction drains their energy, and they need to spend time alone recharging themselves.

People who prefer extraversion will usually behave in a friendly manner and appear open. Those who are more introverted usually do not actively seek out others and may appear to be in their own world; yet, this doesn't mean they are incapable of friendliness or that they are shy or snobbish. They are often skilled with people; however, they prefer smaller numbers of people, fewer interactions, and an opportunity to get to know people well. Interestingly, shyness, defined as timidity in a social situation, can be experienced by both preferences.

The other three pairs of preferences are as follows.

Sensing/Intuition. If your preference is **sensing (S),** you tend to be realistic, practical, observant, and good at remembering and working with a great number of facts (Myers, 1993). If you prefer **intuition (N),** you value and use your imagination, have new ideas, and enjoy solving problems (Myers, 1993). In their perceptions, sensors (S) are concrete and attuned to details while intuitives (N) are visionary and ablaze with possibilities and ideas. When working on a task, sensors (S) prefer a systematic step-by-step procedure and

Can you pick out examples of extraversion and introversion? Even around familiar people, personality differences influence social behavior and enjoyment at business social functions.

don't seem to be bothered by repetition. Intuitives (N) prefer to devise their own methods, will work on several steps or projects at once, and prefer variety. Those with an intuitive preference become bored with routine.

What types of job situations would satisfy a sensor (S)? What about an intuitive (N)?

Thinking/Feeling. If your preference is **thinking (T),** you use logic and decide impersonally. The other way to decide is through **feeling (F).** You consider anything that matters or is important to you or to other people and decide in a personal way (Myers, 1993). The difference is between "head" and "heart" decisions. One who has a clear thinking preference views emotions as more of a problem than as part of a solution (Keating, 1984). This person can be oblivious to other people's feelings, while the opposite (a strong feeling person) can "bend over backward" to avoid hurting anyone. Either can be problematic. People with both preferences can care a great deal about people and believe that their decisions are based on the "right" motives. Caring from a "T" is more apt to be sympathy and from an "F" empathy (Jeffries, 1991). The two preferences can clash or complement each other; clashing is probably more common. In the career world those with a thinking preference have an easier time making the tough decisions. The "feelers" agonize over choices, especially those pertaining to sensitive areas. Ideally, you can use both preferences appropriately.

Imagine you are a company executive who has to decide which employee to terminate. The choice is between two females who have equal levels of work performance. The only differences are that Jennifer is a single parent with two children while Stephanie is single with no children and has been with the company six months longer. What will you do? If you have a thinking preference, you will probably decide almost immediately that Jennifer will be fired. Objectively, seniority makes the difference. If your preference is feeling, you will want to retain Jennifer because you "feel" for her, or you will try to come up with a way to keep both employed.

Judgment/Perception. Judgment (J) means that you prefer living in a planned, decided, orderly way, wanting to regulate life and maintain control over events (Myers, 1993). Planning and preparation are typical behaviors. Judgers (J) seek closure and prefer to reach a decision or judgment quickly. If you like living in a flexible, spontaneous way, wanting to understand and adapt to life (Myers, 1993), your preference is **perception (P).** You often "go with the flow" and like to keep your options open. Key words are *organization* for the judging preference and *adaptability* for perceivers (Jeffries, 1991). Paul, a strong judger (J), said, "I like the idea of someone throwing me a surprise party, but I want to be prepared for it." He added, "I live by my planner. I take it everywhere, even parties." In contrast to Paul, a perceiver (P) probably wouldn't have a planner or would be like Kari who admitted, "I did buy a calendar diary but don't bother to use it!" In the workplace, people of these two extremes can have difficulty getting along. The judger (J) probably views the perceiver (P) as disorganized or flighty, while the perceptive one could become frustrated with what appears to be an overly organized and inflexible co-worker.

Think of behaviors associated with the judgment preference that contribute to career success. How can the attitudes and actions of a perceiver also be of value?

Think about which of the preferences in each of the four categories sounds like you. The combination of the four choices becomes what is called **psychological type,** which provides a broader concept of who you are. Remember that if your preferences are, for example, extraversion, intuition, feeling, and perceiving (ENFP), it doesn't mean you don't have and can't use the opposite preferences as well. However, to do so requires awareness and deliberate intent. Your four preferences interact with each other in a unique way, and each type has a blend of useful behaviors as well as potential pitfalls. Knowledge of type can be especially helpful in determining a satisfying career field, in finding a job that fits you, and in helping you capitalize on your strong points.

You may be able to take the MBTI or a similar test in a class or workshop. Doing an online search of Myers–Briggs Type Indicator shows a number of inventories and exercises that can indicate your preferences. The book *Please Understand Me* (Keirsey & Bates, 1984) includes a questionnaire that yields scores in the four categories. Remember that with any measurement, the results may vary for a number of reasons. Taking the test more than once and being honest in answering the questions will give you a more reliable profile. The indicator identifies a preferred trait and is not intended to exclude other possibilities. For example, in comparing personality to handedness, you may have a strong preference for using your right hand while being able to use your left one, too.

Several books based on the MBTI are especially applicable to careers (see Recommended Reading at the end of the book). They can help in making career choices, learning about your strengths and weaknesses, and gaining insight into the personalities of other people. For example, in the past, a co-worker was annoying to me because he focused on one thing at a time and forced me to wait for his attention until he was completely done with the present task. With an intuition preference, I tend to involve myself with more than one activity at a time (which can be a disadvantage). After learning that he, as a strong sensor, needed to concentrate on one task, which is just another way of doing things and certainly "right" for him, the annoyance decreased considerably.

Personality typing indicates people's strengths. If the two preferences are close, you probably are comfortable using either one. This indicator is not intended to pigeonhole people or arm them with excuses for behaviors. In certain situations, using the lesser preference is advisable. For example, if someone says, "I can't help that I'm disorganized. My preference is perceiving (P)," a good response would be, "You also have a judging (J) preference into which you can shift."

Review the four job scenarios at the beginning of this section. Can you see how each person's personality preferences were creating hardships? Jason is extraverted, and his job severely limits his contact with people. Abby, with a strong sensing preference, doesn't function well when she isn't able to complete one task before moving to another, and she prefers routine to variety. It is obvious that Ming is more of a thinker while Bryan, with a feeling preference, feels an affinity with their employer. Two employees with a judging preference, Emily and Jeff, resent the behaviors of a perceiver. Discover how aware you are of personality preferences by completing the personality awareness activity at the end of the chapter.

Another personality theory (Holland, 1997) classifies people into six different groups that can then be matched to career fields. An inventory, Holland's Self-Directed Search (SDS), reveals your type, which could be realistic (R), investigative (I), artistic (A), social (S), enterprising (E), or conventional (C). See Figure 1.2 for a description of these. You can read more and take the Self-Directed Search online for a nominal fee (www.self-directed-search.com) or discover your top three preferences, known as the Holland Code, by engaging in "The Party Exercise" in the book *What Color Is Your Parachute?* (Bolles, 2003). You can also find the exercise online by clicking on Career Interests Game at the University of Missouri Career Center's Web site (http://career.missouri.edu). The more you know about your personality, the more prepared you are to succeed in your career.

Just from the names of the groups used by Holland (1997), suggest some career fields for each.

All aspects of personality aren't revealed through inventories. Self-knowledge includes appraising all personality traits that can help you design a successful career. Several of these are identified in this and other chapters. Whatever your personality is, you can build on the strengths and alter the weaker aspects.

FIGURE 1.2 A brief description of the Holland personality typology.

	Personality Type					
Attribute	Realistic	Investigative	Artistic	Social Helping	Enterprising	Conventional
Preferences for activities and occupations	Manipulation of machines, tools, and things	Exploration, understanding, and prediction or control of natural and social phenomena	Literary, musical, or artistic activities	Teaching, treating, counseling, or serving others through personal interaction	Persuading, manipulating, or directing others	Establishing or maintaining orderly routines, application of standards
Values	Material rewards for tangible accomplishments	Development or acquisition of knowledge	Creative expression of ideas, emotions, or sentiments	Fostering the welfare of others, social service	Material accomplish-ment and social status	Material or financial accomp-lishment and power in social, business, or political arenas
Sees self as	Practical, conservative, and having manual and mechanical skills—lacking social skills	Analytical, intelligent, skeptical, and having academic talent—lacking interpersonal skills	Open to experience, innovative, intellectual—lacking clerical or office skills	Empathic, patient, and having interpersonal skills—lacking mechanical ability	Having sales and persuasive ability—lacking scientific ability	Having technical skills in business or production—lacking artistic competencies
Others see as	Normal, frank	Asocial, intellectual	Unconventional, disorderly, creative	Nurturing, agreeable, extroverted	Energetic, gregarious	Careful, conforming
Avoids	Interaction with people	Persuasion or sales activities	Routines and conformity to established	Mechanical and technical activity	Scientific, intellectual, or abstruse topics	Ambiguous or unstructured undertakings

Source: Adapted and reproduced by special permission of the Publisher, Psychological Assessment Resources, Inc., from the *Dictionary of Holland Occupational Codes*, Third Edition, by Gary D. Gottfredson, Ph.D., and John Holland, Ph.D. Copyright © 1982, 1989, 1996. Further reproduction is prohibited without permission from PAR, Inc.

Self-Concept: Your Image of Self

Each of us has a mental representation of ourselves known as **self-concept.** It can include (1) present descriptors drawn from the four developmental areas of self; (2) **ideal self,** or the image of what you would like to be; and (3) **self-esteem,** the value placed on the self.

Your current self-description and ideal self may be similar or quite different. Because of unrealistic standards, you may have an impossible ideal. If so, that image is more hurtful than helpful. Mark describes himself as overweight, short, eager to learn, impulsive, shy, and generally unhappy. His ideal self, which he is quick to tell about, is muscular, tall, eager to learn, patient, friendly, and always happy. Which of his ideal descriptors could be useful? Which are just potentially damaging? Knowing what you can and cannot change and formulating a possible ideal self are helpful.

Describe your ideal self. Is this a possible self?

Also beneficial is to realize that achieving your ideal self isn't a requirement for high self-esteem or happiness. Instead, as you come closer to your ideal, set your goals even higher. Employers tend to doubt anyone who thinks he or she has reached the highest pinnacle of selfhood. "When I ask applicants about their weaknesses, I'd better get a response. Nobody is perfect," said one business owner. A healthy attitude is to recognize that striving to better oneself is a lifelong process.

Comparing your present descriptors and ideal self helps assess your level of self-worth. Self-esteem can be thought of as a point on a scale ranging from very low to very high; it goes beyond acceptance of self and is a genuine regard for who one is. Some might mistake self-esteem for vanity, conceit, an egotistic existence, and selfishness. Actually, those who fit these descriptors do not have a healthy love for themselves. Self-inflation is usually a cover-up for self-doubt. Genuine love for the self includes self-respect and dignity; it leads to healthy attitudes and behaviors toward others.

Self-esteem affects all aspects of life. Throughout one's career, high self-esteem is a powerful ally. Job seekers with healthy self-worth are more likely to achieve higher interview ratings and receive more job offers than those with low self-esteem. On the job an individual with high self-esteem can accept and profit from advice and constructive criticism. He or she tends to be more motivated, willing to take reasonable risks, and more likely to demonstrate competence. Pride in self leads to high-quality performance.

As one advances, regard for the self continues to pay off. Managers with high self-esteem have less trouble giving up control and delegating responsibility, can tolerate frustration better, and are capable of treating their employees with respect. The willingness to learn new skills and continue to improve stems from feeling good about self.

Our opinion of ourselves, because it touches the very center of our being, is the most significant judgment in life (Branden, 1983). Whatever you can do to build and strengthen self-esteem is highly recommended. Some ideas are provided later in this chapter.

Self-Efficacy: Your Sense of Competence

Closely aligned with self-esteem is a sense of capability or competence, which is called **self-efficacy.** Imagine that you are assigned the task of producing a mailing list. The belief that "I can do this" indicates self-efficacy, and it's easy to see how this is essential to career success. Self-efficacy pertains to a particular event or task, and it isn't necessary to feel competent about everything. However, in areas related to your career, confidence goes a long way. You may remember the story of the little engine who succeeded by saying, "I think I can, I think I can." People with self-efficacy think they can.

Thinking of your own self-efficacy, what skills or tasks come to mind?

Potential employers may not use the word "self-efficacy"; however, expect to be assessed on whether or not they think you have feelings of self-competence. Some caution is in order. As a job applicant or an employee, it is unrealistic to possess self-efficacy about all tasks. An honest "I don't know how to do that, and I'm willing to learn" in an interview and making reasonable requests for assistance on the job are mature behaviors.

"Employees who perceive themselves as capable can work on their own with little supervision; they are highly valued."

NANCY BROWN. R.N., Program Manager, Nebraska Health and Human Services System, Lincoln, Nebraska

Self-efficacy is related to self-esteem; as one increases, so does the other. Throughout your career, being aware of what you can do well and developing additional competencies while having genuine regard for yourself will most likely lead to success and satisfaction. You can now increase self-understanding and compare your self-concept with how others see you by using the activity "How Well Do I Really Know Myself?" at the end of the chapter.

Making Positive Changes

Necessary for career success is the ability to improve oneself. If you are a student, academic success is a priority. What are you doing to ensure that your educational record and work habits will increase your career potential? Read carefully the "Keys to Academic Success" excerpt.

KEYS TO ACADEMIC SUCCESS

Key Advice

- Decide that you want to achieve at the highest level possible for you. Don't settle for a second-rate effort. If you aren't willing to do this, being in school at this time is probably not for you.
- Be realistic. Don't overload yourself with too many courses, especially if you are holding down a job or have family responsibilites.
- Manage time well. Don't just spend time without thinking about how you are spending it. How economically successful are those who just spend money constantly without any thought of how it is being spent? Time management tips are offered in Chapter 8.
- Attend class and show an interest in what is going on there. Ask youself on a regular basis, "What impression am I making here?"
- Ask questions and participate in class. Even if you occasionally give an incorrect answer, your participation will be appreciated, and you can learn from any mistake.
- Spend time working on course requirements. Don't think that you can succeed by just attending classes. If you aren't sure how much time to spend, ask the insructor or professor.
- Divide the work and "learn as you go." Review material after each class. Don't wait to study for an examination the night before. If you have a major project, use action steps suggested in Chapter 3 in "Achieving Your Goals" and get started immediately.
- Be assertive. If you are unsure about an assignment or confused about why you missed a question on an examination, talk to the instructor or professor. Use open communication skills, described in Chapter 2.
- Take responsibility for your own life. Educators, like employers, don't appreciate excuse making and putting the blame on externals. Even if you take a temporary "hit," such as a point penalty for a late paper, handling this maturely will serve you much better.
- Enjoy where you are! People have a tendency to hurry through life ("I can't wait to graduate") and to think that life will automatically be easier and better in the future. Remember that the only time we are guaranteed to have is right now. Use it well!

A common mistake that many students make is to put their current job ahead of college. While loyalty to an employer is commendable, if you almost always choose "going to work" over "going to class," you are probably short-changing your future. Work will always be there while the opportunity to learn and do well in a course will not. Mary Bartels, an academic advisor, hopes that students learn early that during college, they are to become responsible adults and will not only be expected to attend class, but also will need to devote outside time to their studies. "Students who overload themselves often don't do well," she said.

Being responsible is one of the desirable traits valuable in all career fields and useful in every job. Responsibility and other traits make up your **transferable assets.** You probably already possess several of these assets identified in Key Info. Communicate this to potential employers. In some cases, the trait may not be evident. For example, not everybody exudes enthusiasm. If you feel excitement for your career choice and a particular job and don't think it shows, you can verbalize it in an interview. Innovation is another valuable characteristic that may not be obvious. Businesses need new ideas about how to stay competitive, so being creative in this rapidly changing world is a definite asset. Executives say they want forward-thinking applicants who can move into a job without needing a lot of direction. If you don't require a great deal of supervision and can handle most tasks on your own, you are definitely marketable.

Pretend you are hiring employees. What characteristics or traits would you want? Check your list against the transferable assets listed in Key Info.

KEY INFO

Transferable Assets

assertive	creative/innovative
enthusiastic	flexible
responsible	willing to exert effort
dependable	motivated
congenial/friendly	respectful of self and others
able to see alternatives	able to communicate and take criticism
positive	happy most of the time
goal-oriented	stable in mood and temperament
ethical	open-minded
loyal	accepting of diversity
realistic	technically skilled

In recent surveys of employers and program chairpersons at a community college, a number of employable characteristics were evident. Along with the obvious need for technical skills, nearly all listed dependability. Several emphasized flexibility in thought and action. "We look for people who are adaptable to change," says Deputy Fire Chief Dean Staberg.

Instructors of career-related courses are in close contact with employers and know what is wanted. "Individuals need to be able to communicate, to get along with people, to adapt, and to accept new ideas and concepts," says Charlotte Nedrow. Along with adaptability and being a positive team player, Karen Hermsen describes the key ingredient in being hired.

> Without a doubt, employers are looking for a positive attitude and likeability. You can be the best typist, be familiar with the most software programs, or be the most skilled in any particular field, but if you don't come across as a person who is easy to get along with, you probably won't get the job.

Three business administration instructors agree:

- "Interpersonal skills are probably even more important than technical skills due to the fact that most dissatisfaction and firings are because of personality conflicts."

  Nancy Krumland

- "Companies emphasize the ability to interact well with others. It's important to develop strong interpersonal skills while learning to understand and value differences."

  Pat Galitz

- "Interpersonal skills are at the top of the list of qualities desired by employers."

  Sheryl Piening

Most Desired Capabilities (Daniel, 1998)

A study of corporations found that the three most desired capabilities are communication skills, interpersonal skills, and initiative.

Possessing self-discipline and demonstrating a solid work ethic are impressive and generally hard-to-find characteristics, in the opinion of Leonard

Murphy, a partner in an accounting firm. He voices the opinions of several employers:

> Many people are looking for jobs although they may not be willing to really work. Some people just want a paycheck. If they show up and put in eight hours, they think they're being productive. Those who actually do want to work and to produce are greatly appreciated and will be rewarded.

Knowing what employers want gives you an advantage. Above all else, the self you present must be a likable one.

DEVELOPING AN INTERNAL LOCUS OF CONTROL

Even though most people think they take responsibility, excuses are plentiful. "I know I was late, but . . . " or "If she had left me alone to do my work, I would have finished" or "I was so depressed I just couldn't come to work" are some examples. In a classic study of executives who had experienced high degrees of stressful life events, having what is called an internal locus of control contributed to their psychological hardiness and ability to counteract stress (Kobasa, 1979). An **internal locus of control** is the belief that you are in control of your life as opposed to thinking that external factors are responsible. Are you more likely to take responsibility for your own behaviors, which include all shortcomings, or to blame someone or something else?

The value of feeling in control is supported by studies linking it to improved health (Moyers, 1995), happiness (Myers & Diener, 1995), and improved attitude (Lam & Schaubroeck, 2000). Employers want individuals to be responsible in many ways, and they appreciate those who take responsibility for their actions. "I didn't finish the project on time because I did not plan well and start on it early enough. I regret that and have learned from my mistake" is refreshing and much preferred to a commonly heard excuse: "The project didn't get finished because I'm so busy and just didn't have time." The reality of life is that we all have the same amount of time, and in almost all cases, the project could have been completed. What happened is that there wasn't time left over to do so.

What's the difference between an excuse and a reason? The latter is a statement of fact and indicates self-responsibility. While an excuse can be factual, a "that should get me off the hook" presumption is also included. Excuse making can be detrimental to career success. Not only is making excuses an annoying habit, but those who make excuses also deny themselves the opportunity to learn and grow. Excuses are like antacids that bring temporary relief but do not contribute to long-term success and happiness (Hanna, 2003).

GEECH®

By Jerry Bittle

GEECH reprinted by permission of United Feature Syndicate, Inc.

When you verbally or mentally blame external sources, challenge your thought. Even if you couldn't control the situation, you had a choice as to how to react. When you make a mistake, admit it and resolve to make any needed changes. Chris had a problem with getting to work on time. He said, "I would either blame my faulty alarm clock, the weather, or the traffic, but never myself. When I finally 'woke up,' I realized that I could buy a different alarm clock and could leave for work early enough to take care of both bad weather and heavy traffic. I was responsible for being late, and now I'm in control and can be on time!" Check your locus of control. Then decide that you want to be "in the driver's seat of your life"!

BECOMING ASSERTIVE

Nobody is born assertive so all of us must learn it. **Assertiveness,** defined as the ability to maintain one's legitimate rights and to express thoughts and feelings in nonthreatening ways, is valued in today's work world. In contrast to aggressive behavior that is threatening and controlling or nonassertive behavior that is meek and passive, assertiveness is likely to have a positive outcome. Research reveals that interviewers are most likely to employ assertive applicants (Gallois, Callan, & Palmer, 1992).

How does a person become more assertive? Cognitive restructuring that rids you of fear and anxiety can be especially helpful. You may need to convince yourself that you can be assertive. For example, a thought process may be: "Just because I've been aggressive and abrasive in the past doesn't mean I have to continue to be. I can adjust my behavior and become assertive."

If you fear embarrassment or rejection and feel intimidated, a simple technique can be used to sap the strength of the fear-provoking thought (Butler, 1992). When you think, "What if he gets upset when I state my opinion?" change it: "So what if he gets upset when I state my opinion." Another idea is to ask yourself, "What is the worst thing that can happen if I say or do this?" Usually, the worst isn't all that bad, and your fear is relieved.

Thinking is a powerful beginning; however, the key is to employ assertive actions. Assertiveness can be learned from **modeling,** observing, and then copying the behaviors of an assertive person. If you have an opportunity to role-play assertiveness, do so. For most people, assertiveness requires changes in both verbal and nonverbal behaviors.

- Verbalize with "I" statements such as "I would like," "I don't want," "I think or believe." This assertive language indicates responsibility for your own thoughts and feelings. You will learn about "I" statements in Chapter 2.
- Use a calm and even tone of voice and maintain a moderate rate and volume.
- Make reasonable requests and set reasonable limits, then express these clearly and calmly to others.
- Learn to say no to what you don't want and yes to what you do. Because saying no is difficult for many people, how to do so is covered in Chapter 2.
- Use direct eye contact, appropriate facial expressions, an open body position, confident body stance, and calm and controlled body movements. Avoid threatening gestures such as pointing.
- Be willing to take reasonable risks. Begin with a slight risk and give yourself credit for trying.

Think of assertive behaviors you possess. Then take the assertiveness inventory at the end of the chapter.

As with all learned skills, practice will make assertiveness easier. The path is not necessarily an easy one. As one becomes assertive, others may resent and feel offended by this "new" person, especially if the previous nonassertive behavior served their purposes. "I tried to be assertive with my co-worker, and it led to a confrontation. I'm ready to give up," confessed Hannah. She would be better off practicing her new assertiveness in situations where success is likely and then approaching the co-worker with renewed confidence.

"In order to succeed, a person has to take chances. I struggle with this, but it's true. There's an old sports analogy: You never make a shot you don't take."

MITCH HALL, Senior Project Manager, Financial Analysis, Domino's Pizza, Inc., Ann Arbor, Michigan

BUILDING AND STRENGTHENING SELF-ESTEEM

Before you can raise or bolster the value you place on yourself, you may need to eliminate some obstacles. Some people are handicapped by extreme insecurities, psychological disorders, or drug abuse. Just getting through the day can be a struggle; thus, they fail in attempts to improve themselves. Professional counseling is usually necessary to elevate them to a level where they can take advantage of self-esteem building. The payoff is invaluable. "A decision to be *for* yourself, not against yourself, is the beginning of an entirely different life," says Debra, a college student.

Basic to self-esteem is living consciously. Your degree of alertness and level of functioning are determined by such choices as how much sleep to get (seven to eight hours is highly recommended) and the use of alcohol and other drugs. Those who walk around "in a fog" are not in a position to build their self-esteem.

An analysis of how your self-esteem developed can be quite helpful. All of us have been criticized or put down even by those who love us. Parents use what resources they possess and almost never intentionally hurt their offspring; yet, hurt can occur. Teachers, coaches, and other school personnel can diminish self-esteem because they don't know better ways to direct the lives of others. Sometimes supervisors and co-workers say and do hurtful things because of their own frustrations. Recall any negative comments you have received. Consider the possible reasons. Could it have been because of the person's own feelings of inferiority or lack of self-esteem? Was he or she just being hateful? Did the person have good intentions? Decide what to do with all that has been said and done to you. The past can be a valuable basis for learning and growing; use it in that way and discard any useless self-destructive messages.

Do you concentrate on your strengths? A tendency is to key in on weaknesses and become bogged down. While recognizing drawbacks is beneficial, it's not wise to dwell on them. Focusing on your potential and thinking positively empower the self. A boost to self-esteem can come from the regular use of **affirmations,** which are positive self-thoughts.

What do you like about yourself? Do you listen well? Do you have a nice smile? Are you considerate? List your strong points.

Demonstrating your strengths is even more rewarding. Whatever you do well, be sure to do it! If you have athletic talent, join a team or simply play for enjoyment. If you're talented in some type of craft, make something as a gift. Accept all compliments and don't put yourself down if your attempts aren't perfect. Getting involved in worthwhile activities is a boost to self-esteem, and these are also extremely valuable assets in your career development. Brent participated in an environmental cleanup project, which made him feel good, and eventually impressed an interviewer. Giving to others is a gift to yourself.

Making constructive changes improves your present self and ensures a better future. Make an attainable yet challenging ideal and improve one developmental area of yourself. The goal-setting information in Chapter 3 will be helpful. Any positive change in yourself means an increase in self-esteem.

Building and maintaining high self-esteem is easier with the help of positive, supportive people. If you find yourself around others who tend to be "downers" about themselves or others, seek other company. Being with people who affirm you and modeling after those with high self-esteem are effective esteem boosters.

Name at least two friends or acquaintances who are positive and supportive. Spend time with these people!

Changing your thoughts, or cognitive restructuring, is a useful self-esteem-building technique. Begin by tuning in to your **self-talk,** the thoughts you have about yourself. Are those thoughts realistic and generally affirming or are they distorted and damaging? If self-talk is unnecessarily negative, reframe or restructure it using these four steps.

1. Identify an untruth, distortion, or belittlement.
2. Determine the truth and the facts.
3. Use this way of restructuring: Just because (*the truth/facts as given in Step 2*) doesn't mean (*the untruth, distortion, or belittlement you were thinking as identified in Step 1*).
4. Give yourself an affirmation.

As an example, pretend you didn't get a job you really wanted. Your immediate thought is: "They must not have liked me. I'll never find a job better than that one." The use of cognitive restructuring follows.

1. They must not have liked me. I'll never find a job better than that one. (*Identify this thought as a belittlement and a distortion.*)
2. I didn't get a job I really wanted. (*This is the truth/fact.*)

3. Just because I didn't get a job I really wanted doesn't mean they didn't like me and that I won't find a job that is better. (*This shows the use of the restructuring formula.*)
4. I will make an excellent employee, and I'll just keep looking. (*This is an affirmation.*)

Freeing yourself from the distorted thought allows any number of positive ones. You can even think as did Sarah, "It's the company's loss. They missed out on a terrific employee!" Remember that what you think determines much of your life. Several books include ways of building and strengthening self-esteem (Bloomfield, 1996; Hanna, 2003; McKay & Fanning, 2000). Additionally, courses and seminars can help improve your self-concept. We weren't born with self-esteem. Rather than blame others for where we are now, we can overcome the past and build and strengthen self-esteem in the present. A basic question is to ask yourself if you are being as kind and supportive to yourself as you are to a good friend. If you aren't, why not become your own best friend?

Sharpening Your Basic Skills

Companies today are facing a skills gap more pronounced than ever before. Three types of skills are definitely needed:

- Basic analytical, communication, and organizational skills (includes reading, writing, and arithmetic)
- Technological skills
- Interpersonal skills

Before beginning your career, assess your competencies and learn or sharpen basic skills. A primary one is writing. Throughout your career, the ability to write correctly and clearly will be a significant asset. Additionally, individuals have a major handicap if they lack reading or mathematics skills. If you are deficient in any of these areas, enroll in relevant courses. "Until students have learned to use proper written and spoken language in every facet of their lives, they aren't prepared to enter the work world and be successful," says Larry Hubka, Ph.D., Chief Academic Officer/Director of Education, Quest Education Corporation.

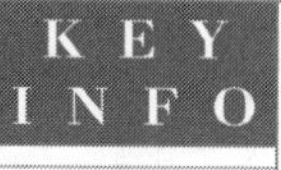

"Good writing is one of the two key abilities I focus on when hiring; the other is the ability to read critically. I can train people to do almost anything else, but I don't have time to do this."

Richard Todd, Federal Reserve Bank as cited in Fisher (1999)

Another beneficial course is public speaking or speech. You may not be expected to make presentations before large audiences; however, most occupations require small group communication. A speech course will also aid in job interview preparation. A definite asset, even though it may not yet be considered basic, is fluency in a second language. Successful coursework typically increases career and job possibilities.

Because computer skills are required in almost every job, taking courses in the basic technology is essential. Not having computer skills today is as much a liability as inability to read and write was a few years ago. Coursework in word processing and spreadsheets will make you even more marketable. You can learn how to use standard office machines either on a job now, from volunteer work, or through coursework. "Learn to use technology that will make you more efficient," is the advice of Lisa Patterson, CPA. Even though equipment varies from one company to another, being familiar with basic operations is a plus.

Of the basic skills identified so far, which do you possess? In what areas, if any, could you use instruction?

When young professionals were asked what they now know that they wish they had known while they were preparing for their career, Lyn Patterson, Staffing Coordinator for an employment company in San Diego, California, advised, "Develop as many basic skills as possible. These are expected of you from the first day and include composing letters and memos, operating copy and fax machines, and using a computer."

Another strong recommendation is to cultivate multiple skills. You may not see the connection between office skills and your chosen career field; however, most employers will be impressed with a variety of abilities. Additionally, you could be surprised. Angie, who was hired as a radiological technician in a clinic, found herself handling several word processing and billing tasks. She was rewarded verbally and financially for her versatility.

Worthy to note is the need for sales skills in a variety of fields. "New employees are typically surprised to learn that accountants must be able to sell. Competition is keen for clients, and we make a concentrated effort to

Computer skills are considered almost as basic as reading and writing in today's job market.

bring in new business," says Lisa Patterson, CPA and Senior Manager for Ernst and Young LLP. Technicians in fields that range from automotive maintenance and repair to graphic design find themselves acting as informal sales representatives for their employer.

Then because the world is changing so rapidly, willingness to learn and to adapt is essential. For example, the software that you now use could become obsolete and, at a minimum, will be updated on a regular basis. Develop a mental attitude of curiosity and openness and be sure to let a potential employer know that you want to continue to learn throughout your life. Definitely, you don't want to give the impression that you know everything. If you can convince an employer that you have needed or desired capabilities and are willing to keep updated, you will have an advantage over other applicants.

"Most people start in entry level jobs that demand bottom-line competencies. Applicants today are expected to have office skills even if they aren't applying for administrative assistant positions."

Lyn Patterson, Staffing Coordinator, The Eastridge Group, San Diego, California

Evaluating Your Career Potential

After analyzing yourself in the four developmental areas, assessing your personality, and beginning to make any needed changes, a practical evaluative tool is to develop a balance sheet of assets and liabilities (see "Assets and Liabilities" at the end of the chapter). Think of **assets** as strengths, skills, and positive experiences that will help you get the job you want. **Liabilities** include drawbacks, weaknesses, skills you lack, and negative experiences that you would rather a potential employer not know. A balance sheet benefits you in several ways.

- You can devote more time and energy to the actual job search because you've compiled all the basic information.
- You'll have a clearer idea of which careers and jobs are best for you.
- Your self-esteem and confidence will be strengthened.
- You'll know what to emphasize (assets) and what may need changing or explaining (liabilities).

What do you think would be considered liabilities to employers? Potential employers will try to uncover any evidence of negative behaviors from your past

KEY INFO

Bothersome Employee Behaviors (Cormack, 1992)

excuses	theft	vandalism
tardiness	poor quality work	personal conflicts with other employees
absenteeism	sabotage	personal conflicts with supervisors
carelessness	accident proneness	tolerance of negative behavior in others
falsification	loitering	
quitting	resistance to change	
poor service	not following rules	

record. Concerns of employers from years ago that are still true today are listed in Key Info "Bothersome Employee Behaviors."

If, before you begin your serious job search, you can change any problematic behaviors, "brush up" on skills, and acquire experience, do so. But what if this isn't possible? "I was fired from a job once. I can't change that," was a dour reply from a career seminar participant. You can either avoid revealing a drawback or explain to and convince a potential employer that the negative actions will stay in the past. The key is to plan how to discuss all liabilities. Most of us don't like to be caught "off guard," and during a job interview this is particularly uncomfortable. "Have you ever been fired?" is the question. If you have, which is a better response?

- Uh, no.
- Uh, yes.
- Well, I was, but it wasn't my fault.
- Yes, I have. When I was in my first year of college, I had a job in a restaurant. To be honest, I tried to take too many classes and was overwhelmed. I wasn't as productive at work as I could have been, and after I was late to work two times, the owner said I was no longer needed. Even though it was painful, I learned a great deal from that experience.

Knowing how to explain a liability on an application and rehearsing what to say before an interview might even increase your chances. After a practice session in a career development class, the interviewer said, "I would be inclined to hire that young man on the basis of his response about his prison sentence." When the student, who had been quite worried about his blemished record, was told that he might have gotten a job because of the positive way he discussed this liability, he and I both had a good laugh.

A successful career path does not begin with your first job. Instead, it begins with *you*. Who you are, how much genuine regard you have for yourself, and what you have to offer in a career field determine the course of your professional life. You can successfully design a career by understanding, improving, and expanding yourself.

KEY POINTS

- Career development begins with self-knowledge.
- Four development areas of the self are physical, mental, emotional, and social. Exploring the whole self is a valuable step.
- Making positive physical changes in appearance and health is beneficial to career success.
- Striving to do your best academically, being willing to learn, developing problem-solving skills, and maintaining a positive attitude foster a strong mental self.
- Understanding the emotional self, learning to express emotions constructively, and being able to change what you feel are hallmarks of a mentally healthy individual. Emotional intelligence is a major asset.
- The ability to interact with and relate to others in a positive way is essential in all career fields. Interpersonal skills are invaluable assets.
- Understanding your own and others' personalities can be extremely helpful. The eight preferences and four types revealed by the Myers–Briggs Type Indicator® provide insight. Holland's theory of six types is also very useful.
- The self-concept consists of self-descriptors, ideal self, and self-esteem.
- Self-efficacy, a belief in your capability to perform a particular task, is a definite asset in all aspects of a career.
- Employers are seeking certain traits and skills in employees. Knowing what these are will enhance your chances in the job market.
- Developing an internal locus of control helps you direct the course of your life.
- Assertiveness is highly desired in today's career world. People are not assertive at birth; they must learn to be.
- Those who succeed in developing and strengthening high levels of self-esteem are usually successful in their careers.
- Basic skills such as writing, reading comprehension, mathematics, and communication are necessary in order to get and keep jobs.
- Developing a balance sheet of assets and liabilities is an important early step in successful career development.

ONLINE RESOURCES

Career and college information: www.adventuresineducation.org

Mapping Your Future: www.mapping-your-future.com

My Future: www.myfuture.com

Self-knowledge tests: www.queendom.com/tests

Related to Myers–Briggs Type Indicator®

The Keirsey Character Sorter and the Keirsey Temperament Sorter: www.keirsey.com

Personality Type: www.personalitytype.com

Temperament Sorter Description: www.advisorteam.com

Type? (personality): www.knowyourtype.com

Related to Holland's Theory

John Holland's Self-Directed Search: www.self-directed-search.com

The Career Interests Game: http://career.missouri.edu

KEY STEPS

SELF-APPRAISAL

Understanding yourself is necessary in designing a satisfying career. Before you read the book and complete the other activities in this section, honestly rate yourself using this scale. Then compute a score. Do this again after you've read the book.

5 = Perfect (couldn't improve)

4 = Very good (almost to the desired level)

3 = Average (could be improved)

2 = Below average (could be much better)

1 = Poor (needs a great deal of improvement)

_______ 1. How well do I really know and understand myself, including my personality, interests, and skills?

_______ 2. How much regard do I have for myself?

_______ 3. How would I rate my attitude about life?

_______ 4. How well do I handle my emotions and cope with stress?

_______ 5. How well do I know and understand my values?

_______ 6. How satisfied am I with my career choice? (If you haven't chosen one, score as 2.)

_______ 7. How well have I researched career fields and job opportunities?

_______ 8. How would I rate my writing skills?

_______ 9. How prepared am I to participate in a job interview?

_______ 10. How well do I get along with people?

Total your scores and divide by 10 to get an average score. If you have less than a 5.0 average, this book will help you. If you scored a 5.0 (perfect), you can benefit from learning about perfectionism!

My average self-appraisal score is: _______________

Honestly reflect on what you hope to gain from this book. How can it help you as you design your career?

PERSONALITY AWARENESS

Circle what you think (or know) your four MBTI preferences to be. For each, describe some of your behaviors that support that choice. If you have no supporting behaviors for one, explain why you think you are more like the opposite preference. You may use other paper in order to elaborate.

Extraversion ____________ Introversion ____________

Sensing ____________ Intuition ____________

Thinking ____________ Feeling ____________

Judgment ____________ Perception ____________

- Identify a personality trait you especially like in yourself and that is related to one of the preferences. Write the preference, how it helps you, and for what reason(s) you are satisfied with it.

- Do the same with a personality characteristic in yourself that could be disadvantageous. Be sure to name the preference that is related to the characteristic.

HOW WELL DO I REALLY KNOW MYSELF?

Use the information in this chapter to complete the first inventory about yourself (three pages). Have another person fill out the second three-page inventory about you. Do not work together. The object is to compare the two inventories.

DESCRIPTORS: Describe yourself in the following areas of self using at least four descriptors for each.

PHYSICAL (appearance, condition of body, health)

____

____

MENTAL (abilities, preferred ways of thinking and learning, interests, attitude)

____

____

EMOTIONAL (usual or general feelings or typical ones in certain situations, description of mood)

____

____

SOCIAL (behaviors around others, preferred social activities)

____

____

If you were to achieve your ideal self, would these descriptors be different, and, if so, in what ways? Use other paper, if needed.

Physical: ______________________________

____

Mental: ______________________________

____

Emotional: ______________________________

____

Social: ______________________________

____

COMPLETE THE FOLLOWING SENTENCES.

The career field that interests me most is

Two of my marketable skills or talents are

Three characteristics or behaviors I appreciate in myself are

One thing I would like to improve about myself is

I am proud of myself for

A career goal I have for myself is

What do I value? (Name at least five.)

What would I do with one million tax-free dollars? (Try to account specifically for all of it. Use other paper, if needed.)

During an average weekday, how do I spend my time? (Account for all 24 hours.)

The X on the continuum below shows how I assess my attitude.

VERY NEGATIVE | NEGATIVE | AVERAGE | POSITIVE | VERY POSITIVE

How do I rate my current level of self-esteem?

1 = very low 2 = low 3 = average 4 = high 5 = very high

One belief I have about myself (self-fulfilling prophecy) is:

I have self-efficacy about (list three specific tasks, talents, or skills):

HOW WELL DOES ANOTHER PERSON KNOW ME?

Please answer the following questions about ________________.

My relationship to this person is as a (an) ________________.

DESCRIPTORS. Describe this person in the following four areas of self using at least four descriptors for each.

PHYSICAL (appearance, condition of body, health)

____

____

MENTAL (abilities, preferred ways of thinking and learning, interests, attitude)

____

____

EMOTIONAL (usual or general feelings or typical ones in certain situations, description of mood)

____

____

SOCIAL (behaviors around others, preferred social activities)

____

____

If this person were to achieve his or her ideal self, would these descriptors be different, and, if so, in what ways? Use other paper, if needed.

Physical: ____

____

Mental: ____

____

Emotional: ____

____

Social: ____

____

COMPLETE THE FOLLOWING SENTENCES.

A career field that interests this person most is

____

____

Two of this person's marketable skills or talents are

____

____

Three characteristics or behaviors this person appreciates about him- or herself are

____

____

____

One thing about self this person would like to improve is

____

____

One thing about self this person is proud of is

____

____

One of this person's career goals is

____

____

What does this person value? (Name at least five.)

____

____

____

____

____

What would this person do with a million tax-free dollars?

During an average weekday, how does this person spend his or her time?

Thinking of attitude as a broad outlook on life, place an X on the continuum to describe this person.

VERY NEGATIVE — NEGATIVE — AVERAGE — POSITIVE — VERY POSITIVE

Thinking of self-esteem as a value placed on self or genuine regard for who one is, what is this person's current level of self-esteem?

1 = very low 2 = low 3 = average 4 = high 5 = very high

THANK YOU VERY MUCH FOR YOUR HELP!

HOW ASSERTIVE AM I?

Answer the following as yes, no, or unknown (i.e., neither yes nor no, or about half the time).

_______ 1. I usually express my anger in constructive, nonthreatening ways.

_______ 2. My posture and manner reflect confidence.

_______ 3. I maintain steady eye contact.

_______ 4. I use "I" statements when expressing my opinion.

_______ 5. I am flexible and willing to compromise.

_______ 6. I tell people no in a pleasant way when I don't want to do something, and I say yes when I do.

_______ 7. I maintain my rights and don't let others take advantage of me.

_______ 8. I do what I think is best rather than follow others.

_______ 9. When someone is being offensive or annoying, I tell him or her.

_______ 10. I listen with an open mind.

The more yes answers you had, the more assertive you are. Select any behaviors that you lack and strive to develop them.

Describe a past experience in which you were assertive or one where assertive behavior would have been advantageous. Be sure to describe your actions.

____

____

____

____

____

____

____

____

____

____

____

____

ASSETS AND LIABILITIES

Read in Chapter 1 about evaluating yourself by developing a balance sheet of assets and liabilities. Next to each of the categories below, list your assets in the left column and your liabilities in the right. For example, for educational experiences, assets are diplomas, degrees, specialized training, certification, licensure, scholarships, a high grade point average, and the like. Lack of any of these and any evidence of weaknesses in education and training are liabilities. Be very complete and use other paper, if necessary. This activity can serve as the basic groundwork for designing your career and will help in all stages of a job search.

	Assets	**Liabilities**
Interests	__________	__________
	__________	__________
	__________	__________
Skills	__________	__________
	__________	__________
	__________	__________
Educational experiences	__________	__________
	__________	__________
	__________	__________
Work experiences	__________	__________
	__________	__________
	__________	__________
Volunteer work	__________	__________
	__________	__________
	__________	__________
Personality characteristics	__________	__________
	__________	__________
	__________	__________

	Assets	**Liabilities**
Work habits	______	______
	______	______
	______	______
Personal and professional goals	______	______
	______	______
	______	______

Select your top two assets and your top liability (if any) in each category (16 assets; 8 liabilities) and write them below. Then choose six major assets and three liabilities and write them at the bottom. Practice discussing your assets so that you can use them to answer interview questions such as: "Why should we hire you?" and "What do you have to offer?" Decide how you could explain your liabilities in a positive way. If you have any that can be changed before your job search, set a goal to do so.

Assets		**Liabilities**
______	______	______
______	______	______
______	______	______
______	______	______
______	______	______
______	______	______
______	______	______
______	______	______

Final List	**Assets**	**Liabilities**
	______	______
	______	______
	______	______
	______	
	______	
	______	

2

Communication is the key to career success.

Interacting Positively with Others

Positive interactions are needed and desired by well-adjusted individuals. The previous chapter and other resources can help you develop the best possible self, which then allows you to positively connect with others. More than any other characteristic, the ability to interact with and relate to others determines the extent of career success for almost everyone. Executives who eventually failed did so most often because of an interpersonal flaw, not a technical inability (Gibbs, 1995). Technology's impact on the workplace puts everyone's "people skills" to their greatest test. Your interpersonal skills and ability to communicate could make or break your career success (Carrig, 1999).

"Having strong 'people skills' is a necessity. At work you relate to everyone from the clerks to the president of the company. And if the clients or customers don't like you, you'll soon be out of a job."

LISA PATTERSON, CPA and Senior Manager, Ernst and Young LLP, Los Angeles

Being Open-Minded

Interacting and establishing relationships require an openness to the prospect of meeting and getting to know others, including people who don't look, think, or act as you do. When you appreciate **diversity**—the differences and variety in human beings—your professional life is enriched, and career success is much more likely.

FIRST IMPRESSIONS

Immediate judgments, known as **first impressions,** are unavoidable. These are based on physical appearance and overt actions. Place yourself in an office setting at the beginning of a job interview. The interviewer, an older, sophisticated-looking woman, is reading some notes when you enter. After a minute, she looks up and in a cool tone of voice says, "Good afternoon. I'm Ms. Thomas." Her handshake is overly firm. What would be your impressions? How would these differ if the interviewer greeted you immediately with a bright smile, said, "Hello. I'm Sally Thomas and I'm delighted you are here," and gave you a pleasantly firm handshake?

Allowing a first impression to dictate the course of an interaction or the ensuing relationship is not recommended. For any number of reasons, people are not always what they seem to be. After analyzing an impression, it's best to let time and involvement determine how realistic it was.

ACCEPTANCE AND APPRECIATION

Entire books have been written about diversity, the presence of differences. Diversity in a society means that a variety of groups are present; often, these are racial and ethnic groups. This brief coverage can help you examine some of your attitudes and, hopefully, show you that one of the greatest handicaps to career success is an inability to accept and appreciate differences. It's easy to be prejudiced; yet, the key to success is to eliminate these negative feelings and develop an egalitarian attitude, a belief that all people are equal.

Generalized ideas about groups of people are **stereotypes.** Whenever there is a difference, stereotyping is possible. Even though some stereotypes present a positive picture of a group, the typical ones focus on the negative. In all cases, stereotypes can limit people or place unrealistic expectations upon them. Reducing an individual to a label based on his or her category is misleading and insulting.

Check to see how quickly stereotypes come to your mind. Think of a group, then a stereotype about that group.

The tendency to generalize is especially common when the individual is outside one's own group. One day during a class discussion, a white male student volunteered to tell the reason he was prejudiced. "When I was a kid, three black kids came into my yard and beat me up. I hated them for it, and I've hated all black people since then." Obviously, he had suffered from a bad experience and had generalized from it. He was asked to use his imagination and pretend that the three boys had been white. Then he was asked, "Would you now hate all white people because three white boys beat you up?" His quick answer was, "Well, no." Because he knew that members of his own race were diverse, he didn't generalize.

Negative stereotyping usually leads to **prejudice,** an unfavorable attitude and feeling that others are inferior or less than you in some way. What often accompanies it is a feeling of dislike, disgust, or hatred. Prejudice is learned from others and by generalizing from a negative experience. Prejudice is insensitive and illogical; career-wise, being prejudiced is a detriment to success.

Related to prejudice is **discrimination,** which is unfair treatment of people. Because discrimination is usually observable behavior, it can be outlawed. Yet, covert and subtle discrimination is still practiced and is often based on prejudice. Discrimination in the workplace is discussed in Chapter 8.

Ideally, you do not make decisions based on stereotypes, do not harbor prejudices, and do not discriminate. If your thinking is stereotypic and you have negative feelings about certain people, act in your best interests and challenge these thoughts and feelings. The following questions can help (Hanna, 2003).

- *Is my thinking reasonable and rational?* If you take pride in your mental abilities, you will want to eliminate inaccurate and unreasonable stereotypic thinking. Refuse to accept the idea that all African Americans or Anglo Americans, Catholics or Protestants, old people or young people, and heterosexuals or gays are one way.

Diversity is the norm in today's workplace.

- *Am I being fair?* How would I feel if I were the victim of prejudice? Most human beings are concerned about justice and fairness. Discrimination is unfair, and even the thinking that can lead to it is usually unjust.
- *Am I basing my impressions on knowledge of an individual or only on the person as a member of a group?* Negative labeling can keep us from getting to know the "real" person. Moving from a collective impression, which is a stereotype, to an individual analysis is the key. Being free of prejudice means your positive or negative feelings about a person are not based on preconceived labeling.
- *Can I come up with a single good reason to contribute to prejudice in the world?* Individuals and societies suffer from prejudice, and ultimately, everyone is harmed.

In the work world, stereotyping and prejudice create problems. Most employers aren't impressed with fixed, inflexible ways of seeing the world. Those who stereotype and label are perceived not only as negative and lacking in knowledge but also as rigid thinkers. As one employer related: "I realize the applicant was from a rural area where there isn't much diversity, and, perhaps, he hadn't been educated about it, but when he used the term 'colored people,' it was a definite turn-off."

Lack of prejudice does not mean blindness to differences. A person can be aware of diversity in race, ethnicity, sex, age, sexual orientation, religion, and even personality preferences; the key is to not let differences stop you from relating. You can learn from diversity and even enjoy it. Sameness can be boring.

The U. S. Census Bureau projects that within the next few years racial and ethnic minorities will make up nearly one-half of all Americans (Sabo, 2000). The workplace is already a mosaic composed of different colors, cultures, and types of individuals and, obviously, will become more so. Additionally, you will likely have diversity experiences because of international travel and interactions. More than two million North Americans work for employers in other countries (Chaney & Martin, 2000). According to Jan Wulf, who teaches Business Communication, anyone in a career field needs to know about cultural diversity on international, national, and local levels. She points out that awareness and sensitivity are needed in four general areas of diversity: language (verbal and non-verbal), religion, treatment of women, and food. "Specific coursework related to intercultural differences is extremely important," she says. A chapter in the book *The Power of Positive Confrontation* (Pachter, 2000) provides invaluable information about international etiquette. All kinds of diversity provide opportunities for expansion of self. The concept of **multiculturalism**—recognition and appreciation of cultural differences—benefits society and its individual members. If you have not done so, seek opportunities to learn about different groups of people. The ability to view differences as gifts and opportunities is an invaluable career asset.

Using Assertiveness

Positive relationships of all types thrive on assertiveness, the ability to maintain legitimate rights and express thoughts and feelings in nonthreatening ways. When one person is passive and allows another to dominate, a relationship suffers. Moreover, few people enjoy working with an aggressive individual who wants to dominate and take advantage of others. He or she may prevail; however, the price is high.

A situation can warrant a mild, moderate, or intense degree of assertiveness. Begin with a mild approach—a simple explanation of circumstances and a request for a change. If that doesn't work, you can use a moderate approach that sounds more direct. Only when necessary and after you have weighed the possible consequences would you use the intense level.

Let's look at some possible situations. Another employee named Josh and you share a computer terminal; actually, he uses it much more than you do. It is Friday afternoon, and you want to develop a memo before you leave. The assertive approach would be to say, "Josh, I'd like to talk with you for a few minutes." Then when you have his attention, begin at the mild level:

> *Over the past few weeks I'm having difficulty completing some work because the computer is not available. I realize you, too, are busy, and I'd like for us to schedule computer time so it's fair for both of us. I have a memo to do this afternoon.*

Remember that your body posture, eye contact, and tone of voice need to reflect confidence, poise, and openness. In most cases, this assertiveness level would be effective.

A more difficult situation involves a supervisor. Debra has scheduled you to work late several days in succession. You are experiencing a high level of stress and actually feel ill. After requesting an opportune time to discuss the matter, begin by stating the extra efforts you have already made. Express a willingness to be a good team member, then use the mild assertiveness level.

> *I am now at a point where my effectiveness and productivity are low, and I feel ill. I would appreciate it if you could find someone else to handle the extra work right now as that seems to me to be in everybody's best interest.*

Hopefully, your request will be met. However, if it isn't, you can move to the moderate level.

> *I realize that you are in a bind, and I wish there were an easy solution. I think it's only fair that I be given some relief. I prefer not to continue working late right now.*

Before using the intense level, consider the possible outcomes. The worst case scenario would be to lose your job, so be sure you are prepared. Generally, a supervisor can handle intense assertiveness.

> *I have given this a great deal of thought and know that I have reached my limit. Even though I want to help and certainly prefer to continue in this job, I am not going to continue to do extra work at this time. I'll be willing to do more again in the future.*

The intense level is risky. Yet, a supervisor who would terminate you because of your assertiveness is not the person for whom you deserve to work. Additionally, people who don't seem to be able to ever say no invariably end up with pent-up resentment that is physically and psychologically damaging.

Learning to say no is difficult for many people. A basic step is to decide that doing so is acceptable. A cognitive technique can be useful. Ask yourself, "What's the worst thing that will happen if I say no? How does that compare to what happens to me when I say yes and resent it?" Then, continue to think, "What if the person becomes angry with me because I say no? How bad will that be?" Keep telling yourself that you have the right to say no.

Once you have decided to decline, you can practice how to say it. Of course you can just say the two-letter word nicely; however, most people feel more comfortable with other kinds of statements such as one of the following.

- "I have decided not to take on any more right now."
- "I would like to say yes; however, this time I'm not going to do that."
- "I've been doing some time management work and prioritizing, and right now other things come first."
- "Thanks for asking; however, I'm not going to participate right now."
- "Believe it or not, I'm going to say no."
- "I have a hard time saying no; this time I'm going to stick with it."

Saying no firmly and politely is assertive behavior. A balance between saying no and saying yes is reasonable during your career life. See how assertive you are and in what areas you can improve by reviewing "How Assertive Am I?" at the end of Chapter 1.

How we act, interact, and react with people affects all aspects of life. Learning and applying positive interpersonal skills will create the successful career you desire.

Communicating: The Key to Success

Foremost among all relating skills is the ability to communicate. **Communication** is defined as a complex process of interaction through which two or more individuals share information in an attempt to understand. With positive, effective communication, you can build rewarding relationships and dramatically affect your career.

When you think of communicating, what behaviors do you include? Look around you. If you are in the presence of another person, communication is taking place.

What exactly transpires as we communicate? Usually, we think first of speaking or talking; for some, communication is identified only with talking. "He doesn't communicate," was used to describe a man who rarely talked.

Talking certainly plays a key role in communication; however, equally or even of more import is listening. Nonverbal behaviors, even if nobody is talking or listening, definitely have a critical impact. More than any other factor, communication determines the quality of interactions and relationships. Even though most people are born with the ability to speak and hear, communication skills must be learned.

The Importance of Communication

- Identified as the most essential skill for the workforce of the twenty-first century by a group of human resource professionals (Sabo, 2000).
- Lack of skills cited as the single most prevalent reason that people do not advance in their careers, according to the *Wall Street Journal* (Cole, 1997).
- At the top of the desired list in the hiring of new employees (Daniel, 1998).

Active listening and communicating directions clearly to others were identified as interpersonal skills most needed yet most lacking by Pat Galitz and Nancy Krumland, business administration instructors. Often in troubled relationships, communication is identified as the most problematic factor; conversely, it is credited as the most strengthening factor in successful relationships. Career success is virtually impossible without positive communication skills. Lack of effective communication skills most often leads to problems. According to Richard Ross, a college dean and former senior vice president of a savings and loan association, "Difficulties arise because of a lack of understanding between a person delivering services and either a customer, client, or student."

"Employers say our students possess needed technical skills. What is often lacking is the ability to communicate in a positive, clear, and effective manner."

SHERYL PIENING, Management and Human Relations Instructor, Southeast Community College, Milford, Nebraska

As communication takes place, individuals are continually sending, receiving, interpreting, and reacting. Ideally, the communicators will create and share a common meaning. Unfortunately, misinterpretation is often the case. Ways to avoid problems are covered later in this chapter.

Because communication is so consequential, one might expect it would be formally taught; rarely is this the case. More commonly, we are left to pick it up however we can. If communication skills are left to amateur teachers who learned from other untrained people, it is no wonder that difficulties are common.

CHARACTERISTICS OF A POSITIVE COMMUNICATOR

Several of the same qualities that enhance career potential are beneficial when communicating. A positive attitude and having genuine regard for others come from your own healthy self-esteem and create an environment for positive communication. Honesty in communication means authenticity, an invaluable quality in healthy exchanges. Honest communicators don't mislead or try to manipulate, and they create a climate of trust.

Openness and willingness to share about oneself are essential. A closed person who isn't willing to learn about others or who is reluctant to disclose information is a poor interpersonal communication candidate. Expressiveness of emotion enhances health and well-being, and it also helps people be better communicators. Being interested in others and appropriate self-disclosure are definite assets. A good communicator knows when and how much to share and to ask.

Flexibility is also needed. Rigid individuals aren't enjoyable to be around and are usually frustrating conversationalists. Being closed-minded is detrimental to a give-and-take communication process. Opinions can be stated in flexible ways, as will be discussed later.

A sense of humor, while not a necessity, separates good communicators from outstanding ones. Having a sense of humor does not mean telling one joke after another. Instead, you see humor in life, add a witty spark to conversations, don't take yourself too seriously, and appreciate the humor of others. It's important to demonstrate sensitivity and avoid sarcasm.

Finally, being understanding and capable of making reasonable interpretations is needed in order to achieve a shared meaning. Locked-in thinking, the tendency to see things only one way, causes communication problems. Being able to see several alternatives and showing that you want to understand another's point of view contribute to an affirmative atmosphere. You can check your communication characteristics by completing an activity in Key Steps at the end of the chapter.

BECOMING A POSITIVE LISTENER

Were you taught to listen or were you just told to listen? For most of us, we were just told; in fact, we were probably told several times! Listening is not a given. Instead, it is an art that is learned and that can be improved.

Perhaps you actually learned some listening skills; however, for most of us, being able to hear meant that we were expected to know how to listen. Kurt Yost, an executive director of a banking association, commented:

> I spent years in school learning about history, math, and science. In my career I spend most of my time communicating, much of which is listening. How much training did I get in listening? None. If they taught it, I missed it.

Actually, most of us missed it because listening usually isn't taught. Of all the language arts learning experiences in our schools, listening is the most neglected.

"Listening is the most important communication skill. When you let another person know by your listening that you really want to understand, that is very flattering to him or her."

JEANNE BAER, President, Creative Training Solutions, Lincoln, Nebraska

What is involved in listening? When someone says, "I heard you," is that listening? Actually, hearing or taking in of auditory sounds is only a part of **listening,** which is the active process of hearing, interpreting, and then providing feedback.

Removing Barriers

Other obstacles, along with a lack of training, can get in the way of positive listening. You can eliminate barriers after you recognize them. The most common ones are lack of interest and preoccupation. If you aren't interested in what someone else is saying, you have choices determined by the circumstances. You may force yourself to listen, you may only pretend to be listening, or you can be honest and tell the person you are not interested. Obviously, if the communication pertains to your job, you are better off listening and trying to develop an interest.

We can be preoccupied for any number of reasons, including thinking about other more pressing or interesting subjects and experiencing certain emotions or high levels of stress. A common source of preoccupation is self-imposed. Someone says, "I can listen to you while I'm doing this." It's possible to do more than one thing at a time; frequently, however, the concentration needed to listen isn't adequate. Not only is it rude to engage in another activity when listening is expected, the chances are that valuable information will be missed or misunderstood. Full attention is required if you are going to do your best listening.

The environment is full of potential barriers. Noise can interfere with conversation. Tim has frustrating conversations with a supervisor who leaves the office door open. "It's hard to concentrate because people are coming and going, the telephone is ringing, and other conversations are taking place." Distraction can also be visual or related to temperature and air flow. Listening situations deserve an environment free from diversions.

An interesting obstacle is our own psychological filter made up of preconceived ideas, moods, assumptions, labels, stereotypes, past experiences, degrees of self-esteem, emotions, hopes, and memories. We often let a clogged filter determine our level of listening. As selective listeners, we can hear only half or less of what is being said. For example, if you know the opinions of a co-worker, you are apt to "tune out" him or her. A major problem can occur at work if you assume that you already know what to do and don't listen carefully to directions. Just as a homeowner periodically checks a furnace filter, examining your psychological one is a good idea. You may not be able to entirely eliminate all the "dust," yet being aware and discarding whatever you can will enhance your listening abilities.

Do you know that you can listen at a faster rate than a person can talk? Figures vary; however, the average rate of speech is about 125 to 175 words a minute, while the brain thinks at the rate of 500 to 1,000 words a minute. Because of this, listeners are likely to mentally finish the speaker's sentence and predict what is coming. During the time difference the mind can wander, which creates a definite barrier.

The listener's intentions can be an obstacle. People can listen only enough to gain an advantage. They may want to persuade individuals to adopt their ideas or to manipulate others in some way. Instead of truly listening, they are thinking and rehearsing what they will say, and they frequently interrupt in their haste. Some want to use information in harmful ways, as in the case of gossip. Certainly we listen for different reasons; however, those interested in becoming positive listeners resist having negative intentions. Eliminating all barriers sets the stage for the best possible listening.

Improving Listening Behaviors

Positive listening is assuredly active, not passive. "Bumps on logs" make terrible listeners! We can improve our listening by focusing on body position and behaviors.

Do you appear to be listening? Think of what a good listener does.

The way you position yourself in relation to the speaker makes a major difference in the communication exchange. A distance of 1.5 feet to 4 feet is comfortable for most people. Speaking and listening at a similar eye level sets a positive tone. If one stands while the other sits, the exchange is likely to feel unequal, and the one seated is at a disadvantage. Of utmost importance is to face the speaker. Turning your body away carries a message of disinterest or disgust, or both, and severely lessens your involvement. Sitting so you are across from the speaker and leaning slightly forward demonstrate attentiveness.

Adopting an open, attentive posture indicates interest, openness, and involvement. Sitting with legs and arms crossed, slouching, and leaning away from the speaker give negative impressions. Instead, a positive listener sits with hands at the sides or on the lap. A slumped posture may be comfortable, yet if you are truly interested, your body usually reflects this by a generally upright posture. It's important to appear relaxed, as well. The next time you are in a classroom or another listening situation, periodically check body position. What impression are you giving?

Maintaining steady eye contact in the American society is expected. Usually, conversations don't start until eye contact is made. Employers often have negative impressions of applicants who don't "look them in the eye." Poor eye contact may be interpreted as a lack of confidence or as a sign of dishonesty. However, direct eye contact may be culturally discouraged and looking down is then considered a sign of respect. Often, job candidates from other countries or cultures are surprised to learn that they are expected to look directly at the other person.

> *"Direct eye contact is the most essential nonverbal behavior in getting a job and will make a difference throughout one's career."*
>
> **NANCY BROWN,** R.N., Program Manager

How can a person develop steady eye contact? It's helpful to realize that direct eye contact does not mean staring fixedly nor does it even require looking directly into the other person's eyes. If you are within the comfortable distance zone mentioned earlier, you can focus anywhere on the face including the forehead, nose, mouth, or chin. Looking at the speaker's face for about three-quarters of the time in glances lasting from one to seven seconds is sufficient. Incidentally, as a speaker, you may look at the listener about half the time and glance away more often. Even though it may sound silly, ask a family member or friend to assess your eye contact and to help you improve, if necessary. Awareness and reminders to yourself will usually lead to better eye contact.

Responsiveness is delivered to a great extent by changes in facial expression. A "poker face" is helpful in a card game, yet is generally useless and often demeaning in the communication process. A positive listener reacts to what is being said by registering appropriate thinking and feeling responses. About 20,000 different facial expressions are possible (Carl, 1980), so it won't be overly difficult to change yours! Maintaining an interested, pleasant look will enhance your standing in all encounters. Joel commented, "I know it's important to smile, but I hate the way my teeth look." He finally decided that getting his teeth fixed was worth the price he had been paying in decreased interactive skills. You can ask a family member or friend to honestly evaluate your facial expressions.

A positive listening behavior is nodding the head. An affirmative nod shows the speaker that you have heard and understood and usually that you also agree. A nod can motivate and energize a speaker, so "nodders" are wonderful to have in an exchange. Even a side-to-side nod indicating confusion or disagreement is helpful if the objective is to arrive at a shared meaning. Nodding can be developed and, initially, can seem fake and mechanical, yet, after time, feel natural. It is possible to nod too much as a student discovered from a videotaped practice interview. "I nodded so much that it looked as if my head would fall off," she said as she vowed to decrease her nods by about half. Other body movements such as tilting the head to the side or shrugging the shoulders can also provide helpful feedback.

Touching is not usually thought of as a listening behavior; however, when appropriate, it can be quite effective. Generally, the arm is considered to be a neutral or nonvulnerable area and usually acceptable. Touch can be a gesture of warmth and concern; it can also be perceived as seductive, impertinent, annoying, or degrading. Examine your reasons for touching and be sure they are positive ones. Professionals can use touch to be supportive and more effective, and in certain settings, it is quite appropriate. Counselors and therapists show concern and support while those in health-related fields are even expected to touch a patient in their job-related duties. A pat on the hand, arm, or shoulder, a squeeze, and even a hug, in proper circumstances, add a dimension to the listening process.

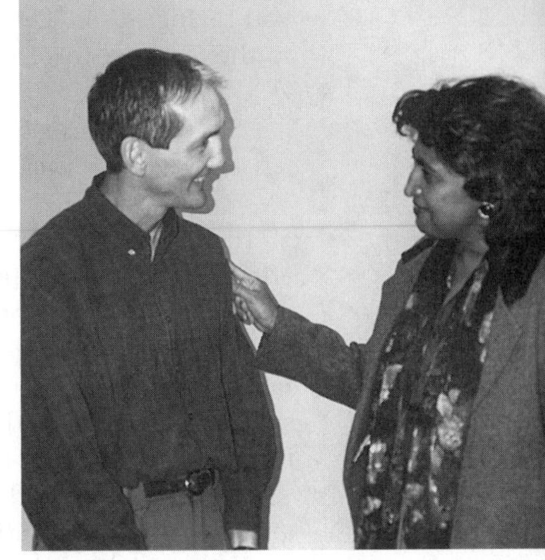

Active listening skills create a positive communication climate.

Of the active listening behaviors identified so far, which ones do you use?

Generally, listening is a nonverbal activity, yet verbal responses are signs of a positive listener. These can vary from a simple word such as "oh," to a statement such as, "That's great," or "I had never heard that." Be careful that you don't overuse these as too many interrupt the speaker's flow. "Really," "I know," or "I understand" said after each of the speaker's sentences is distracting and annoying. Questions that encourage a speaker to continue or to expand are excellent responses. "What course of action did you take?" "What is the company's policy on that?" "What motivated you to pursue this career?" are examples. If you are a positive listener, your questions do not move the conversation in a different direction. Note the difference in these two exchanges.

1. SPEAKER: *I'm upset because she didn't give me the day off.*
   LISTENER: *Did she just forget?*

2. SPEAKER: *I'm upset because she didn't give me the day off.*
   LISTENER: *Well, did you hear that she fired Joe?*

When you ask questions that move the conversation in the same direction, you are telling the speaker that what is being said is of interest and you want to hear more. That's affirming!

Verbal responses can include more than short comments or questions. Restating what you thought was said in your own words is **paraphrasing.** Using such lead-ins as "It sounds like," "In other words," "You mean that," "What I hear you saying is," or "Let me make sure I understand what you mean," you don't add to the message; instead, you repeat the meaning as you understand it. For example:

SPEAKER: *This job is really getting to me.*
LISTENER: *It sounds as if your job is really stressful.*

Paraphrasing may seem clumsy, yet with practice, it becomes easier. The benefits are worth the initial discomfort. People like to be understood, and they appreciate your attempt to do so. Paraphrasing can keep anger and other emotions from escalating, calm a stressful situation, decrease the possibility of misinterpretation, and aid you in remembering what was said. In the previous dialogue, the speaker could agree that the responsibilities are stressful, state that there are difficulties with people at work, or describe exactly the reason.

Going a little further than paraphrasing is **clarifying,** which includes restating and questioning in order to get more information. "Do you mean that your responsibilities are overwhelming right now?" or "Do you feel differently now than you did a few months ago?" are examples of clarifying. You can also tell the speaker your interpretation. "It sounds as if you support the seat-belt law," or "I'm getting the impression that you are depressed" can show both interest and concern.

Feedback includes all behaviors that indicate listening. **Verbal feedback,** specifically, is responding with what you, as the listener, think, feel, or sense. The best feedback is offered in an honest, nonthreatening, and supportive way after the speaker is entirely finished. This is the time to let the speaker know how his or her words and actions have affected you, and it can be a "golden opportunity." Sasha asked her supervisor if she could leave early for a dentist's appointment.

The response was a brusque reply, "If you need to," which seemed to match a facial expression of annoyance. Instead of retreating, Sasha clarified by asking, "Are you sure you don't mind?" The supervisor looked surprised and said, "No, why do you ask?" Sasha then described the facial expression and tone of voice and was heartened to hear a chuckle and, "I probably looked and sounded annoyed because I was thinking of a meeting I don't want to attend after lunch. I'm glad you said something because I certainly don't want to give the wrong impression."

Assertiveness is helpful when it comes to clarifying and providing honest feedback. Because of the complexity of human behavior, misinterpretations are common. Such variances as tone of voice, volume, facial expression, and body position may be meaningless and still create ill will. Positive listeners are committed to being clear and sharing a common meaning.

Knowing what not to do when listening deserves attention. Interrupting is common and especially hard to avoid for those who enjoy talking. If you know that you are guilty of jumping in before another is finished talking, make a strong effort to keep still. Certain sounds and actions are also disconcerting. Some of these include rolling of the eyes, sighing, yawning, pulling back the corners of the mouth, and drumming of a finger on a table or desk. Any behavior that indicates disinterest, insensitivity, or disdain is rude and is to be avoided. How would you rate your listening skills? Take the inventory "How Well Do You Listen" at the end of the chapter and honestly grade yourself.

Using Specific Types of Listening

Even though all listening is active, specific types of listening are most effective in different situations. Using **receptive listening** means that you resist certain behaviors and remain quiet until the speaker is completely through. As mentioned earlier, interrupting is to be avoided. Even if you don't interrupt, be careful about the following.

- *Judging or putting down the speaker.* Keep critical, judgmental, and admonishing reactions to yourself.
- *One-upping.* Avoid jumping in with your own comment or story that is more dramatic, more interesting, better, or worse than the speaker's. One especially disturbing lead-in, used far too often, is "That's nothing." What the person has told you is something as opposed to nothing, and is to be acknowledged as such.
- *Advice giving and problem solving.* Even though advice and solutions can be helpful, most of us respond too quickly and don't allow the person to finish. What can happen is that the entire story isn't told, or, in many cases, the speaker is denied a healthy release of emotion.

Empathic listening means awareness of the speaker's emotions to the point that the listener feels similarly. A listener uses nonverbal and verbal responses to show empathy. Saying "I know exactly what you feel" is not recommended. Telling the person that you understand the reason for the feeling or that you have a strong sense of what is being felt is more realistic. In the past, empathy was not expected in the work world. Today's supervisors and employees are usually encouraged to demonstrate empathy, and the listening role affords a tremendous opportunity to do so.

"In order for us to help patients, communication skills are mandatory. With all the emotions that can arise when someone is in the dental chair, we must possess the talents to effectively handle each situation. We must also demonstrate empathy and develop rapport. These go deeper than just understanding a person."

JAMES SAHLING, D.D.S., P.C., Lincoln, Nebraska

More controlling than either receptive or empathic is **directive listening,** which consists of directing the exchange, usually by asking questions. A good job interviewer will use directive listening to learn about job candidates. Both the speaker and the listener share the responsibility of information gathering. New employees may use this type of listening to elicit needed information and later to learn new skills and understand policies and procedures.

Different types of questions are used depending upon the circumstances, and experts have ranked them according to desirability (Miller, Wackman, Nunnally, & Miller, 1992). Least desirable are "why" questions. People often react with defensiveness and tension when confronted by "Why?" One woman commented, "I hate it when my supervisor comes in and invariably asks me, 'Why are you doing that?' or 'Why are you doing it that way?'" Other ways of asking about reasons are less likely to be negatively received. "How did you decide to do that?" or "What were your reasons for that choice?" are possibilities.

Listening is of great significance in the communication process. If it is one of your strengths, you have an advantage, and it would be wise to let potential employers know of your listening skills. Throughout your career life, listening will be a significant asset.

DEVELOPING AN OPEN STYLE OF VERBALIZING

Even though you can send a great deal of information without talking, speaking is of primary importance in the communication process. Both what is said and how it is presented deserve attention. During your entire career, others will assess you on both. The most powerful tools in this society are words, according to Harvey Mackay (1993), international speaker, author, and CEO of his own business. He contends that upgrading your communication skills is the surest way to open the door to a job or to jump-start a stalled career.

Have you ever thought about the way you deliver your message? **Style** refers to how one verbalizes. Communication styles affect how the speaker comes across and usually the type of response. The two general types are closed and open. Note the difference in the following comments.

> CLOSED STYLE: "*This company doesn't care about the employees. Nobody is paid enough, and you never get the recognition you deserve. The managers should take a good look at the way they always act around the employees!*"
>
> OPEN STYLE: "*I don't think the company shows enough regard for the employees. As far as I'm concerned, most of us aren't paid the salary we deserve and seldom is recognition given when it's deserved. I think managers would be wise to examine their behaviors around their employees and to make constructive changes.*"

Essentially, the same message was delivered, but the listener's reactions would likely be different. The **closed style** uses definite comments that leave little room for a reasonable response. Positive exchange is stifled because of its absoluteness, finality, forcefulness, and all-inclusive/all-exclusive language. Opinions stated as inflexible truths invariably foster a negative communication climate, whereas the **open style** is refreshing and encourages discussion. One's point of view is stated in a flexible manner that invites a reasonable, positive response. Rather than offending or "turning others off," open communicators attract people and are more likely to develop and maintain positive relationships.

To change the closed style to one of openness requires awareness of the three types of closed communication. Then it's a matter of following certain guidelines as you rephrase.

Recognizing dogmatic type. Think of statements that sound "definitely definite," rigid, and inflexible. A **dogmatic** communicator sounds like a final authority and expresses opinion as fact. Read the closed style example about the company not caring about its employees, and note that each statement is dogmatic. Incidentally, if the person had said, "This company does care about its employees," it would still be dogmatic! How a comment is stated, not its content, makes it dogmatic. Most people do not realize how definite their opinions often sound.

Think of some dogmatic statements you have used or heard recently.

Using "I" statements. The basic technique of open communication is the use of **"I" statements.** These eliminate the dogmatic element, and because a person is speaking for self, they are considered assertive language. "I" statements can be divided into two categories: actual "I" statements in which the word "I" is used within the phrase (see Figure 2.1) and phrases that convey an "I" meaning (see Figure 2.2). Notice that "I know" is not considered an "I" statement because if used correctly, it is fact, not opinion. Unfortunately and incorrectly, people do use it when expressing an opinion as in, "I know this company doesn't care about its employees."

Actual "I" expressions or phrases that give an "I" meaning can be used at the beginning of a statement, in the middle, or even at the end. Be careful of the inflection in your voice when using an "I" statement. If you say, "***I*** think" or "in *my* opinion," the value of the openness is lost.

Use an "I" statement to change any dogmatic statement you have used or heard.

Recognizing commando type. A second type of closed communication is commonly used. The use of forcing, pressuring words and phrases such as "should," "have to," "must," "ought," and "need to" are typical of **commando** statements. They

FIGURE 2.1 Actual "I" statements.

I think	I like	I want
I believe	I consider	I feel
I feel that	I prefer	I am or was

Note: An opposite could be made of each by inserting *don't* or another appropriate word.

FIGURE 2.2 "I" statement phrases.

In my opinion	In my way of thinking
As far as I'm concerned	My thoughts are
It seems to me	To me it appears/it appears to me

leave little, if any, room for alternatives. Notice the authoritarian, commanding nature of these statements.

You should get a job.

He needs to go to college.

She has to apply to more places.

Consider how you generally react to forcing words, especially when they are preceded by the word "you." Most of us become defensive. This type of statement can evoke unhealthy responses of defiance, resistance, or passivity. In the closed style example at the beginning of this section, the commando word is "should."

Think of a commando statement you or someone you know has used.

Being tentative and flexible. In order to avoid commando statements, eliminate the forcing word or phrase, and reword the statement with a tentative phrase (see Figure 2.3). Also, when giving an opinion, use an "I" statement.

In most cases, an "I" statement would precede the tentative phrase. Following are changes in the commando statements used earlier as examples.

It seems to me you would benefit by getting a job.

I think it's a good idea for him to go to college.

I believe that it's wise for her to apply to more places.

The same point can be made less demandingly and, importantly, in a manner that offers the other person a benefit.

Recognizing grandiose type. The third type can be fun to identify. **Grandiose** statements can be exaggerated, all-inclusive or all-exclusive, and dramatic. Facts are typically distorted.

Following are examples of grandiose words and statements.

everyone–no one

everybody–nobody

Tentative phrases.

I think it would be a good idea if . . .	It seems to me it could be helpful to . . .
I believe he could benefit from . . .	In my opinion, it would be wise . . .
I think you might want to consider . . .	As far as I'm concerned, it's better to . . .

all–none

always–never

everything–nothing–anything

only

every

The *only* way to learn about computers is to take a class.

She's *always* late.

Nobody is paid enough.

You *never* get the recognition you deserve.

The last two statements are taken from the closed example about the uncaring company at the beginning of this section.

Grandiose statements are almost always inaccurate. For example, even though it may seem true to say, "*Every* time I wash my car, it rains," it probably isn't. However, if the grandiose word is accurate, you may use it. Perhaps it has actually rained every time! Incidentally, the next time you are tempted to say, "There was *no* way I could get to class or to work," hopefully, someone will remind you that there probably was a way. Awareness of grandiose use is the first step in improvement. Then you can make use of accurate words.

Do you recall your use of any grandiose words? Were they used accurately?

Adding or replacing with qualifiers. In order to be truthful, replace or modify the grandiose word with a qualifier (see Figure 2.4). If an opinion is being offered, use an "I" statement. Following are the rewordings of the grandiose statements that were given as examples.

I think that a good way to learn about computers is to take a class.

It seems to me that she's usually late.

FIGURE 2.4 Qualifiers.

often	rarely	hardly ever	most	nearly
usually	seldom	possibly	many	almost
frequently	infrequently	some	several	probably
generally	sometimes	few	quite a few	in general

In my opinion, most employees here aren't paid enough.

I believe you rarely get the recognition you deserve.

Often, a statement will contain all three types. "Everybody should work a while before going to college" is dogmatic because it expresses opinion as fact, the "should" indicates commando, and "everybody" is grandiose. A better way to get your point across and not change the meaning to any great extent is to say, "I think that it would be a good idea for most people to work a while before going to college."

Open communication is worth the time and effort (a dogmatic statement, by the way; however, these are permitted in textbooks)! To become an open communicator, carefully listen to yourself, then reword mentally and aloud any closed statements. After practice, open communication becomes natural. The activity of identifying closed communication then using open communication in Key Steps at the end of the chapter is good practice. See how well you do! As you pursue your career path, open communication will open doors of opportunity.

Closed communication indicates a closed mind.

INCREASING YOUR VERBAL EFFECTIVENESS

In addition to using an open style, you can improve your speaking by expressing yourself effectively. Old patterns can be discarded as you practice new ways of getting a message across. Being direct and straightforward by speaking in an assertive way instills trust. Using veiled statements or sarcasm shows a lack of communication skills. Effective communicators do not ask a question when a statement or request is more candid. "Why are you making so much noise?" is better replaced with "I would appreciate it if you would make less noise." They also avoid overusing what are called wishy-washy words, such as "kind of" and "sort of," which sound overly indecisive. Even the use of "I think" when you really do know something is not recommended (Pachter & Magee, 2000).

Ineffectiveness often results in confusion. Clarity comes from selecting your words carefully and being specific about what you think and want. The ability to verbalize in behavioral terms prevents misinterpretation or confusion problems.

For example, you may say, "I want you to respect me." What does respect mean in behavioral terms? How do you and the other person know when respect is being demonstrated if you don't specifically describe it? Many words are vague and have several meanings. Employers in many fields want their employees to be articulate and able to explain their procedures to customers, clients, or patients. Effective communicators attempt to be clear and precise when they want to make a point.

"Firefighting is a communicative profession. Being able to get your message across is a definite asset."

MARK MUNGER, Captain, Lincoln Fire Department, Lincoln, Nebraska

Effectiveness is decreased by hurting another person or appearing superior to others. Instead, you can be a supportive communicator by avoiding derogatory labels, sarcasm, unnecessary comparisons of two or more people, judgmental comments, and threats. Effective communicators are not out to prove points or win; instead, they want to be encouraging and promote understanding and good will.

Effective communication is also hindered when the speaker meanders, gives too much detail, or overuses fillers. Making one's point efficiently is often the best course. Notice the distraction in the following.

Well, you know—I go to college—you know—and—uh—it's been a good experience—you know. Uh, I've really—like you know—learned a lot—you know—and think I—uh—well—basically—you know—would be a good employee.

From the playground to corporation conference rooms, in all walks of life, the phrase *you know* is heard. *Uh, well, like,* and *basically* are also common. A **filler** is a word, phrase, or sound used for no other reason than to replace silence.

Listen to yourself talk. Are you using a filler?

Actually, any word or phrase used repeatedly can be annoying. "I'm going skiing this weekend," she says. "COOL!" is the reply. "My significant other is going, too," she adds. "COOL!" is heard. "We may be able to stay in my uncle's condo there." "COOL!" again is the reply. Keep in mind that too many "COOLS" may cool the conversation! Another bothersome insertion of a word involves unnecessary qualifying words, such as "kind of" (often spoken as "kinda"). Kelli was explaining her reasons for not handing in an assignment.

> I kinda got involved in another project that took a lot of thought. So I kinda lost track of time. I want to make up the work if I can cause I'm kinda interested in making psychology my career.

Is it any wonder that it was difficult to take seriously what she was saying?

Being descriptive can enhance conversations. However, too much unnecessary detail is inefficient and likely to bore a listener. In a job interview, Kate was asked about a past job. Ten minutes later she was still describing every specific duty and how she had learned to do each one. It was no surprise when the interviewer yawned.

Applying what you learned from Chapter 1 about personality preferences can greatly increase your effectiveness. To "reach" other people, you need to deliver a message in the way they will hear it. Following are some very useful tips (Tieger & Barron-Tieger, 1998). When speaking to:

- Extraverts—Keep the conversation moving and let them talk.
- Introverts—Give them time to reflect and don't finish their sentences.
- Sensors—State one topic clearly and present facts in a step-by-step fashion.
- Intuitives—Talk about possibilities and ideas and don't overwhelm them with details.
- Thinkers—Be organized and logical and don't repeat yourself.
- Feelers—Mention points of agreement and talk about "people" concerns.
- Judgers—Allow them to make decisions and be organized and definitive.
- Perceivers—Give them choices, don't force a decision, and be open to new information.

As you can see, effective communication takes knowledge, thought, and practice. The rewards are plentiful, and you will have grateful listeners!

MONITORING THE CONTENT OF A MESSAGE

Spoken or written words and sentences make up **content.** Considering all your comments and conversations, think of all the topics you cover during the day. Even though some of these exchanges lack depth, talking with others is a significant part of life. This section can help you in providing information to others and in responding to comments.

Becoming aware of content. A positive communicator is authentic and sensitive and wants to avoid potential pitfalls identified in the following paragraphs.

The words you use reveal your attitude, values, and personality and directly influence the impressions you create.

Semantics, the meaning of words, is a challenging area that includes vocabulary, dialect, and specific word images. Building your vocabulary can prevent some embarrassing situations. Also, you can help others by being sensitive to the challenges of anyone who is learning English as a second language. In a career development class, a Vietnamese man looked disturbed when the instructor told the students how important it was to sell themselves to a potential employer. Later he said, "Selling myself is bad." His confusion was understandable. The many slang terms and multiple meanings of words and phrases can be baffling. What do the following mean to you? What do they literally mean?

- "Don't 'rock the boat.'"
- "There's just too much 'red tape.'"
- "I'll give you the 'bottom line.'"
- "I had to 'eat my words.'"

Within the same language, **dialect,** any speech that differs from the standard, can be confusing. If you have traveled, you have probably encountered differences in dialect. For those from the Midwest, it's hard to believe that not all Americans call soft drinks "pop." As long as the differences don't result in misunderstandings, they can be fun and interesting. Helpful in getting along with others is avoiding the assumption that your way of speaking is the right way. An American tourist was asked, "When you were in England, could you understand them? They just don't speak the 'right' English." The person was reminded that their English is the original!

Probably the most common source of confusion and misconception is each individual's image of the meaning of a word. The mental representations you have of words such as *trust* and *loyalty* may be quite different from those of someone else. "He isn't trustworthy," says a co-worker. What exactly does that mean? Because language is so relative, specificity is vital to effective communication (Caudron, 2000). It's helpful if people use concrete examples for abstract terms and then paraphrase and clarify to ensure a common meaning.

What does honest mean to you? Ask a few others and see if the images are the same or different.

One of the surest ways to sabotage your chances for career success is to use language that indicates prejudice, bias, insensitivity, or lack of knowledge. Whether in a job interview or after employment, anyone who consciously or unconsciously demeans others is likely to suffer. Certain derogatory labels are usually known and can be avoided. What may be more challenging is to recognize more subtle ones. Some of these are calling adult women "girls" or "gals," as well as using "colored" to refer to any race, because it is historically demeaning.

As discussed earlier, improvement in intercultural communication is conducive to career success. Because you will be communicating with people whose first language is not the same as yours, reading books and taking a course are recommended avenues.

The Dilemma of "No" (Krizan, Merrier, Jones, & Harcourt, 2002)

There is not a word for "no" in Thailand, and there are over 20 ways to avoid directly using the word "no" in Japan. When answering a question, most Asians will answer with either "yes" or "maybe." In fact, "yes" to a question may just mean that the person heard it.

Within the American culture, demonstrating an attitude of gender equality means that you use inclusive language instead of the masculine-dominated speech of the past. For example, *chairman* is more appropriately *chairperson* or *chair, fireman* is now *firefighter*, and *policeman* is *police officer*. Use of male pronouns to denote either sex and salutations that begin "Dear Sir," are no longer acceptable. Fair-minded men realize that they wouldn't like it if language reflected female dominance and are committed to the elimination of outdated sexist expressions.

A difficulty in sensitivity is that bias-free language changes and individuals may have their own preferred terms. Whether to use *African American* or *black*, *Anglo American* or *white*, *Native American* or *American Indian* can be puzzling. Likewise, you may not know what title to use or whether to use a title at all. Is it Mrs. Smith, Ms. Smith, Dr. Smith, or just Mary? The wisest choice is to keep up with what is acceptable and then, if in doubt, to ask a person what he or she prefers.

Finally, an awareness of content can help you avoid emotion-packed lead-in phrases such as "When I was your age," "After you've worked here as long as I have," and "Let me tell you," as well as checking your use of slang, vulgarity, and grammar. A common slang term often used in a job interview that sounds extremely unprofessional is *guys*, as in "What do you 'guys' manufacture?" Another unprofessional word is *yeah* instead of *yes*. Many people are offended by vulgarity as well as by certain slang terms. Profanity becomes a definite habit, and you may find it difficult to control in professional situations. Errors in grammar can also be embarrassing and detrimental. "It don't make no difference," he said and found that it made all the difference in the world. He didn't get hired!

Effective communication goes hand in hand with the ability to speak and write a language correctly. Awareness is necessary; if your skills are lacking, do yourself a favor and take a basic course or use self-study resources to improve.

Identifying and using levels of content. What we talk about can be categorized into levels related to depth. After you've read about these, check your understanding in "Awareness of Content" in Key Steps at the end of the chapter.

- *Superficial.* This is made up of conventional comments such as "How are you?" "Isn't the weather great?" and "Have a nice day." Much of our everyday conversation consists of this chit-chat. It's safe and easy, and life would be dreary without it.
- *Basic data.* We often tell facts about ourselves and about others. "I'm an instructor," "I'm married," "I was born in Alabama" are examples of self-disclosure; this is a safe and easy level. "She's the manager," "Mary is getting married next month," "Tom's birthday was yesterday" are factual pieces of information about others. As long as they're not gossip or rumors, these are welcome additions to conversations.
- *Preferences.* We also talk about what we like, don't like, and what we enjoy. "I like to use the computer," "I would rather read than watch television," "I don't enjoy spicy food" are self-disclosing examples. We can also tell about other people's preferences. "She doesn't like violent movies," "Mark would rather write his own reports" are preference statements. These, too, are fairly easy to use in conversations.
- *Ideas and beliefs.* Depending upon the situation and our own personalities, it can be more difficult to converse at this level. In the work environment, new ideas are often welcomed; however, it may be considered inappropriate to discuss certain personal beliefs. When people use "I" statements and make it clear that they are not trying to impose their beliefs on others, this level can be interesting and stimulating. Certainly in your personal relationships, discussing your opinions in nonthreatening ways is positive.
- *Feelings or emotions.* For many people, this is a challenging level. In general, we have probably been told to keep feelings to ourselves. Few of us have had positive experiences revealing our emotions, especially ones of fear, anger, sadness, or disappointment. Because there are several benefits related to emotional expression (Hanna, 2003), learning to reveal, when appropriate, is in your best interests. "I'm concerned because you seem depressed," "I was disappointed when you didn't follow through on that project," "It was upsetting to me when she criticized her supervisor" are "I" statements of feeling that can be quite

useful. Being able to share your emotions with others may not only relieve stress; it also can serve to enhance relationships.

Think of examples of your use of content on each of the levels of content. If one level hasn't been used, what is the reason?

Content from a particular level is best used in appropriate situations and in reasonable amounts. People who discuss only superficial topics or who converse on the deepest levels with mere acquaintances aren't effective communicators. Your career journey will be much smoother if you are aware of content levels and use them to enrich your conversations.

VERBALIZING ABOUT ISSUES

When individuals agree, it's easy to discuss an issue. What if they don't agree or if clarification is needed? Learning about dimensions of awareness (Miller, et al., 1992) and then verbalizing each of these to others are effective in discussions about issues. The five dimensions follow.

- **Sensation** is input we receive through our senses (what we see, hear, smell, taste, and touch). Inaccuracies may occur, so it's important to explain what our input has been. Typically, sensation either is not verbalized at all or is poorly described.
- **Thought** is the meaning, interpretation, or conclusion from the sensory input. Thoughts are subjective rather than objective truths. Interpretations are not "the way things are." They are the way you make sense out of input, and even though an interpretation is real for you, others who receive the same input may come to very different conclusions. Too often, people give only their interpretation of a situation or issue and, to make matters worse, begin their statement with "you," as in "You don't care."
- **Feeling** is an emotional response. An emotion is neither right nor wrong; it just exists. Being able to connect with your feelings and then describe them can be quite useful.
- **Want** is a desire or wish for yourself, for others, and for your relationship together. To agree on a common want is an invaluable step toward resolution.
- **Action** is behavior in the past, present, and future. To describe action is to tell what you have done, are doing, or will do about the issue. It demonstrates a commitment.

When you privately identify each of the five dimensions, you realize what the issue means to you. Then, it's a matter of picking an appropriate time and, with the use of "I" statements, telling the other person about each dimension. For example, your supervisor has criticized you for not completing your work in a timely manner. You could say:

(Sensation)	*"Yesterday you told me I wasn't being productive, and today you said, 'If you can't keep up with the work around here, I'll find someone who will!'"*
(Thought)	*"It seems to me that you are not at all satisfied with my ability to do the work."*
(Feeling)	*"I'm concerned about this."*
(Want)	*"I want to keep the job, and I definitely want to be an asset to the business, so I'm hoping to clarify things."*
(Action)	*"I've rearranged my work schedule and would like for you to share with me any ideas of how you think I can be even more productive."*

You can begin with any dimension and disclose each in a way that is comfortable for you, as long as you remember to use "I" statements. For example, you could say,

I'm concerned because it seems to me you are not satisfied with my ability to do the work. Yesterday and today the two comments you made about my lack of productivity and possibly finding someone who can do the job prompted me to rearrange my work schedule. I do want to keep this job and certainly want to do it well, and I'd like you to give me some ideas of how you think I can be even more productive.

Think of the last time you discussed an issue. What information was relayed and, most importantly, what was left unsaid?

If you're thinking that this is too time consuming and involved, consider how worthwhile clear communication and a positive communication climate are to you. A major problem in the process of communicating is our tendency to relay partial information and leave the person guessing about the rest. For example, in the previous scenario, an employee might say, "You're not satisfied with my work," which may be true but is quite incomplete. Check your skills in the activity at the end of the chapter. Verbalizing dimensions of awareness is not necessary in every situation; however, in discussions of issues, a positive outcome is likely.

"Having excellent communication skills that indicate you are a 'people person' is essential for career success."

SUE COLLINS, Director, KinderCare Learning Center, Lincoln, Nebraska

UNDERSTANDING PARALANGUAGE AND BODY LANGUAGE

The meaning of a message is greatly influenced by other factors in addition to verbalizing styles and content. About 93 percent of an expression is conveyed by vocal changes and nonverbal behaviors (Mehrabian, 1968, 1981).

Using paralanguage. Of utmost importance is **paralanguage,** which refers to the variations in the voice, not the words themselves. Meanings can be changed or enriched in a number of ways. One way is to vary the rhythm or accent a part of a word. "*I* think" or "*I* believe" destroys the openness of an "I" statement. Similarly, inflection, which is a change in pitch, can convey sarcasm or negativity as in "You did *that*?" Inflection can also change a statement into a question. "You like your job" can become "You like your job?" Robert Frost, the well-known poet, said, "There are tones of voice that mean more than words."

Say, "Oh, she's really listening." Did you emphasize "really"? Would you agree that it sounded sarcastic?

Volume and speed are also a part of paralanguage. Consider the different impressions you have of people who talk too loudly versus those who speak quite softly. Meaning can be altered just by changing degrees of volume. The rate of speaking makes a difference in the degree of understanding as well as the interest level of the listener. People who talk too fast are often misunderstood or they overwhelm a listener, whereas slow talkers can easily put people to sleep or be quite frustrating. Practice using a well-modulated voice at a moderate speed and then introduce appropriate variances.

Articulation—or distinct pronunciation—is critical. When a person either mumbles or doesn't enunciate properly, a listener is apt to be confused and annoyed. Over-articulating can give an unfavorable impression. Without intending to do so, you may be using an insensitive blend of loud volume and over-enunciation, especially when you speak to an older person. A receptionist who was guilty of this was reprimanded by a 70-year-old woman who said, "I am quite capable of understanding you and would like to be talked to in exactly the same way as the last person."

Listening to yourself and even hearing a recording of yourself in conversation are helpful. You may be expressing more or less than you think and conveying far different meanings than you realize.

Improving body language. Our nonverbal behaviors and demeanor known as **body language** probably account for more than half the meaning of a message being verbalized. Even by itself, body language relays a powerful message.

Misinterpretations are bound to occur; yet, you can improve your communication skills by paying attention to the message your body is sending and working hard to communicate the one you want to give. It is also highly recommended that you learn the body language of other cultures.

Presentation of self is an attempt to present to others what and how we want to be seen (Goffman, 1959), and much of this is accomplished through body language and dress. Jason came to an interview in a nice-looking, dark gray suit, crisp-looking white shirt, and a fashionable tie. From his polished shoes to his neatly combed hair, he looked the part of a professional. He smiled confidently, looked directly at the interviewer, and responded to the outstretched hand with a firm handshake. He was off to an excellent start before he even said a word!

Personality traits are often assigned to us based on our body language. Just by watching a person's body language, you may think that he or she is aggressive, shy, poised, confident, open, closed, or cocky.

Ask someone how he or she would have described your personality before the two of you ever talked. Are you surprised?

Three areas of body language can be monitored and analyzed. **Body movement** occurs when any part of the body is changed. Variations in facial expression, eye contact, nodding, and touching were discussed in the section on listening.

Common hand and arm movements associated with speaking are **gestures.** These can add to or detract from a message. If you have taken a speech class, you learned the importance of gestures and, hopefully, an appropriate use of them. Interviewers have commented that a stiff, nongesturing applicant is not impressive; however, they realize that gestures can be overdone. "By the time she finished flailing her arms and hands around, I was almost dizzy. I hardly remembered what she said," commented an interviewer. A moderate and appropriate use of hand and arm movements is recommended.

Certain gestures are likely to elicit a negative reaction. A common one is an index finger pointed at another, usually in an effort to accentuate a point. "Pointers" may not realize that this gesture is likely to negate whatever point they are trying to make. Are you aware that arm and hand movements carry different meanings from one society to another? If you plan to travel to or interact with people from other cultures, take the time to learn the meaning of their common gestures.

Body position is the second element of body language. Position or posture is how you sit or stand. You can reflect attitudes of agreement, disagreement, interest, boredom, respect, affection, dominance, subordination, passivity, openness, or closed-mindedness. The student or employee who may be interested, yet appears bored, is likely to be characterized in an unfavorable way. The best posture in the career world conveys self-confidence and competence (Booher, 1999).

Of extreme importance is the impression you give of openness. Without intending to do so, people can look closed by sitting or standing with folded arms. In professional situations, as well as in most personal conversations, you look open when you don't cross your arms, have your feet on the floor (standing or sitting), look squarely at the person, and have a comfortable, yet erect, posture.

Considering just body language, what impressions are you giving right now?

Body language tells its own story.

A final aspect of position has to do with eye level. Try sitting and carrying on a serious conversation with a person who is standing. After a while, it usually begins to feel strange. "I don't like it at all," said one person. "I felt as if I was being 'looked down on,' which I guess I was!" Unless there is a reason to be in a different position, a tone of equality is set when two people are on a similar level.

Have you ever heard about invasion of personal space? The third area of body language has to do with **spatial relationships,** the distance between two or more people. Individuals vary in their personal-space preferences; yet, for the most part, you can follow those identified below in Key Info. For most conversations, the personal zone is appropriate. In formal or business situations, the social zone may be more comfortable. Keep in mind that you can position yourself too close and appear intimidating (or just annoying), or you can distance yourself from another person and appear cold and aloof.

KEY INFO

Spatial Zones (Hall, 1969)

Intimate (actually touching to 1.5 feet apart)

Personal (1.5 feet to 4 feet apart)

Social (4 feet to 12 feet apart)

Public (12 feet or more apart)

If you are surprised about how much is involved in communication, you are not alone. A person remarked, "I never thought about how I appeared to others in terms of body language. I might have worried about how I looked, then I forgot all the rest. Amazing!" Not only is body language amazing, it can also spell the difference between success and failure in many interactions.

A videotape of yourself can help you evaluate both verbal and nonverbal behaviors. As students in a career development class watch themselves during a "mock" job interview, the reactions are predictable: "Do I really look like that?" "I didn't know I did that!" "I'm going to have to sit on my hands." "I sure looked a lot more confident than I felt." If you have an opportunity to see and hear yourself as others see and hear you, take advantage of a special learning experience. Use "Becoming More Aware of Paralanguage and Body Language" at the end of the chapter to become more of an expert in this field.

Communication is much more involved than most people think. Because so little formal instruction is offered, it is up to individuals to examine their own verbal and nonverbal behaviors and to set out to develop or improve the skills they have. Since no other ability will probably play such a critical part in your career success, be sure to give communication the attention it deserves.

KEY POINTS

- Interpersonal skills are a top career asset.
- Relating positively with others begins with an attitude of open-mindedness. Even though first impressions are important, you are wise to reserve judgment.
- Appreciation of both similarities and diversity and a commitment to rid oneself of stereotypic beliefs and prejudice are vital to career success.
- Forsaking aggression and passivity and developing assertiveness skills help build self-esteem. When you use assertive behavior, you gain the respect of others and present yourself as a person of value.
- Communication, a complex process of interaction through which information is shared, is the key to positive relationships and career success.
- The ability to communicate openly, appropriately, and effectively is an essential skill.
- Positive communication skills can be learned.
- One of the most critical requirements in the work world is the ability to listen.
- Becoming a positive listener includes eliminating barriers, improving active listening skills, and using the appropriate type of listening.

- Using an open style of verbalizing fosters a positive communication climate, whereas being effective helps to get your message across and ensure a shared meaning.
- Paying attention to certain elements of content, such as semantics and bias-free language, is a characteristic of a positive communicator.
- Intercultural communication is vital in today's work world. When communicating with someone of a different culture, being aware of diversity in style and content leads to increased understanding that benefits everyone.
- To become an interesting conversationalist and to build relationships, you can use different levels of content.
- Verbalizing five dimensions of awareness is beneficial in clarifying and resolving issues.
- Paralanguage and body language make up a large portion of the meaning of a message and deserve attention.
- Career success is directly related to positive interactions, which require interpersonal communication skills.

ONLINE RESOURCES

Communication tests: www.queendom.com/tests/relationships/communication_skills_r_access.html
Diversity: www.diversityweb.org
Voices of Civil Rights: voicesofcivilrights.org

KEY STEPS

CHARACTERISTICS OF A GOOD COMMUNICATOR

For each of the following, write about one recent behavior or situation in which you demonstrated the characteristic. If you "draw a blank," you will know what needs to be developed.

- Having a positive attitude about others

  ____

- Showing genuineness and authenticity (being my real self)

  ____

- Being open and willing to share about myself with others

  ____

- Expressing my emotions

  ____

- Showing an interest in others

  ____

- Being appropriate in how much I share and how much I ask

  ____

- Demonstrating flexibility (willingness to "give and take")

  ____

- Having a positive sense of humor

  ____

- Being understanding

  ____

- Making accurate interpretations of others' behavior

  ____

HOW WELL DO YOU LISTEN?

Using the scale, answer the following questions.

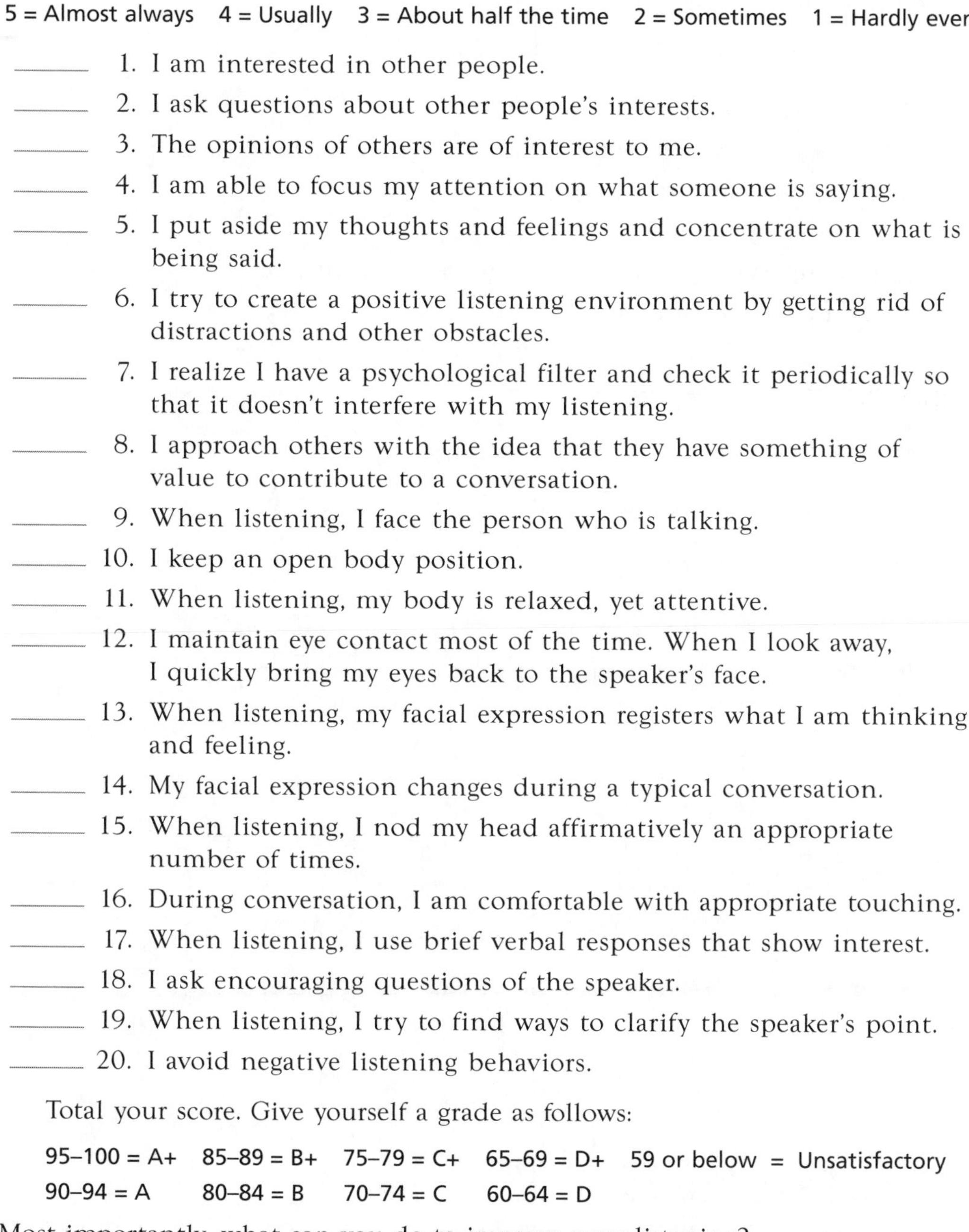

5 = Almost always 4 = Usually 3 = About half the time 2 = Sometimes 1 = Hardly ever

_____ 1. I am interested in other people.

_____ 2. I ask questions about other people's interests.

_____ 3. The opinions of others are of interest to me.

_____ 4. I am able to focus my attention on what someone is saying.

_____ 5. I put aside my thoughts and feelings and concentrate on what is being said.

_____ 6. I try to create a positive listening environment by getting rid of distractions and other obstacles.

_____ 7. I realize I have a psychological filter and check it periodically so that it doesn't interfere with my listening.

_____ 8. I approach others with the idea that they have something of value to contribute to a conversation.

_____ 9. When listening, I face the person who is talking.

_____ 10. I keep an open body position.

_____ 11. When listening, my body is relaxed, yet attentive.

_____ 12. I maintain eye contact most of the time. When I look away, I quickly bring my eyes back to the speaker's face.

_____ 13. When listening, my facial expression registers what I am thinking and feeling.

_____ 14. My facial expression changes during a typical conversation.

_____ 15. When listening, I nod my head affirmatively an appropriate number of times.

_____ 16. During conversation, I am comfortable with appropriate touching.

_____ 17. When listening, I use brief verbal responses that show interest.

_____ 18. I ask encouraging questions of the speaker.

_____ 19. When listening, I try to find ways to clarify the speaker's point.

_____ 20. I avoid negative listening behaviors.

Total your score. Give yourself a grade as follows:

95–100 = A+ 85–89 = B+ 75–79 = C+ 65–69 = D+ 59 or below = Unsatisfactory
90–94 = A 80–84 = B 70–74 = C 60–64 = D

Most importantly, what can you do to improve your listening?

IDENTIFYING CLOSED COMMUNICATION

Use the following letters to identify closed types. If the statement has more than one type, use more than one letter.

D = Dogmatic C = Command G = Grandiose

_______ Employers don't listen to their employees.

_______ He needs to work harder if he wants to get ahead.

_______ She never pays attention.

_______ I think you should be more cooperative.

_______ Her supervisor always finds something to criticize.

_______ All he does is complain.

USING OPEN COMMUNICATION

Rewrite each of the statements above in the open style.

1. ______________________________

____

2. ______________________________

____

3. ______________________________

____

4. ______________________________

____

5. ______________________________

____

6. ______________________________

____

Listen for any example of closed communication in your everyday life. Write it, then reword in the open style.

Ask someone to listen to you for any uses of fillers. Identify the word or phrase.

AWARENESS OF CONTENT

Using the following, identify each statement.

S = Superficial BD = Basic Data P = Preference I = Idea/Belief F = Feeling

_______ I was disappointed when I didn't receive the promotion.
_______ I thought she expressed herself well in the interview.
_______ Isn't the weather great today?
_______ I have held three different jobs so far.
_______ I liked my last job best.
_______ I enjoyed her seminar.
_______ I am concerned about him.
_______ I don't think that was a wise choice.
_______ Good morning. How are you?
_______ I was quite proud after my employee review.
_______ I believe we have a good record of hiring well-qualified people.
_______ I want to eventually live in the Northeast.
_______ I am a nurse.
_______ As far as I'm concerned, she was treated unfairly.
_______ Have a nice day.

Write your own example of each of the levels of content.

Superficial: ____

____

Basic data: ____

____

Preference: ____

____

Idea/belief: ____

____

Feeling: ____

____

USING DIMENSIONS OF AWARENESS

Sensation is given in the scenario below. Write it in the form of an "I" statement next to Sensation, then make up the other four dimensions of awareness and write "I" statements to say them to the supervisor.

Your supervisor has been watching you closely, even leaning over your shoulder, and then checking your work.

Sensation: ______________________________

____

____

____

Thought: ______________________________

____

____

____

Feeling: ______________________________

____

____

____

Want: ______________________________

____

____

____

Action: ______________________________

____

____

____

BECOMING MORE AWARE OF PARALANGUAGE AND BODY LANGUAGE

Watch for examples of paralanguage and body language. Describe some of these below. As much as possible, disregard what is actually being said. Briefly write what could be interpreted just from the paralanguage and body language.

Even though this is not a recommended way to communicate, try it. Carry on a conversation with someone and try not to vary your body language during this time (same posture, facial expression, etc.). Write how it felt and what happened.

Those who want and never do are left wanting.

Getting What You Want

Adults are commonly asked, "What do you do?" Most respond with a job title or an answer that indicates an occupation. Our self-identities are invariably connected to our choices in careers and jobs.

Were you ever asked, "What do you want to be when you grow up?" What was your response?

When you consider how much time people spend pursuing their careers and actually working, it's not surprising that so much of what individuals think about themselves is related to work. Years ago we were told that with technology, people would have considerably more leisure time in the future. That prediction "missed its mark"! The 40-hour week—about 10,000 days of one's life—has expanded. Even more thought-provoking is the concept of "24/7," which means that many people find that they have to be "on" 24 hours a day, 7 days a week (*U.S. News & World Report*, 2000), and often they take work home. It is no wonder that much of life's satisfaction stems from our work.

KEY INFO

Hours Worked Per Week (*Boston College Magazine*, 2001)

Traditional employees: 51.3

Telecommuters: 50.5

Daily flextime workers: 49.5

Seeking Career and Job Satisfaction

Because the relationship between career and job satisfaction and personal well-being is well documented, carefully selecting a career and then designing a satisfying occupational path are necessary. A survey (Koretz, 2000) found that only 51 percent of workers were satisfied with their jobs. Among baby boomers—45 to 54 years of age—satisfaction was especially low at 46.5 percent. Comparing job satisfaction in 21 countries, the United States ranked seventh while Denmark was first (Sousa-Poza, 2000).

Because job satisfaction will dramatically affect the quality of your life, learning what makes a difference is time well spent. Having an interesting job and good relations with one's employer had the greatest effect in a study of 21 nations (Sousa-Poza, 2000). High on the list for other employees were work environment, praise and recognition, and compensation and benefits (*Sales & Marketing Management*, 1999). Another study showed that dissatisfaction came from low income and time required at work (Phillips-Miller, Campbell, & Morrison, 2000).

Although these studies reflect the views of other people, what about you? A first step in determining or confirming what is right for you is to consider career and job separately. Even if you have not decided on a career field, you have probably held a **job,** defined as tasks and duties that a person does for pay on a regular basis. A **career** is a broad field of endeavor that spans a longer period of time. Think of career as a category of possibilities within which you may hold any number of different jobs.

Giving serious thought to career choice comes first. In the past, this was often overlooked. For example, Jack became an electrician because his father had been one, and he was expected to take over the family business. Sue decided to be a secretary because a technical school was located in her hometown, and she did not have other aspirations. Charles wanted to remain in his hometown, so he took a job in a bank and made that his career. My father started with a job in a retail business while he was in high school, then ended up having his own store and staying in the same business all his career life.

While it seems that people are giving more thought to what will be satisfying, some still limit themselves. Females especially are apt to adjust their career aspirations to a male's life. One young woman said, "I always wanted to be a doctor. However, my boyfriend, who is in college, wants me to get through a two-year college and get a job, so I've decided to be a medical assistant." Some men have their own set of challenges. The pressure to be financially successful may lead to career and job choices that aren't satisfying. Also, men, more than women, feel compelled to take over family businesses or farming enterprises even if they don't want to do so.

Simple geography, coupled with fear, can be a hindrance. How many people do you know who have no desire to even explore living anywhere other than where they were born and raised? If you limit where you will live, you limit your career opportunities. Fear is often the cause. Sherri was born and raised in the Midwest and experienced apprehension when her husband wanted to take a job in the East. He persevered and convinced her to move to New Jersey, within a half-hour commute of Manhattan, where she taught sixth grade. It proved to be a wonderful experience that she would have missed because of fear.

Not only are there possibilities throughout the United States, you can even think of international opportunities. One suggestion is to contact companies that have branches in other countries and find out if they can offer you any opportunities. You can find executive search firms and other agencies that specialize in worldwide placements. Any large library is a source of valuable information, as is the Internet (see resources listed at the end of this chapter).

If you're fortunate, you could have an easy way to see if living and working in another country is for you. Susan jumped at the opportunity to participate in a yearlong position exchange with another employee of the same advertising firm. She went to Madrid, and her counterpart came to Chicago. Susan loved it so much that she remained there and became an advertising director for a Spanish company. She enthusiastically endorses her experience: "Living in another country and stepping out of your own culture opens your mind not only to the new culture, but also to yourself. It's a constant journey of discovery and enrichment."

At least, explore other possibilities. In the public library or online, you can find newspapers from major cities, and state and local governments will be happy to send you information. You can also write or telephone the chamber of commerce in any city or access the city's Web site. If you can, spend some time in the possible relocation area finding out whether you like the climate and the social opportunities. Learn about housing possibilities and costs, tax rates, health care, educational opportunities, transportation, cultural and recreational facilities and activities, and anything that could make a difference in satisfaction. After amassing all the data, you may decide to stay where you are or to seek new horizons.

Even though there are numerous career fields and claims of up to 20,000 occupations (Bolles, 2003), many people are unaware of this and restrict themselves. Where do you find this vast array of choices? Libraries have several directories that list and describe both careers and jobs. Because the Internet has so much information, you can spend days and just "touch the tip of the iceberg." One of the most commonly used sources is the *Occupational Outlook Handbook*, available in print and online. It provides detailed information including the nature of the work, working conditions, qualifications, employment possibilities, and future outlook. The fastest-growing occupations are listed under educational/training requirements. Also very comprehensive is the Occupational Information Network (O*NET), which has replaced the Dictionary of Occupational Titles. For a list of these and other resources, see the end of this chapter. A great springboard is a Web site maintained by Richard Bolles, author of *What Color Is Your Parachute?* (www. JobHuntersBible.com). From it you can move through various links, one of which is research. The site also provides guides and tutorials on mastering the Internet and directs you on the use of a variety of online resources. No matter how you make a selection, vow not to limit yourself only to occupations of which you are now aware.

As you are thinking about choices, try not to be pressured or to put limits on your possibilities. Also, keep in mind that what you decide today isn't necessarily permanent; in fact, career changes are quite common. One estimate states the average worker will change careers at least five to seven times and jobs up to 12 times (Shakoor, 2000). Knowing yourself is essential. If you aren't sure who you are, you are likely to choose a career that isn't for you. Several aspects of self are involved. Think of this critical step of career development as putting together a jigsaw puzzle. Each piece makes a contribution.

"Think of hundreds of trees when you consider a career and then consider the vast numbers of branches as jobs. You may be much happier on one branch than another. Expand your horizons."

SUSAN BROWN, Advertising Director, Madrid, Spain

MATCHING YOURSELF TO A CAREER

If you were asked, "What do you want to be?" what type of answer would you give? Most of us would give a title such as teacher, accountant, journalist, or automotive technician. In some cases, this provides information about career expectations; however, it doesn't necessarily spell out exactly what one actually does. When I was in high school, I wanted to be a nurse until a friend of mine reminded me that most of the duties of a nurse were not to my liking! Asking the more revealing question, "What do I want to do?" is an excellent step in selecting a career that can be satisfying. Being able to do what you enjoy creates a stimulating work experience. Keep in mind that it's unlikely that all your career responsibilities will be enjoyable; yet, if a high percentage of your hours are filled with enjoyable tasks, you'll look forward to your time at work.

What are your interests? Do you have any passions? Make a list of your favorite subjects, anything in which you have a special interest.

A student said that he had not yet made a career decision; when asked about absorbing subjects, he replied, "Classic cars and airplanes." On his list of things he enjoyed doing were writing and traveling. He decided to research careers that could combine his passion and what he loved to do. Another good idea is to evaluate academic coursework (Ellis, 2000). Of the classes you've taken, which did you like? Dislike? And, very importantly, why? This can lead you to potential career fields. Identify your interests and skills by completing the exercise "Achieving Satisfaction" at the end of the chapter.

Instead of thinking of what they enjoy, a number of students have in mind only a dollar sign. While money is necessary, you're much better off focusing on more than just wages. Dave Sonenberg, a dean of student services, says that too often the first and only question a student will ask when told of a job is, "How much does it pay?" He challenges students with a scenario.

If I offer you $25 an hour to pick up litter around the campus, most of you could do it. My bet is that most of you would not do it for a long period of time. Why? The *interest isn't there, and earning money won't motivate most of you beyond the "really bored" stage.*

Other factors deserve your attention. Values and what is meaningful will also make a difference. If you highly value money or what it can buy, you will not be satisfied in low-paying professions no matter how much you like the work. The Internet has several sites that provide income information. One that has both general and specific salary surveys is JobStar (see Online Resources at the end of this chapter). As an extra incentive, all but a few of the 50 highest-paying jobs require a college degree (*Occupational Outlook Handbook*, 2002–2003). If such factors as physical and emotional environment, income, outlook, physical demands, security, stress, travel opportunities, and job perks are of interest to you, the book *Jobs Rated Almanac* (Krantz, 2002) ranks 250 careers in these areas.

KEY INFO

Best Jobs Related to Education (Farr & Ludden, 2001)

Associate's degree: Dental hygienist

Bachelor's degree: Computer engineer

Master's degree: Management analyst

Doctoral degree: College/university faculty

Professional degree: Physician

The tragic events of September 11, 2001, led most people to examine their values. Taking on greater significance were spending time with family, helping others, and serving one's country. When surveyed, only 19 percent of people said that making lots of money was important (Yin, 2001).

Having a strong moral code would make it difficult to work in certain career fields that would challenge your sense of ethics. Is prestige of high value? Sociologists have ranked careers on a prestige scale, and if this is of importance to you, acquainting yourself with the higher-status career fields is recommended. If you value upward mobility, certain career fields offer more. How important is leisure and family time? Some careers afford less of this than others. If you feel strongly about a certain cause such as the environment, working in that field is likely to be meaningful.

Your self-esteem level indicates how highly you value yourself. Having a genuine regard for one's self is beneficial in all aspects of life and is well worth strengthening and bolstering. When you consider a career field, ask yourself whether your sense of self will be enhanced. One reason Tim changed careers was that his average record in a high-powered sales career was diminishing his self-worth. "I decided to go into elementary teaching, which doesn't pay nearly as much but is so much more rewarding to me. My self-esteem is strengthened several times a week." To make the connection between values and career choices, use the exercise at the end of the chapter.

Related to values are work orientations (Derr, 1986). Check the following to see which are personally significant.

- Valuing *upward mobility* means you want a career field where you can advance and move "up the ladder."
- Being *secure* is a feeling that your job will last.
- Wishing to be *free* is a desire for independence and the flexibility to "do your own thing" at work.
- Being *high* is a feeling of excitement and challenge in a career field where risks are desirable.
- Being *balanced* is harmony between personal and professional life and adequate leisure time.

The last orientation is a significant one for most people. In fact, the number one career concern for this millennium is the ability to balance family and work demands (Carrig, 1999). Feeling that your life is out of balance is a factor in poor job performance. Even though jobs within a career field can offer more or less of each of the work orientations, knowing what you want before selecting a career is advisable.

"Knowing that I am really making a difference in helping people improve their lives by improving their health satisfies my need to feel that my work has a deeper purpose."

LORI HALL, Vice President, Health Initiatives, American Heart Association, Southfield, Michigan

Personality type plays an instrumental role in a satisfying career. The Myers–Briggs Type Indicator reveals preferences that apply to career choices. For example, someone with an intuitive (N) preference will be much more satisfied in a career field that offers variety and opportunities to use creative ideas. The person with a sensing (S) preference enjoys working with facts, figures, and details, which lends itself to particular careers. One preference can provide some insight; yet, it is the combination of the four preferences, what is called type, that is most enlightening.

Knowing what personality characteristics you possess and which are needed in career fields will aid you in matching yourself with a career field. Ryan Turner, an associate in investment banking, described characteristics that are needed in the financial world. "To succeed, a person must be well-organized, responsible, good at time management, detail-oriented, and assertive. He or she also has to have excellent communication skills, a high level of professionalism, and the ability to manage expectations for self and others." It's no wonder Ryan is so successful, because without realizing it, he was describing himself! Some Internet sites contain personality tests that relate specifically to career and job choices (see Online Resources at the end of this chapter).

For a particularly insightful understanding of personality type as it relates to careers, read *Do What You Are* (Tieger & Barron-Tieger, 2001). The authors devote a chapter to each of the 16 personality types for a thorough look at what would be satisfying and why, as well as a description of each type's strengths and weaknesses on the job. Finding out my type and then reading satisfying career choices confirmed what I already knew: I love teaching!

Your emotions are an integral part of the self and play a major role in career satisfaction. As indicated in the MBTI personality typing, a number of individuals prefer to make decisions based on feelings. While this can be advantageous in certain situations, it creates stress in administrative decisions, especially those involved with hiring and firing. And even though empathy is a desirable trait, those who are overly empathic usually agonize over everyone's problems. Because Beth was very caring and had a clear feeling preference, she thought counseling was the best career choice. Her advisor pointed out some potential problems. Could she leave her clients' problems at work or would she carry them with her everywhere? Would she be so empathic that she would forgo logical suggestions? Similarly, sales careers require people to accept "no" without taking it as a personal rejection, which requires use of the thinking preference. You are able to shift to the weaker preference when appropriate; yet, some people find that extremely difficult.

Related to emotionality is your ability to withstand pressure. Constant deadlines may not fit your personality. Similarly, high levels of stress are "part of the territory" in some career fields. Individuals vary considerably in their coping styles. For example, Jon was a laid-back individual who didn't like pressure and externally imposed deadlines. His first job in a busy printing company was an invaluable learning experience. He developed stress-related migraine headaches and ulcers before he realized that he didn't want to cope with the high-speed world of printing technology.

How much pressure can you stand? Does your "pressure point" fit with your chosen career field?

Obviously, an important consideration in satisfaction is matching your skills and abilities to a career. Even if you enjoy doing something and it matches your values and personality, if you are not adept in this field, you are likely to dislike it. Chris said he enjoyed writing and felt he had good ideas to offer. His personality type indicated that he would fit well into journalism. However, his writing was stilted, uninteresting, and full of errors. He could possibly improve his skills with effort; lacking that, career satisfaction would be unlikely. The fire department in Lincoln, Nebraska, selects firefighters through a process that assesses physical abilities, mental aptitude, values, and personality. According to Deputy Chief Dean Staberg, this method works extremely well. "The firefighters who are selected experience a high degree of success, and we have an extremely low turnover rate. Employees don't usually leave until they retire or die."

Finally, commitment is a key element. How committed to a career will you be? Certain fields require more time, energy, and effort than others. A chief of a fire department caused a few eyes to widen in a class when he mentioned that a firefighting career means spending one-third of your life away from family. It's possible to succeed in some careers with less time and motivation so, again, knowing yourself is essential. For example, people who aren't self-motivated seldom succeed in sales positions. Are you one who wants to own your own business someday? If so, do you realize the high degree of motivation and commitment that is required? A person may think, "I want to be my own boss so nobody can tell me what to do," and have no idea what owning a business means. For those of you who want to learn more about this, see Chapter 6. Degree of commitment is a major factor to consider when you choose a career.

KEY INFO

"Haven't Decided on a Career?"

What Can You Do?

Says Mary Bartels, Academic Transfer Advisor, Southeast Community College, Lincoln, Nebraska:

- Take classes and pay attention to the ones you like the most.
- Enroll in a course designed to help you explore your options.
- If you have an idea, talk to someone who is in that field.
- Use the Internet. A recommended site that lists careers by college majors is www.unl.edu/careers/majors/majors/majors.html.
- Don't panic. As many as 35 to 40 percent of students haven't decided.

MATCHING YOURSELF TO A JOB

After a wise career choice, a specific job selection takes the spotlight. A career selection is similar to deciding what material possession to buy. Let's say you have decided that a new car is preferable to a new boat, computer, or furniture. In a similar way, you might decide that your career field is architecture. Then the focus is on what kind of car, just as the next choice to make is which job in the field of architecture. If you're looking for the ultimate in satisfaction, you won't just look at a few of the usual possibilities. For example, the majority of psychology majors become counselors; however, many other possibilities exist, such as teaching, research, consulting, training and development, marketing, and motivating. Check the end of this chapter for the names of directories and online resources that list thousands of jobs. Finding the job that fits means putting together several more pieces of the puzzle.

As you specifically focus on a job, most of the same career choice aspects are relevant. Consider what you will *do* at work. Even though you select a career based on what you enjoy, it's possible that a particular job is full of less desirable tasks. For example, a creative drafter found herself in a job where she just copied others' drawings day in and day out. She dreaded going to work. A major question to have answered before accepting a job is: "What will I be *doing* in this job?"

Ethical considerations are critical, as well. In every career field there are businesses that use questionable methods. A young man said he quit selling automobiles for one firm because of expected sales techniques that, to him, were dishonest. If your standards and values are not in harmony with what is expected of you, it's unlikely you will be comfortable. Discussed earlier in reference to career choice, another aspect to consider is what you value. If you think it's important to do work that has personal purpose and meaning, a job that just requires routine labor will not be satisfying. An activity in Key Steps at the end of this chapter can help you match values with career and job selections.

A serious consideration is whether a particular job will offer adequate opportunities to raise or strengthen your self-esteem level. Chris realized that her self-worth was enhanced by seeing the end product of her work and from receiving recognition for her efforts. It wasn't difficult for her to understand why she was dissatisfied with a job where there never seemed to be an end to her many tasks for which she received little or no praise. She moved on to a different job because, as she put it, "I had high enough self-esteem to know that I deserved better!"

Before you accept a job, it would be a good idea to look over the work orientations described earlier. How many of the ones you value are aspects of this particular job? For example, a career in journalism or advertising calls for creativity and will usually afford freedom. However, certain jobs within those fields could limit your independence and not provide enough flexibility. Because your job occupies so much of your daily time, having your values and work orientations in harmony with the job description is of immense importance.

Individuals who value being of service to others find satisfying careers in helping professions.

Knowing your personality type can be most helpful in job selection. A drafting job for Scott was particularly frustrating. "I just get started with one project, and my supervisor pulls me off that and puts me on another. I hate leaving one thing undone and going on to another!" His clear sensing preference required the chance to complete one task before moving on to another one. The interruption and change in routine were disconcerting. He found a different job that allowed him to stay with a project until it was completed.

Degree of pressure can vary from one job to another. Even though most jobs have times when deadlines must be met, some seem to be nothing but one deadline after another. On the other extreme, Carlos found himself in a "laid-back" job that demanded little of him, and he was bored because his threshold for pressure was much higher.

Another factor is how well you cope with stress. All jobs can be stressful; yet, certain ones are loaded with stress producers. Finding a job that produces **eustress,** the amount and type of stress that is healthy and good for you, is well worth your time and efforts. Jeanne Baer, president of Creative Training Solutions, said, "Even though most jobs today demand a great deal and can be quite stressful, there is a point when a person really is wise to say, 'Enough! It's not worth my health.'" Ideally, you can find a job that provides you with eustress and, if you find yourself in one where you are constantly "on edge," you will make a healthy decision to leave. Incidentally, *Jobs Rated Almanac* (Krantz, 2002) ranks 250 jobs by degree of stress. Most stressful is U. S. President, one that few of us will ever have to worry about. Rounding out the top five most stressful jobs are: firefighter, corporate executive, race car driver, and taxi driver. Least stressful are musical instrument repairers and florists.

The size and personality of the company deserve attention. You may prefer a smaller company, or perhaps the excitement of a large, dynamic company would be more satisfying. Most workplaces have a "personality" in that the general atmosphere could be friendly and upbeat or extremely professional and serious. Where do you fit?

A job may be right in all other ways and still not work for you because of money. Preparing for a job search means figuring how much salary you eventually want and what your expenses are. If you have an up-to-date budget, the information is there. If you don't, a good resource is *What Color Is Your Parachute?* (Bolles, 2003), which provides an easy-to-fill-out monthly expense form as an exercise on salary requirements. You can come up with a realistic appraisal of what compensation is needed and then eliminate jobs that don't provide that amount.

Do you know how much money you need each month? If you don't, decide to find out!

A major factor to consider is whether the job contributes to your career design. Assessing the learning opportunities in any job to determine if they contribute to your career goals is advised by Harvard Business School professor Linda A. Hill (1994).

Finally, some jobs demand more than others. Commitment and dedication go hand-in-hand. You may be expected to "go the extra mile," which could mean putting in extra hours, coming in on weekends, or assuming additional tasks. If you are not that committed, it's best to avoid those jobs.

"I looked upon the first few years as being in 'boot camp.' Putting in 60 hours a week wasn't unusual; the time and effort spent were worth it to me."

LISA PATTERSON, CPA and Senior Manager, Ernst and Young LLP, Los Angeles

Several young career professionals report that the workload is heavier than they anticipated and that one person is often expected to do the work of two. This will probably not change in the foreseeable future. "A person is often required to perform multiple functions or have dual roles. Versatility, adaptability, and career commitment will prove invaluable in a crowded field," says Jody Horwitz, Vice President of Human Resources, The WB Television Network, Los Angeles. No matter what job you choose, more will probably be expected of you than in years past; yet, because of variations in the necessary degree of commitment, you will have some latitude in how dedicated you want to be.

An invaluable resource in your job search is the book *Best Jobs for the 21st Century* (Farr & Ludden, 2001). It lists the best jobs overall and, more specifically, by various criteria such as personality, interests, geographic location, age, sex, and level of education. For example, at the level of an associate's degree, the best jobs are dental hygienists, registered nurses, paralegal, and legal assistants. Of all jobs, the best paid are dentists, physicians, aircraft pilots, and flight engineers. Almost half of the top 15 jobs are in the computer field, followed by those that are health related. The authors underscore the value of education by pointing out that over 75 percent of the best 50 jobs require a four-year degree. The book also provides detailed descriptions of the 500 best-paid jobs.

BEING REALISTIC AND PRACTICAL

Getting what you want, in a sense, is following your dream. However, dreams do not become realities if certain realisms aren't considered. "I've wanted to be a firefighter since I was a little kid. It's all I've ever wanted," said Jeff, who had just found out that his visual deficiencies were such that he would not realize his dream. Being realistic about your own limitations, as long as you don't restrict yourself unnecessarily, is essential.

Practicalities are also important. While predictions are risky, it is clear that certain occupations will be hard-pressed to survive. Employment projections from the Bureau of Labor Statistics are readily available online (see end of chapter). Among the occupations predicted to have large numerical decreases within the next decade are farmers and ranchers, order clerks, bank tellers, insurance claims and policy processing clerks, word processors, and typists. On the other hand, the fastest-growing occupations are in computer technology, followed by desktop publishers, personal and home care aides, and medical assistants; the largest job growth will occur in the occupations of combined food preparation, customer service, and registered nurses, according to the online 2002–2003 *Occupational Outlook Handbook*. You can also find information about fastest-growing occupations by level of education and training.

Another realistic consideration is where you want to live and the type of lifestyle you wish to maintain. If you wish to own your own above-average home, look at whether your career path will support that. Find out what housing will cost in your favored geographic location. Wherever you want to live, check to see what income will provide your desired lifestyle, then, if necessary, make adjustments either in your career, desired lifestyle, or geographic location. An excellent resource is *Places Rated Almanac* (Savageau & D'Agostino, 2000), which rates and ranks 354 metropolitan areas in the United States and Canada in the following areas: costs of living, transportation, jobs, education, climate, crime, the arts, health care, and recreation. The metro area that ranks the highest in terms of percent increase in new jobs and number of new jobs created by the year 2005, as well as number of jobs with above-average pay, is Phoenix–Mesa, Arizona. You can go online and take advantage of tools such as the Salary Calculator (www.salary.com or available at most career Web sites) to find out how much money you would need to make in order to live in a new location.

Even though men are more apt to consider lifestyle factors, doing so is highly recommended for both sexes. For example, during college at UCLA my daughter Lisa decided that she wanted to live in Los Angeles with an above-average lifestyle and, along with other considered factors, decided to become a certified public accountant. Her position as a senior manager with a large accounting firm makes her lifestyle possible. It is unwise for females to believe that someone else will always provide for them or that they will have the financial help of a partner.

Visualize the lifestyle you wish to have. Will your career choice and available jobs support this?

If this sounds involved, that's because it is! Yet, when you consider how many other life choices are influenced by career and job satisfaction, the relationship between professional and personal satisfaction, and the actual time spent at work, your attention to these choices is imperative. How much satisfaction you get from your career and job will directly affect all other aspects of your life. Designing your career means knowing yourself well, considering and exploring all feasible choices, then choosing wisely. If you have put the puzzle pieces together correctly, you will enjoy the end result and certainly are deserving of a high level of satisfaction.

Achieving Your Goals

Most people have heard so much about goal setting, they tend to "tune out." Hopefully, you won't because if you are going to get what you want, you will have to set and achieve goals.

GETTING MOTIVATED

Most of us carry around a collection of internal messages about goals: "You should have goals," "You'll never get anywhere if you don't set goals," and "It's a good idea to have goals." Then we also have specific goal messages such as "My goal is to become a pharmacist," or "I should go into business." The language of goal setting makes a difference. Notice that some of the messages sound forced and pressured and lack a sense of personal commitment. Replacing words such as "should" with "want" generates motivation and enthusiasm. If you want to graduate from college, you are more likely to do so and enjoy the process than if your thoughts and words are "I should" or "I have to."

In a career development class, Daryl Rivers, president of his own company, said, "Human beings will if they want to and won't if they don't. I want employees who want to work and will be enthusiastic about it." Personal desire for a goal creates a powerful motivating force. But, instead, the goal may belong to someone else, as in the case of Michael. "My parents always wanted me to go into engineering, and even though I don't really want to, I went along with them. After three years in college, I am even more convinced it is a poor choice for me. It's hard to disappoint them though." Yet, in order to experience career and job satisfaction, you must set and pursue your own goals.

ASSESSING GOALS

Once you are sure that you really want a certain career goal, analyze it realistically. In addition to asking whether the goal is yours, can you answer the following with a "yes"?

- Is the goal in accord with my values and beliefs?
- Is this goal compatible with what I want in my personal life?
- Do I have enough motivation to achieve it?
- Is the goal realistic and attainable?
- Do I have the capabilities it requires?
- Is the goal focused and well defined?

In designing a career you will have a major career goal related to the occupation you choose and other goals to help you get there. A goal of completing your formal education will lead to a position in a career field that can, eventually, enable you to achieve your ultimate career desire.

FIGURING OUT THE "HOW"

This is the stage where so many falter. Setting a goal is easy compared to carrying it out. A student completed a goal-setting exercise by writing, "I'm going to be rich and retire by the time I'm 35." I smiled as I wrote, "Good luck," and then added, "HOW?" It's wonderful to have wants and goals; however, if you don't know how to achieve them, they can easily become frustrations.

Eliminating obstacles. Even if people have an idea as to "how," they may be hindered by self-imposed obstacles (Brinkerhoff, 1994). Some of these follow.

- *Pessimism.* If one's attitude is one of "gloom and doom," feelings of hopelessness and helplessness prevail, and little is done. Developing a strong internal locus of control, discussed in Chapter 1, is beneficial.

- *Optimism.* Strangely, the opposite mental attitude can be a detriment. "I can do anything" isn't realistic, and if a person is overly optimistic, the results are usually disappointing.
- *Procrastination.* Putting off activities until later is a serious problem if it's a chronic behavior. Learning why you procrastinate, identifying the repercussions of doing so, and then taking necessary steps to accomplish even the small bits are remedies for this destructive habit (Hanna, 2003).
- *Lack of money.* Conducting a job search isn't terribly costly. However, it does require funds, and this isn't the time to "pinch pennies." For example, why order cheap paper for a resume instead of the heavier weight, which is usually only a few cents more? If your money is limited, try to cut costs for a while in other areas, such as fewer soft drinks, alcoholic beverages, candy, and cigarettes. Your health will benefit as well!
- *Lack of time.* Remember that we all have the same amount of time—24 hours a day. Instead of using this as an excuse for inaction, figure out how you can take time away from other activities and use it to succeed academically and professionally. Fifteen minutes here and there add up.

Feeling overwhelmed by a lofty goal is another major obstacle. An especially helpful technique is to pinpoint, or set, goals with realistic numbers attached. Breaking the goal into attainable, measurable action steps converts a towering mountain into a small hill. Likewise, having a way to measure accomplishment can spell the difference between success and failure. For example, just saying that you want to exercise is less likely to bring about results than, "I'm going to walk a mile a day." The realistic numbers in pinpointing also include completion dates for both the goal and each action step. Being able to chart your progress and reward yourself for smaller achievements along the way will be energizing.

Acting on a goal. A plan must include measurable actions if a goal is to be achieved. Thinking about writing this book was somewhat overwhelming, even though I'd already written one. Knowing that the plan would have to be action driven, a key initial step was to write an outline. That achievement then motivated me to begin the actual manuscript. "Little by little" can move mountains, so don't sabotage yourself by feeling overwhelmed and failing to act. Think of a goal and do the activity at the end of the chapter to show that you understand the process.

The following plan has an ultimate goal of sending out 25 resumes.

- I will compile a list of at least 25 employer addresses and telephone numbers by February 1.

- I will write or telephone each of the companies and request information about the company and get the name and address of the person to whom resumes are sent by February 7.
- I will gather the needed information to develop a resume by February 10.
- I will compose the first draft of my resume by February 12.
- I will have Stephanie read my resume draft and make suggestions to me by February 18.
- I will contact my references and ask permission to use their names by February 18.
- I will type the final copy of my resume by February 22.
- I will select resume paper and have 30 copies made by February 24.
- I will compose a draft of a cover letter by February 25.
- I will have Stephanie read my cover letter and make suggestions to me by February 27.
- I will type addresses of 25 companies on envelopes by February 28.
- I will type the 25 individual cover letters by March 2.
- I will take the resumes/cover letters to the post office, have each weighed to ensure sufficient postage, and mail by March 4.

If you miss an intermediate date on the way to the final goal, simply revise it and stay on task. Of benefit is to write these steps in a checklist format. Marking each completed step provides satisfaction that is motivating. This may seem a bit tedious; however, you are much more likely to achieve the goal by March 4 than if you carry around the nebulous idea of beginning a job search. Remember, you can let time slip away by not doing what is necessary to reach a career goal, or you can begin to take those essential action steps.

In the resume-sending plan, find each action word and the measurable pinpoints.

Researching Careers, Jobs, and Employers

After you have become familiar with yourself and have a good idea of a desired career, yet before you set specific job-seeking goals, learn all you can about that career field, the jobs that are available, and the employers. As in all major decisions, people who amass information are in a better position to make sound judgments. House buyers usually spend a great deal of time and effort learning all they can. Your career decisions deserve as much, if not more, consideration.

WHY RESEARCH?

Information can confirm your career choice or reveal meaningful questions. Research will clarify job expectations and let you know what is required of you. Because job satisfaction is so critical, you want to match yourself to a job. How can you do this without research? Additionally, finding out about potential employers helps you narrow your list of desirables so you can focus on the jobs you really want.

Most important, employers are impressed by applicants who have taken the time to find out about their businesses. "When a job candidate shows me that she or he knows about us, that's a major plus. Those who know nothing are unimpressive," said an interviewer. Motivated job seekers are well prepared, knowledgeable, and persistent in their approach, and it will spell the difference between getting what you want or settling for less. Knowledge really is power.

HOW TO RESEARCH

The answer to the question "Where do I get information?" could be "Anywhere you can!" However, some sources are more credible than others.

A library, especially at a college or university, contains numerous resources such as the following. Typically, there is a special career counseling or development area.

- Directories such as the *Occupational Outlook Handbook, Encyclopedia of Business Information Sources,* and *Standard and Poor's Register,* which provide trends, definitions, profiles of occupations, and information about companies
- Books on career development, specific parts of the job search such as resume writing, and specific career fields
- Trade journals and magazines about all aspects of career development
- Newspapers from major cities
- Videotapes about careers and job-seeking skills
- Access to the Internet
- Software that can provide occupational outlooks, job-seeking suggestions, and job-search tools
- Actual human beings who are career counselors are there to provide services, often free, if you are a student of that particular institution

Spending time in a library may sound grueling, yet it will pay off in many ways.

The Internet is an amazingly plentiful source of career information. The most common uses of the Internet follow.

- Research career fields and occupations, employers, geographical areas, and even yourself through various personality and interest/skill assessments.
- Learn about all aspects of career development, such as writing resumes and cover letters, interviewing, and salary negotiation.
- Search for job openings.
- Post your resume.
- Find career counseling and job-hunting help.
- Make contacts.

The Internet has virtually exploded with thousands of career sites. Additionally, online services such as America Online and Yahoo! offer their own resources. To find your way through the maze of possibilities, what are called gateway sites can be extremely beneficial. For example, the Riley Guide (www.rileyguide.com) has an index of job-hunting resources and other extremely useful information on all aspects of career development. Rather than strike out on your own, invest in one of several Internet job-hunting books. One of the best is *Job-Hunting on the Internet* (Bolles, 2001). Another is *Career Exploration on the Internet* (Gabler, 2000) that describes and provides addresses for more than 500 sites.

What are the advantages of using the Internet? If you have your own computer, the immediate answer is the convenience factor. Instead of going to a library, you can access massive amounts of information from home. "Massive" describes another advantage: If you have not used the Internet in your career development, you will be amazed at the magnitude of what is at your fingertips. As a word of caution, the sheer size can also be overwhelming. Imagine being from a small town remote from any large city and suddenly being transported into the heart of New York City amid its towering buildings with resounding masses of people and vehicles converging on you. Accept that you can feel disoriented, and realize how important it is to focus so that you don't meander aimlessly from one Web site to another. Treat it as an adventure and seek to make it a productive use of your time and energy.

An added benefit is to become more skilled in computer use and in navigating the World Wide Web. Many employers expect applicants to be proficient in this area. If you don't have your own computer, hopefully, you can use someone else's system. Most schools provide students access to the Internet. Many public libraries offer free Internet use. As a last resort, you can pay for time at a specialty store or cyber cafe. However you do it, being able to use online resources keeps you up with the competition or gives you an edge. At the end of this chapter is a partial list of both library and online resources. In later chapters you will read about the use of the Internet in other aspects of your career design.

How much do you know about the Internet and online services? If your experience is limited, what can you do to change that?

A good source of job information is a company itself. You can write to or telephone a company and ask for information to be mailed. Most will provide you with brochures or packets of material. Very important for future use is to get a copy of the job application and ask for details about the job-seeking process for this particular company. Be sure to volunteer to pay for the postage. Again, the Internet is an avenue for company information either through company profiles in career Web sites (see the end of this chapter) or by accessing the company's own Web site.

It may be even better to go in person to get information. Conducting what are called **informational interviews,** designed solely to learn about the business and your career field of interest, is highly recommended. Having visual and auditory information, in addition to written materials, can be especially beneficial. Also, you are in an excellent position to make a positive impression in a much less formidable situation than a job interview. For a required career development course project, Steve visited an architectural firm and talked with the head of the drafting department and two other employees. "It was great," he reported. "I learned so much, and I think they were impressed. The head of the department asked me to contact her when I was ready to graduate."

Steps in conducting an informational interview include:

- Decide on businesses in which you have a keen interest.
- Identify the individuals whom you want to interview.
- Write or telephone for appointments, making it clear that your only purpose is to learn. Find out how much time the person has available. You may also request a tour if that is appropriate.
- Prepare questions. These should be related to the company, products, and the career field of interest. You can find a sample of topics at the end of this chapter. Refrain from asking questions that have obvious answers or seeking information that you can readily find elsewhere. Often, the interviewee is willing and even pleased to offer information about his or her own career path and give advice. You will want to request names of other companies and individuals who would be valuable sources of information.
- Conduct the interview. Dress as you would for a job interview. Record the information you receive either in writing or with a tape recorder, or both.

If you want to record, be sure to get the person's permission. It is advisable to bring out a resume only if the person requests one. Because this was set up as an information-gathering interview, obvious job seeking will probably diminish your credibility. Stay within the time limits and express your sincere appreciation for this opportunity.

- Follow up with a thank-you letter to the person you interviewed. Also, you benefit yourself by sending either a letter or a note to anyone who was helpful, such as a receptionist or a tour guide. If you were impressed by the interviewee, an excellent idea is to write a letter of praise to his or her supervisor or to the owner of the business.

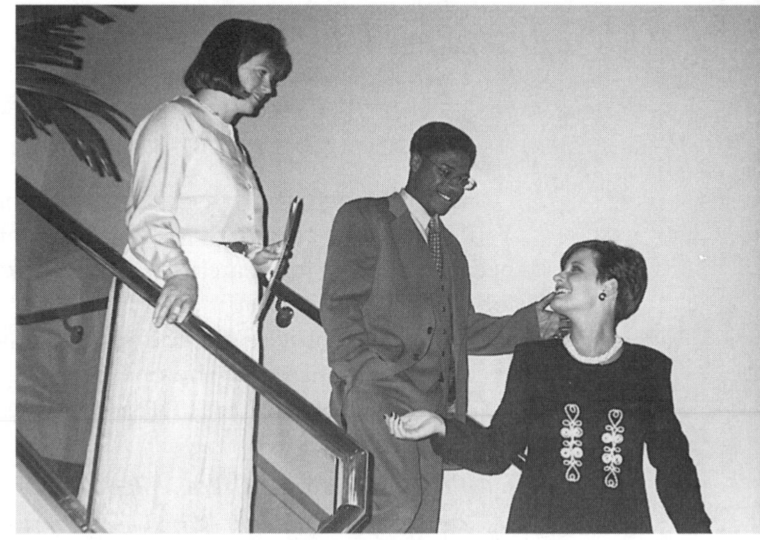
A tour of a company provides firsthand information and contacts.

Informational interviews take time and effort, yet probably no activity is more conducive to a successful job-search conclusion.

Even more informative than a short visit is **job shadowing,** spending a day or so observing a person on the job. Obviously, this will be scheduled ahead of time, and it's imperative that you not interfere with the person's work. Being a "shadow" means maintaining a low profile as you gather valuable information. Whether you conduct an informational interview or spend a longer time in job shadowing, send a sincere thank-you note.

If the company is a public corporation, you can get an annual report from investment services and brokerage houses. The Better Business Bureau in the particular city is another source of information about the company's reputation and record. You may also contact any of the more than 22,000 trade associations representing different industries and occupations. The *Encyclopedia of Associations and National Trade and Professional Associations of the United States* lists various associations.

Word-of-mouth is a commonly used resource. Talking directly with employers and employees can yield helpful information. You might also talk with customers or clients of particular businesses; however, be cautious of personal opinions and assessments. Other people's ideas can be enlightening; yet, restricting your information to word-of-mouth is not recommended. Later you will read about using personal contacts to actually help you find a job.

Planning and Conducting Your Job Search

Imagine this scenario. It's Sunday morning, and Tony is reading through help-wanted ads. He is disgruntled because there are only four interesting ones; he circles each in red ink. On Monday morning he makes a telephone call as directed in the advertisement and mails three resumes. Then he waits—and waits—and waits. He may play a waiting game forever in today's world of work.

"Job seekers have to take the initiative and be very resourceful."

JEANNE SALERNO, Director of Professional Development, Kutak Rock Law Firm, Omaha, Nebraska

Learning actual job-seeking skills is one of the best investments you can make. You may have the highest qualifications of any candidate yet be overlooked because of poor job-search methods. Make a commitment to become proficient in job-seeking skills. Reading and applying the ideas in this book is one way to do so. Other possibilities are courses, seminars, workshops, reading, and by accessing online sources listed at the end of this chapter. Expect to invest time and energy in this endeavor, which is the preliminary stage.

How much job-search training have you had? What have you read? Your answers can tell you what would be wise to do.

Getting to the actual search, you may have heard the advice of many in the career development field: Make your job search a full-time job. Yet, how many people do you know who work seven or eight hours a day at job seeking? Regardless of the time spent, the key to a successful job search is activity. Of course, random or frivolous activity is pointless, as in the case of Matt. He spent hours mailing 150 resumes, what is called "the shotgun approach"; then he settled in to wait. "I put in lots of time and effort," he said, "and all I have to show for it are two rejection letters and three that say they'll keep my resume on file. The rest didn't even respond." This type of activity proved fruitless and resulted in a depressed young man.

Even though experts once recommended sending as many resumes as possible with the idea that a certain percentage would generate results, the reality is that the results are "slim to none." Mailing out numerous resumes at random is effective in getting a job for only 7 of every 100 job hunters (Bolles, 2003).

To help make your job search seem like a job, set the stage. Successful job hunters have a "professional spot" even if it's just a desk where everything pertaining to the search can be found. Spend time there every day as you would on a job. Be sure you have a telephone line that is seldom used except by you plus an answering machine with a professional-sounding personal message. When making return calls to applicants for my husband's company, I was appalled to hear, "Hey, guy, be cool. This dude's out doin' some damage. Catch ya later!" I'm not sure who "caught him" later; he definitely did not hear from us again!

What kind of activity leads to success? If you haven't yet formulated goals and objectives, it's time to do so. Knowing what you want limits your list of potential employers, which saves you time and effort. The shotgun approach may sound good; yet, if 50 of those companies don't have what you want or if you don't have what they want, you have wasted your time. Having goals and objectives also shows that you are in charge of your career.

FINDING POTENTIAL EMPLOYERS

After researching and deciding what you want, it's time to take the initiative. Action is key. You might think that Tony in the scenario at the beginning of this section took the initiative and acted when he responded to four advertisements. The problem is that this was all he did. Later you will read more about newspaper advertisements.

A good first-action step is to develop a list of employers from your research. Then you can focus all aspects of the search on this particular group. The list contains those you want to work for and ones who have reason to hire you, in order of priority. If an employer fits both criteria, it ranks at the top of your list. Don't overlook small companies. Many job seekers limit their job search to names they recognize. The number on your list is up to you; however, be reasonable because you can always add to it. This list can come from a variety of sources as listed in Key Info.

As a practical matter, have an organized system for your list of employers, such as index cards. Relevant data include name, address, telephone and other numbers, name of the person in charge of hiring, and a brief profile of the business. In addition to cards, accordion-file folders with a slot for each potential employer can hold brochures and other information. If you have not yet contacted the employer directly to request materials, this is the time to do so.

The more alert and curious you are, the more possibilities you will find. Before graduating from a desktop publishing program, Tom saw an article in the newspaper about a new printing company opening soon. He sought further information, then mailed a resume and a cover letter (mentioning how he knew about the company). His reward? He was one of the first local people hired! Most of the sources in Key Info "Sources of Employment Leads" are self-explanatory. A few merit special attention and some explanation.

KEY INFO

Sources of Employment Leads

- Directories of employers
- Directories available from a chamber of commerce
- Career development books
- Trade publications, newsletters, and magazines (advertisements and articles)
- Newspapers from any location of interest (news articles, business advertisements, and classified ads)
- Classified telephone directories (Yellow Pages from any desired location)
- Online sources
- College career and placement services
- College program or department
- Career days or fairs at colleges and universities
- Government reports and listings
- Word-of-mouth

SEEKING HELP IN YOUR JOB SEARCH

If you are a student, definitely take advantage of the college placement office. Its major purpose is to aid students in finding employment. According to Lynn Willey, Placement Specialist at Southeast Community College, services include keeping an applicant aware of full-time positions, providing help with resumes and cover letters, setting up mock job interviews and giving feedback, maintaining a library of corporate information, and coordinating job fairs throughout the year. She says, "Students are pleasantly surprised as to what is available. There is no charge for either current students or alumni. Those who are active in their job search will use the placement service as one tool. We're proud of our high placement rate for graduates!"

Because numerous employers contact a college placement office when they're hiring, if you're not registered, you are probably missing out on major opportunities. A placement staff person can be an invaluable ally because he or she, as a representative of the college or university, wants you to find a job. Most placement offices are a part of a larger career counseling department and try to match students' interests, values, and skills with career areas through informal discussion and inventories. Not all placement services are free; however, in most cases, the fee is nominal and certainly could be well worth the expenditure. Incidentally, if you use the service, remember to send a thank-you letter.

Difficult career decisions are easier with the help of a professional college placement office.

Usually, a college program or department can provide contacts and job leads. Be sure to let the program or department chair and other faculty know you are seeking employment. Typically, employers are in contact with these people and may even be serving on advisory committees for the program. Don Mumm, head of a laboratory technology program at a community college, commented, "The employers with whom we're in contact are actually 'standing in line' for candidates. In the past six years close to 100 percent, if not 100 percent, of our graduates found jobs in their field, and most of them were directly through our program." Take advantage, as well, of special events such as career days or job fairs. Usually, employers are there in person to offer information firsthand, and you have an opportunity to talk personally with representatives.

If one is available, have you registered with your college placement office? Have you discussed employment with a program or department chair, a professor, or an instructor?

Government agencies can be valuable sources of leads. States and cities, eager to attract residents, will assist you in finding potential employers. Writing or calling the mayor or city manager's office will probably be well worth your effort. Also, check the city's Web site. Marita decided she wanted to relocate to a warmer climate and chose a city in Florida. She went online to request information about the area, specifically regarding employment, and was overwhelmed with the response. "I really felt as if the city wanted me to move there, and I already feel welcome." Online sources and directories are listed at the end of this chapter.

Have you ever received a name of a potential employer or a job lead from a personal contact? This question is almost guaranteed to be answered "yes."

Word-of-mouth can provide more information about employers than any other source, and 33 percent of job seekers find jobs this way (Bolles, 2003). A list of possible contacts is given in Key Info "Word-of-Mouth Possibilities." To increase your contacts, suggest that each person mention your job search to others. No matter whom you are with, mention career and job aspirations. Leads can come from anywhere!

As you look at Key Info "Word-of-Mouth Possibilities," make your own list of any names that come to mind.

USING YOUR NETWORK

Personal contacts can become even more beneficial if you are **networking**—establishing contacts who may be helpful. Even before the job search begins, you can meet new people and ask for business cards or at least their names, addresses, and telephone numbers for professional reasons. Ted, whose career field was accounting, had a file of 82 names before he graduated from college. One of the ways he met so many people was by joining and participating in professional organizations, a highly recommended way to increase your network.

KEY INFO

Word-of-Mouth Possibilities

- Immediate or extended family members
- Friends and friends' family members
- Other students (college and high school)
- Members of a religious group
- Teachers, instructors, professors
- Former employers and supervisors
- Co-workers
- Acquaintances such as an insurance agent, banker, attorney, dentist, dental hygienist, doctor, nurse, hairdresser, minister, priest, rabbi, real estate agent, sales clerk
- Members of special-interest groups such as bowling teams, hobby clubs, or craft groups

The Internet can help you locate contacts from whom you can receive information and who may actually help you find a job. The book *Job-Hunting on the Internet* (Bolles, 2001) has a chapter devoted to sites where you can make such contacts. Also, check the sampling of Web sites given at the end of this chapter.

Networking can help you get a desired job, advance in your career, or change directions. The old saying, "Who you know, not what you know, makes a difference" is not entirely true; however, the first part, "who you know," certainly is. In a study, up to 51.8 percent of graduates got their jobs through informal channels (Villar, Juan, Corominas, & Capell, 2000). One man asserted, "I don't want to be hired because I know somebody; I want to be hired on the basis of my abilities alone." He was assured that even Albert Einstein found a job after graduation through the father of one of his classmates (Fisher et al., 1977). Besides, you are unlikely to be hired, even with the best personal contact, unless you are qualified. The "what you know" is a necessary part of being hired for most positions. The key is to "get your foot into the door," which a person can often do for you. Finding the person who can hire you through your contacts has the highest job-search effectiveness rate of 86 percent (Bolles, 2003).

Additionally, those in your network can provide career education, information, and encouragement and may serve as role models and references. If someone gives you a job lead or if you think you may want that person to serve as a reference, ask permission to use her or his name. Whether you get actual ideas for jobs, each name you collect could benefit you in the future. Get active in the networking process!

FINE-TUNING YOUR INFORMATION

Once you have an initial list of employers with information about each one, scrutinize it. If you don't have the name of the person who could hire you, call the company and ask for the name. This is usually the supervisor or head of the area in which you want to work. You may be told to apply or send your resume and cover letter to human resources (formerly called "personnel"); yet, you want to make sure the person in charge of the final decision also has your information. Using the name of the human resources director is a "nice touch." Definitely use the name of the hiring person. Be sure to get the correct spelling of each one's name even if it's common. Even "Smith" can be spelled "Smyth" or "Smythe."

Then study each potential employer and identify reasons you would be needed and ways you can help the business achieve its goals. This is one of the most basic elements of successful job seeking and the one that is too often overlooked. Employers are most likely to hire an individual who will be of benefit to the business. Generally, job seekers fill their minds with "What can the company do for me?" instead of "What can I do for this company?" In a competitive world, employers want employees who will give them an advantage, and if you want to be hired, you must convince them that you can do this. On the index card for each employer, write down the ways you could benefit the company (see example). The more you know about the employer's needs and how your abilities will match, the more likely you are to be hired.

Accent Enterprises	Owner: Mark Caldwell
334 South Rose Street	Telephone: 612-728-1940
St. Paul, MN 55111	e-mail: accent@aol.com

Small company of 16 employees involved in real estate management and renovation of houses

Needs: office organizational skills, computer word processing and spreadsheets, and renovation estimate expertise

SELECTING REFERENCES

You may have thought about this before; however, once you know specifically what employment you plan to seek, you are in a better position to select your references. This critical part of the job search deserves serious thought followed by appropriate action.

References can be divided into two general categories: professional and personal. Following are suggestions for each.

Professional references. Select people who know of your work capabilities—attitude, abilities, and performance. A final group of three, four, or five is satisfactory; however, you may want a larger pool from which to draw. If your research has been complete, you will know which ones are likely to be most impressive to which employer. As a result, you may not use the same group of references for each position. Continue to update this list as you make more professional connections.

Obviously, if you have demonstrated skills that are necessary in the job for which you are applying, anyone who can document this is a top reference candidate. Even those who are aware of your transferable skills can be quite helpful and should be included in the top group of possibilities. Think of:

- Past or present supervisors
- Co-workers
- Those you have supervised
- Customers or clients
- Professors, instructors, and teachers

Using the list of possibilities, think of several references.

Other professional references could be people with whom you have had business dealings or have worked in a professional or volunteer organization, such as bankers, sales representatives, insurance agents, and community leaders.

Personal references. Sometimes requested on an application are personal references, those who can attest to your character and can document certain desirable characteristics. Preferably, these individuals would have credibility in their profession or in the community. Most important is to know the ones not to select. Do not use relatives, people you have known less than a year, clergy (unless you have worked with that person, which would qualify her or him as a professional reference), or "significant others." In checking references, an employer called and talked to what sounded like a young female. He asked, "How do you know this applicant?" She replied, "Oh, he's my boyfriend." The unimpressed employer was left with the question, "Is this all he could do in terms of a reference?" A key point is that unless an application specifically asks for personal references, use only professional ones.

I'm delighted your wife wants you to work, but do you have any other references?

CONTACTING AND USING REFERENCES

After you have a list of possible references, the next step is to contact each one personally and ask permission to use him or her as a reference. This point cannot be overemphasized. Even if you inform the person later, not asking first is a major mistake in the job search. Not only is it considered impolite, it can backfire. A career counselor told of receiving a telephone call about a former student who had used her name without permission. "I honestly could not recollect anything about the person so I couldn't help. In fact, I'm sure it hurt the person's chances." An aspect to consider is whether you can expect a positive recommendation. If you don't know for sure, ask about the quality of the recommendation. The "Contacts and Resources" activity at the end of the chapter encourages you to make necessary contacts, including references.

KEY INFO

How Can You Effectively Use References?

- Ask permission.
- Give the person specific information about any position you are seeking.
- Keep in touch and show appreciation.

Many job seekers collect letters of recommendation and supply these to potential employers. While these can be helpful, they aren't as effective as an unsolicited letter directly from the reference. Before being contacted by an employer, a reference can either call, write, or e-mail a letter of recommendation. Do not ask one person to do this every time you apply; however, if there is a position you especially want, this is appropriate and will likely be impressive.

These references can also be used on an application and with a resume and cover letter. Will all your references always be contacted? The honest answer is no, not always. Yet, in many instances, they will be. Strong, positive recommendations from respectable individuals can spell the difference between being considered and hired or being just an applicant who eventually is rejected.

MAKING DIRECT CONTACT

Even if an employer doesn't appear to be hiring, the direct approach is highly recommended because it works. The idea is to be ahead of the competition or at least at the same level. Most effective is to arrange to see the person who can hire you. This is done by using your contacts—either having the appointment set up for you or using the name of the person to "get your foot in the door." A creative approach to job hunting with an 86 percent success rate (Bolles, 2003) is a process of deciding what you have to offer and where you want to use your skills, then going after the employer who interests you the most whether or not there is a known vacancy. Because most employers aren't impressed when someone just appears at the door, you are advised to telephone or mail resumes and cover letters to well-targeted employers, or both. Follow-up is definitely recommended.

If you have excellent telephone skills and want to contact employers more quickly, you may opt to use an effective three-step method. To begin, if you don't know who is answering or if it's obviously an operator or a receptionist, introduce yourself by name and then ask to speak to the person who could hire you (use this individual's name, which you should already know). If the person is not available, you are better off finding out what time to call again. Leaving your name and telephone number may yield nothing, or the person may call back when you are not there or not in a position to talk. Julie had left her name and telephone number, and when the potential employer returned her call, she was embarrassed because her two children were both crying loudly in the background. Another reason is that throughout the job search, a good idea is to "keep the ball in your court"; in other words, you want to stay in control as much as possible.

When you are talking to the person who can hire you, proceed as follows through the three steps.

1. *Greet the person by name and then give your name.* "Hello Mr. (or Ms.) Ross. This is Kevin Grant."
2. *Mention at least one of your assets (a reason why the person would be interested in hiring you) and, if you can, the contact person who is the connecting link.* "I will graduate in June with a degree in landscape architecture and have worked throughout college for Jacobs Landscape Design in Seattle. I understand that you are expanding in this area. The creative work I've been doing, I think, would be of interest to you. Jane Larson thinks it would be a good idea for us to talk." Or, you can lead in with: "Jane Larson, my previous employer, suggested that I call you."
3. *Tell the reason for your call.* "I'm very interested in a position with your company in the area of landscape design."

Some might question the reason for the second step. "Can't I just introduce myself and tell the person why I'm calling?" Certainly you can; however, what you have to offer is most significant. Another practical reason has to do with memory. If a person receives several calls a day, specific information is likely to be remembered. "Oh, yes, I remember. He said he worked for Jacobs Landscape Design, and that company hires only the best."

Just as important as what to say is what not to say. One of the worst openings is also one of the most common. *Don't* begin with any of these:

- Do you have any openings?
- Are you hiring?
- Do you have any positions (or jobs) available?

Those questions are quite likely to get a response of "no." When you make a direct contact, you don't want to provide an opportunity for an easy rejection. And even if an employer had an opening, the caller has done nothing to be impressive.

A day-care center director put it bluntly, "If I pick up the phone one more time and hear, 'Do you have any openings?' I think I'll just scream."

The three-step direct method will result in one of several replies. Because you have exerted time and effort to make this telephone call, you don't want to go away empty-handed. Following are employer replies (given from most to least positive) and a recommended response.

1. EMPLOYER: *I am in need of someone in the near future and would be interested in discussing the position.*

   APPLICANT: *Except for Mondays and Wednesdays when I have classes, I'm available at your convenience. In the meantime I'll mail you a copy of my resume.*
2. EMPLOYER: *Your qualifications sound great; however, we aren't hiring right now.*

   APPLICANT: *I'm sorry to hear that; I'd like to send you my resume to keep on file for future openings.*
3. EMPLOYER: *We aren't hiring right now, and I don't see any chance of it in the foreseeable future.*

   APPLICANT: *I'm sorry to hear that because I'm very impressed with your company. Do you know of anyone else who might be hiring in the near future?*

The request for another contact may sound strange, yet employers also network and are usually willing to be helpful. If you do get a name, ask if you can tell how you received it. Practice this method with "Making Direct Contact" at the end of the chapter.

No matter which reply you receive, you can be pleased that you did get something for the time. Also, you may be like Sara, who was told that the hospital was not hiring in her field and probably wouldn't be in the foreseeable future (the third reply). Two weeks after she made the call, she received a call from the head of the respiratory therapy department:

> *Sara, if you haven't yet taken a position, I'd like to talk to you. I just received a surprise one-month notice from a technician who is moving to another city. I was quite impressed with our telephone call and remembered your qualifications. Now I do want your resume and would also like to schedule an interview.*

If Sara had not made direct contact or had just asked if the hospital had openings, this would not have happened.

E-mailing a potential employer using this same three-step method can work well, too. The disadvantage as compared to telephoning is that you then have to wait for a response. Other types of direct contact are by regular mail or fax machine. The next chapter covers presenting yourself in writing.

A common, yet usually ineffective, way of finding a job is to rely only on newspaper advertisements.

USING ADVERTISEMENTS AND ONLINE JOB POSTINGS

Remember Tony and his Sunday-morning circling of classified ads? When most uninformed individuals decide to look for work, this is how they proceed. While it would be foolish not to use the classified ads, some facts are good to know. One is that a high percentage of jobs available are not even advertised, which means you are missing out on many opportunities. Often, an employer doesn't need to advertise, and probably doesn't want to deal with the usual overwhelming response. Classified ads are costly for smaller companies so they, too, would rather find applicants other ways.

Another reason not to rely on this method comes from thinking about what others are doing on that same Sunday morning. Picture hundreds of others circling the same ads as Tony. When you respond to an ad, you have a great deal of competition. Typically, an employer receives many responses as a result of an advertisement, and its effectiveness rate in getting a job ranges from 5 to 24 percent (Bolles, 2003). The higher the job level, the less effective is this method. Besides the degree of competition, employers probably won't be as impressed by a responder as they will be by an "activator." Check a current classified-ad section to see how many job openings would be of interest to you. Go online and do the same.

Online job postings also have the same handicaps. The sheer numbers sound impressive. For example, America's Job Bank (www.ajb.org) claims to have thousands of new jobs posted every day. Employers also list openings on their own Web sites, and going directly there is preferable to using a general posting site. If you have a specific company in mind, you can either search for it by its name or use a site such as DirectEmployers Association (www.directemployers.com) that lists companies and provides addresses and links. A partial list of job posting sites is provided at the end of this chapter. Chapter 4 covers electronic resumes and online posting.

Does online searching sound like the answer to every job seeker's dream? Before you begin to believe so, consider some cautionary advice. Even though the numbers are impressive, they still represent only a small fraction of total jobs available. Additionally, postings often remain long after the position has been filled. Ultimately, your chance of finding a job through a posting site is low. If you are looking for a computer-related position, it is 45 percent effective; however, it drops to only 2 percent if you're seeking something else. In fact, at least one expert believes it is the worst way to hunt for a job (Bolles, 2001). Still, as one of several job lead sources, it's wise to make use of the Internet. Sites are identified in special Internet or online search books listed in Recommended Reading at the end of the book; several sites are listed at the end of the chapter.

UTILIZING PLACEMENT SERVICES

Various types of placement services are available, each with advantages and, in some cases, a few drawbacks. Even though the already-discussed college or university placement service will not guarantee you a job, its effectiveness is fairly high. You have nothing to lose, except a small amount of money if the service is not free, and everything to gain by registering. You're advised to make contact several months before your anticipated graduation date and check with the office on a regular basis.

What are commonly called employment agencies are of two general types: public and private. Depending upon the agency, you could receive help in identifying potential employers, researching companies, improving specific job skills such as interviewing, determining appropriate salary figures, and preparing for employment tests.

Public agencies, operated by state and local governments, offer free services. These are part of a federal network called United States Employment Service. Registration involves paperwork. This may be well worth your time, although you will want to use it as only one source among others. Most agencies have current job listings and hotlines you may call; most important, they will put you in contact with any employer who is looking for help.

Private agencies are in business to match employers with applicants. They are paid either by employers or applicants (or both), and you'll want to know who is liable for the fee. Read carefully and ask questions about any contract before you sign. Applicants pay only if they accept positions through the agency. Typically, the fee is a percentage of your salary. Avoid signing a contract that demands "exclusive listing or handling," which binds you to a fee even if you find a job elsewhere.

Agencies are similar to real estate agents who are paid by a homeowner when a house is sold. Most claim they can find applicants better jobs at higher salaries faster than the applicants could on their own. If this is so, it could be a worthwhile investment of money. Others question their effectiveness. Of those who walk in the door of a private agency, 5 to 28 percent get jobs (Bolles, 2003). If the employer pays the fee, the applicant obviously has no cost; however, in these cases, the agency is working for the employer, not the applicant. This could mean an agency will try to pressure you into taking a job just to collect a fee.

Is it wise to use a private employment agency in your search? An advantage in using it is that you have control over acceptance of a job and, thus, over having to pay for the services. If you are in a hurry to find a job, you may opt to use an agency immediately, or you can save it for a last resort, especially if there is a fee. Regardless, research the agency and be sure it has a good reputation in the area.

After you have been on the job for a while, you may be contacted by an executive-search firm staffed by what are called **headhunters.** These firms find employees for companies so the normal case is that they would contact you; however, if you are well qualified and seeking a higher-level position, you may take the initiative and contact one.

If you are not successful in finding full-time employment, you can consider working for a temporary-help agency. You might choose to do this as a method of research. Job seekers benefit in many ways. The most obvious is that you are being paid while gaining both information and experience. Having access to all the different companies serviced by a temporary agency can help a job seeker decide which is most desirable. For example, Nicole wanted a job in the entertainment business. She "temped" and had the opportunity to work a few months at several major television networks. Other temporary work that has value is summer employment or a part-time job during the school year, ideally in your career field. However, any job you do well adds to your credentials. Additionally, the fact that you are using your time productively will impress a potential employer.

KEY INFO

Why Seek Temporary Employment?

According to Jennifer L. Yester, CEO, A + The Employment Company, Burbank, California:

- People can "try out" jobs first.
- Temping often leads to full-time employment.
- Temporary work can help a person earn money while pursuing other careers.
- For career changing, temping offers the opportunity to learn a new industry and get paid for the training.

SEEKING INTERNSHIPS, VOLUNTEER WORK, AND SPECIAL PROGRAM HELP

Whether you're still in school or actively seeking work and having no success, you can take advantage of methods that have worked for many. **Internships,** sometimes called work-study programs, are cooperative efforts between employers and schools. For the potential job candidate, they provide opportunities to gain experience, valuable information about the career field and companies, and excellent contacts. In most cases, you also get scholastic credit. "Internships are a great way to gain 'real-life' career experience to see if you really like that type of work," says Lori Hall, Vice President, Health Initiatives, American Heart Association.

"Students are wise to look upon internships and other part-time employment as a long-term investment in their future rather than just as a way of earning money."

MARCIA PHELPS, Ph.D., Director of Career Development Services, University of West Florida, Pensacola, Florida

Even if you are like Jessica, who participated in a yearlong work program and discovered that early childhood education was not for her, you will have gained valuable information. The good news is that many college students today are being paid upward of $20 an hour, and some even receive stock options and other benefits. Employers view internships as an effective recruiting tool and an opportunity to give students a trial run for future employment, according to *Newsweek* (2000). Obviously, paid internships are preferable; however, don't disregard an unpaid opportunity that could reap major dividends later. In a survey reported in *Newsweek* (2000), 86 percent of students reported that the educational value of an internship was of top priority, and 88 percent said that they believed internships were instrumental in their getting a job. A study confirmed these expectations. Students with internships were more apt to be employed upon graduation (Knouse, Tanner, & Harris, 1999).

Volunteer work, whether when you are still in school or when you are having difficulty finding exactly what you want, has the following advantages.

- You can improve skills and learn new ones.
- You will add to your experience. Incidentally, employers today are likely to assess unpaid work in the same way they do paid experience.
- You can make valuable contacts.

- You can develop helpful references.
- As with temporary work, you could get a paid position.
- Employers are almost always impressed by volunteerism.

The last reason was underscored by a deputy chief of a city fire department when he told a class, "If I don't see any indication of volunteer work, you have fallen a degree in my estimation. Obviously, volunteer firefighting is preferable; however, I'm impressed by any type of volunteer activity."

In order to locate volunteer activities, check for a community volunteer clearinghouse or center or find names of nonprofit organizations in the yellow pages. You are unlikely to get or keep even a volunteer position unless you are qualified and eager to work. Most organizations know that a poor volunteer is worse than none.

Special programs that provide information and help are available through local, county, or state governments, community colleges, universities, and organizations. If you are middle age or older, the American Association of Retired Persons (AARP) has member programs that either put people to work or sponsor workshops that foster job opportunities.

HANDLING REJECTION

Almost certain in any career is being told or receiving in writing: "Sorry, but your qualifications and the position were not the best match. Good luck." It may be worded differently, yet the meaning is the same—you were not considered or selected. What is your reaction? Most of us struggle with rejection.

So what can one do? Accept the idea that nobody wants to be rejected. Instead, most people believe that always getting what they want makes life wonderful. The reality is that life will never be that way, and we wouldn't be truly happy if it were. The line of life is a series of ups and downs, and well-adjusted individuals learn to use the low spots to enhance the highs. Valuable lessons are learned in the trenches, the dips of life (Hanna, 2003).

Before beginning a job search, examine how you handle rejection. Ask yourself honestly: On a scale of 1 (very poorly) to 5 (very well), where would I rank myself? If the answer is a 4 or 5, you are probably ready to strike out on your quest. If it's lower, you would be spending your time wisely by learning how to deal with a rebuff. Not doing so can lead to depression and other unpleasant emotions, giving up, or becoming desperate and accepting any job to avoid the pain of further rejection.

As in life, rejection in a job search is usually inevitable and can occur at any step of the process. In general, not getting an interview is disappointing, yet applicants are more likely to take it personally if they are not hired after being interviewed. Similarly, not getting a bite while fishing can be discouraging, yet having a big fish on the line then losing it is enough to make a person weep!

The most important thought to maintain is that being rejected for a job is not personal. If, after an interview, you don't get a job you really want, cognitive restructuring techniques can transform negative feelings into hopeful ones. Instead of thinking, "Because they didn't hire me, something is wrong with me," change it to: "Just because they didn't hire me doesn't mean something is wrong with me. Evidently, in their minds the position and I didn't match. The company missed an opportunity to get a first-rate employee." Then choose to move forward to a better job selection.

Another useful technique is described in *Guerilla Tactics in the Job Market* (Jackson, 1993). Visualizing the job search as a series of "no's" followed by a "yes" is not only realistic, it's hopeful. Also comforting is to realize that this is the path almost every effective job hunter follows.

Getting what you want in a career and jobs requires a great deal of initiative, time, thought, and activity. Determination in the wake of rejection is essential. Those who are willing to invest in the effort are likely to succeed and feel satisfied with this extremely important aspect of their lives.

KEY POINTS

- Because so much time is spent on your career and because career satisfaction is closely related to life satisfaction, you are well served by spending time and effort on its development.
- A career is a broad field of endeavor while a job consists of tasks and duties on a day-to-day basis. In both, satisfaction is essential.
- Individuals can limit career and job choices and are benefited by expanding their range of possibilities.
- Through self-understanding and career research you can match yourself to both a career and a particular job.
- Having realistic and practical aspirations and keeping up to date on various occupational fields increase your chances for career success and satisfaction.
- Getting motivated, assessing your goals, and then acting upon them are highly recommended and will yield results.

- Researching careers, jobs, and employers is a critical part of total career development.
- Numerous sources of information exist, and an effective job search takes advantage of as many as possible. A library holds a vast store of career material; online sources are also plentiful.
- Using a school's career counseling and placement services and your own program or department is effective in making career decisions and job searching.
- From a potential list of employers, making direct contacts is highly recommended. Responding to advertisements and online job postings, while not effective on its own, is still advisable.
- Seeking and making use of references and networking can result in job leads and career advancement.
- Temporary work has benefits that include experience and potential permanent jobs.
- Students can benefit from internships and other types of employment while in school.
- Volunteer work is a definite asset.
- Learning to handle rejection is necessary because most job searches include some negative results. Most important is to not take job rejection personally.

ONLINE RESOURCES

Gateway Sites (indexes of major job sites plus career help)

The Riley Guide: www.rileyguide.com

Job-Hunt: www.job-hunt.org

Career Resource Center: www.careers.org

Research (career fields, companies, and salaries)

Adguide: www.adguide.com/college

AllBusiness: www.allbusiness.com

America's Career Infonet: www.acinet.org

America's Job Bank: www.ajb.org

Bureau of Labor Statistics' Projections: http://stats.bls.gov/news.release/ecopro.toc.htm

Campus Career Center: www.campuscareercenter.com

Career Builder: www.careerbuilder.com

Career Journal from the *Wall Street Journal*: http://careers.wsj.com

The Career Key and Major to Career Converter: www.unl.edu/careers

CompaniesOnline: www.companiesonline.com

DirectEmployers Association: www.directemployers.com

Europages, The European Business Directory: www.europages.com

Federal Jobs Central: www.fedjobs.com

FlipDog: www.flipdog.com

Hotjobs at Yahoo!: http://hotjobs.com

Informational interviewing: www.quintcareers.com/informational_interviewing.html

International opportunities: www.escapeartist.com

JobBankUSA: www.jobbankusa.com

JobHunters Bible: www.jobhuntersbible.com

JobReviews: www.jobreviews.com

JobStar: http://jobsmart.org and http://jobsmart.org/tools/salary/sal-prof.htm

Monster Board: www.monster.com

National Organization on Disability: www.nod.org

Networking: networking.monster.com

O*Net Online: http://online.onetcenter.org

Occupational Outlook Handbook: http://www.bls.gov/oco

Salary Wizard: www.salary.com

Volunteer information: www.serviceleader.org

WetFeet: www.wetfeet.com

KEY STEPS

ACHIEVING SATISFACTION

Under the following columns, list as many as you possibly can. Stretch your thinking and consider all aspects of your life.

WHAT I LIKE TO DO	WHAT I DO WELL
______________________	______________________
______________________	______________________
______________________	______________________
______________________	______________________
______________________	______________________
______________________	______________________
______________________	______________________
______________________	______________________
______________________	______________________
______________________	______________________
______________________	______________________
______________________	______________________
______________________	______________________
______________________	______________________
______________________	______________________

Identify a career field—preferably, the one you have chosen.

____

Now circle any entries from both columns that would be used as one pursues this particular career.

If you have a job now, or before you take a job, do this same activity and compare it with the specific job duties.

The more you do of what you enjoy and are good at doing, the more satisfied you will be!

MATCHING VALUES TO CAREER AND JOBS

Using numerals from 1 (most important) to 16 (least important) rank the following values in the order of importance for you.

_____ 1. prestige

_____ 2. self-worth

_____ 3. excitement

_____ 4. security

_____ 5. moral code/ethics

_____ 6. meaningful causes

_____ 7. accomplishment

_____ 8. pleasant environment

_____ 9. advancement

_____ 10. health

_____ 11. power

_____ 12. flexibility

_____ 13. financial security

_____ 14. service to others

_____ 15. family/balance

_____ 16. leadership

How many are possible within your current career choice?

____

____

Now go back to "How Well Do I Really Know Myself?," the activity in Key Steps for Chapter 1, and write below the five values you listed. Then add any from the other person's inventory that are true for you.

____

____

____

From this list, check those that you think will be possible to uphold and are in harmony with your chosen career field. If you are considering a particular job, be sure to pay attention to how your responsibilities and duties will coincide with your values.

SETTING AND ACHIEVING A CAREER GOAL

Think of a short-term career goal. Using the information from Chapter 3, complete this page. Give yourself credit for reaching a goal.

My short-term career goal is:

____

Final date of completion:

____

1. Evaluate this goal by answering the questions in the section of this chapter titled "Assessing Goals." Identify any potential problems. Read the section that discusses obstacles and decide how you will deal with any that might get in your way.

____

____

____

____

____

2. Draw a series of stair steps, then write a specific action and date by each. Use pinpointing to make them measurable.

RESEARCHING POTENTIAL EMPLOYERS

Contact an employer in a chosen field of interest and arrange an informational interview. Develop questions in the following areas and add some of your own to the list. If possible, also take a tour of the business. Be sure to write a thank-you letter to the person you interview.

- History of this company or business
- Current business projects, activities, services
- Working conditions and benefits
- Organizational scheme ("chain of command")
- Decision-making procedures, use of teamwork
- Strengths and challenges
- Future outlook
- Interviewee's career path, including the present position
- Interviewee's likes and dislikes about the job
- Typical workday
- Responsibilities of positions in this career field
- Requirements and desired characteristics for positions
- Salary ranges and benefits
- Advancement possibilities
- Expected changes for this career field
- Specific advice for you in this career field
- Names of others in the career field
- How one would go about seeking a job with this employer especially in terms of types of resumes and cover letters (a recommendation is that you review Chapter 4 beforehand)

List additional questions.

____

____

____

____

____

____

____

CONTACTS AND RESOURCES

Do yourself a favor and complete the following important steps.

1. Begin to develop a list of potential employers. Consider making a file card on each, as described in this book. Then you can group the cards in whatever way is most useful (alphabetically, geographically, by job title, etc.).

   ____
   ____
   ____

2. If you have not yet done so, visit a college career and placement center to see what is offered. Register in your college or university placement office.

3. Spend five to ten minutes and write below every name that comes to mind to include in your network of contacts.

   ____
   ____
   ____
   ____
   ____
   ____
   ____
   ____
   ____
   ____

4. From the list, select at least five, if not more, who would provide impressive recommendations. Write their names below. Then, contact each one and ask if he or she would serve as a reference.

   ____
   ____
   ____
   ____
   ____

MAKING DIRECT CONTACT

Using the three-step method of direct contact by telephone and the recommended responses, write *what you would say* in each of the following situations.

- You are interested in employment at Henderson and Associates and are calling for the first time. You do not know the name of the person who can hire you. A receptionist answers the telephone.

____

____

____

____

____

- You are calling to talk with Margaret Henderson at Henderson and Associates because you would like to work there and she is in charge of hiring. A receptionist answers the telephone.

____

____

____

____

____

- You have called Henderson Associates and asked to speak to Margaret Henderson. She is in charge of hiring, and you are now speaking directly to her.

____

____

____

____

____

- You have been told by Margaret Henderson that there is an open position.

- You have talked with Margaret Henderson and have been told that there are no current openings.

- You have talked with Margaret Henderson and have been told that there are no future prospects for hiring.

Writing is a powerful communication tool.

Presenting Yourself in Writing

The ability to present yourself positively in writing is a critical part of your job search. Why? Unless you go in person or speak to the person who can hire you by telephone, your first impression will be a written one. If you don't succeed at impressing the reader, this particular job search is over. Resumes, cover letters, and applications are key elements in "getting your foot in the door." And, even if these methods aren't your initial way of approaching, presenting yourself in writing will, at some time, be expected. Generally, an employer will not take the time for an interview unless you, in writing, have set yourself apart from the competition.

Developing Your Resume

Entire books have been written on this subject, and you are encouraged to read several. You can also get help on the Internet (see Online Resources at the end of this chapter). Then it will be up to you to decide exactly what advice to take. From years of researching resume writing, one thing is clear: There is different advice, and, in some cases, disagreement among the experts. This section includes suggestions from different sources. Consider the recommendations you will find here. The rest is up to you!

WHAT IS A RESUME?

You can think of a **resume** as a marketing piece or an advertisement for yourself. In the academic field, a resume is called a **vitae** and includes all published works, which usually makes it longer. Years ago there was only the formatted resume prepared on a typewriter or computer and furnished in hard copy. In today's world of high technology, you are wise to have other types that are discussed later in the chapter.

Resumes are not autobiographies; nor are they personal in the sense of describing your private life. The purpose of a resume is to impress a potential employer and get you an interview, which you accomplish by clearly stating what you can do for the employer. Anything that could possibly hinder or detract from this should not be included.

REASONS FOR RESUMES

In order to be competitive, a resume is a necessity because employers either require or at least expect one. Your resume needs to be at least as impressive and preferably more so than others. In the unlikely case that a resume is not required, your having prepared one can be a major advantage.

A key benefit is that a resume forces you to gather and clarify self-information. You will then be much more prepared for other aspects of a job search. Also, a resume, unlike an application, lets you present yourself in the most favorable way.

If you consider why you take notes in classes or for what reason you might write a person's name, the reason is to remember it later. Something in writing jogs the memory. Employers use resumes for the same reason, and having one on file helps you be remembered. An interesting benefit is that resume preparation can raise one's confidence. Said Todd, "After I read all the things I can do and have done, my self-esteem is higher."

Additionally, you can use your resume as a written advertisement with your entire group of contacts. Ask each one to try to give it to someone who might be interested. With knowledge of its many benefits, look on a resume as an opportunity to present yourself in the most favorable way, realizing that what you are is worthy of pride.

RESUME REQUIREMENTS

Where does one start? Not surprisingly, the recommendation is to develop a traditional, formatted resume. Then you can alter it so that it can be used electronically. Even though experts aren't necessarily in agreement about all aspects of resume writing, certain "absolutes" are clear and apply to all types of resumes.

- The resume has a neat, professional appearance and must be in typeface.
- No negative information is given.
- All words are spelled correctly. Because the spell-check function in word processing programs will not catch certain errors such as the word "to" used for "too," have someone with excellent spelling skills proofread your resume. In addition, using correct grammar, punctuation, and sentence construction shows that you are adept in the language and that you care enough to be error-free. As an employer put it, "Employers conclude that if you make errors in your written communications before you are hired, you will make even more mistakes on the job." Even though perfection may be hard to achieve, a resume should be perfect.
- The content is brief. Experts differ on whether a one- or two-page resume is better; however, it's rare if anyone suggests longer than two pages. A vitae that is used in academia could be an exception to this if you have a number of published works.
- The writing is clear, concise, and easy to read.
- All information is true. Dishonesty on a resume is a guaranteed way either to not get hired or to be fired if the truth is learned, which it usually is.
- It is evident what the candidate has to offer the employer. Self-serving resumes are a waste of time.

- A poor resume is worse than no resume at all. Decide that yours will be excellent.

(Thomas, McMasters, Roberts, & Dombkowski, 1999).
One-page resumes are more influential in interview selections than are two-page ones, according to research.

"A tiny lie on a resume can destroy all credibility. A misspelled word or grammar error shows lack of thoroughness or pride in one's work."

LOIS KEMBLE, Cooperative Education Coordinator (retired), Southeast Community College, Lincoln, Nebraska

TYPES AND FORMATS OF RESUMES

As mentioned, a successful job search requires different types of resumes. One is the traditional "human eye" formatted variety that is to be read by someone. This is usually mailed or, in some cases, delivered personally to an employer. Today's job seekers may be overwhelmed by the variety of other ways resumes are sent and received. A potential employer may ask that you send your resume by e-mail. Since most businesses do not want to receive attachments, this requires converting the original one into plain text, which is explained later. If a company uses a scanning system, you will need to develop a type suitable for that technology. A successful job seeker will carefully research what has been called the electronic resume explosion (Washington, 2003). Obviously, technology is ever changing so it is absolutely necessary to regularly educate yourself. Several books deal only with electronic resumes (see Recommended Reading at the end of the book), and Web sites contain updated information (listed at the end of this chapter). Figure 4.1 clarifies a number of resume types.

All types of resumes can be powerful communication tools giving you an opportunity to be impressive. Regardless of which type you create, one of the first important decisions has to do with **format**—the way any type of resume is organized. The primary differences are in the order of listings and emphasis. The best choice depends upon you, your background, and what you have to offer. In this

FIGURE 4.1

Resume types.

- *Traditional or formatted:* Created with word processing then printed. It has an attractive graphic design and is intended to be read. This type is sent by mail, delivered personally, or sent as an e-mail attachment *only* if requested by the employer. Because of viruses, most employers will not open attachments.
- *Plain text:* (also known as text format and ASCII format): Used when sending a resume as text within an e-mail message or storing in a resume bank. This universal format is one that all computers recognize.
- *Scannable:* Created so that scanners can "hit on" key words. It is virtually free of formatting features. This type can be mailed or transmitted electronically.
- *Electronic or eResume:* Sent through cyberspace and not printed on paper. This type is used when e-mailing, posting at Web sites, and pasting into online forms.
- *Web resume and Web portfolio:* Less common than the others, these are types of personal Web sites that contain your resume and links to other documents that can help you make a positive impression.

section are descriptions and samples of different formats: chronological, functional, combination, and targeted.

As the name implies, the **chronological format** follows a time sequence and emphasizes dates. Positions are described beginning with the present or most recent, regardless of how relevant they are. After your job history, you tell when and for how long you were employed. See Figure 4.2 for a sample chronological resume. Consider the reasons you would choose this format.

An employer's shocked and amused reaction to a resume is not what a job seeker wants!

- Because it is the most common one, employers are comfortable with it. Many believe that dates are valuable information, and they expect to see them.

FIGURE 4.2

Sample chronological format.

KELLY L. HALL
2226 Parham Place
Ann Arbor, Michigan 48104
(734) 770-5546
klhall@yahoo.com

OBJECTIVE
Youth psychological counseling that requires expertise in understanding and helping young people achieve psychological well-being.

QUALIFICATIONS
- B.A. in Psychology with high distinction
- Youth counseling certification
- Counseling experiences with children aged 6–17
- Desire to continue to learn and expand current level of skills

EXPERIENCE

2003–*present*
Counselor, Youth Services
Larchmount Clinic
Ann Arbor, Michigan
- Counseled 16–20 children a week.
- Trained two new counselors.

1998–2003
Teacher Aide
Early Childhood Education Center
Columbia, Missouri
- Guided young children in development and craft activities.
- Provided art therapy sessions for five children.

EDUCATION

2003
B.A., Psychology
University of Missouri, Columbia, Missouri
GPA: 3.98

2002
Assisted with research on teenage drug abuse.
University of Missouri, Columbia, Missouri

AFFILIATIONS
American Psychological Association
Psi Chi Honorary Society
Student Senate President

- If your work history is stable with jobs of average or longer duration, this format focuses on a major asset.
- If your progression has been steady and in the direction of career objectives, achievement is evident.

Knowing the reasons you would want to consider another format is quite useful. A chronological resume is *not* in your best interests if you have had:

- Several jobs (the number varies depending upon your age)
- Jobs of short duration
- Unexplained gaps in your work history

Thinking of your own history, does it include any of the reasons to avoid the chronological format? If not, this is probably the best choice.

The **functional format** emphasizes experiences and skills, not dates. Chronological order is not required, so the resume writer can prioritize the value of the experiences and describe those first. See Figure 4.3 for a sample functional resume. Following are its advantages.

- You have an opportunity to highlight what you can do.
- The potential employer is not "hit in the face" with chronological liabilities. If you have unexplained gaps or several jobs of short duration, this is not evident.
- Relevant experiences can be described first even if they occurred early in your work history. For example, Kevin was applying for a job in radio broadcasting, and he had once had a similar position. Since then, he had worked at two other jobs. The chronological format would force him to describe the unrelated jobs before the broadcasting position. Using a functional resume, he could begin with his broadcasting experiences.
- Any of your skills that are assets for the particular position can be grouped together. This gives more validity to your qualifications.

Can you think of any reason a functional format would be a better choice for you?

As the name suggests, a **combination format** is both functional and chronological. Skills and experiences are functionally highlighted then are followed by a brief chronological listing of employment history and education. The advantage is the opportunity to emphasize what you can do for an employer while not avoiding what most want to know—dates and duration. See Figure 4.4 for a sample combination resume.

FIGURE 4.3 Sample functional format.

MICHAEL A. NEWTON

5424 Forest Avenue | (310) 552-2624
Santa Monica, California 90276 | mnew@earthlink.net

OFFICE MANAGEMENT

- Established procedures to improve office efficiency.
- Maintained payroll and tax records.
- Communicated with customers personally and by correspondence.
- Scheduled three crews on a weekly basis.

ACCOUNTING

- Set up and maintained a computer accounting system that resulted in a 20% saving.
- Prepared tax returns for a 20-employee company.

SALES

- Sold computers and related products for large electronics firm.
- Earned recognition for outstanding sales record in one year.

SUPERVISION

- Promoted after one month of employment to supervise three other crew members in pouring and finishing concrete for residential driveways.

EDUCATION

Associate of Science Degree, Business Management, 2003
Valley Community College
Riverside, California
GPA: 3.78

HONORS AND ACTIVITIES

Who's Who in Junior Colleges
President of Student Senate, Valley Community College
Dean's List (all semesters)
Volunteer, Red Cross

Sample combination format.

FIGURE 4.4

MARY A. MARTINO

4432 South Patton Avenue (802) 445-3829
Montpelier, Vermont 05156 (802) 330-9210
mmartino@juno.com

OBJECTIVE: Firefighter

EXPERIENCES

- Volunteer firefighting experience for six years
- Leadership experience as head of firefighting team
- EMT certified and advanced CPR training
- Associate of Applied Science Degree with Highest Distinction
  Fire Protection Technology
  GPA 4.0
- Relevant coursework in psychology, sociology, and interpersonal relations
- Volunteer experiences at rehabilitation center and with Meals-on-Wheels
- Customer relations responsibilities for large insurance company
- Retail sales with record for highest productivity for two consecutive years

EDUCATION

Associate of Applied Science Degree with Highest Distinction 2004
Fire Protection Technology
Rosemount Community College
Montpelier, Vermont

EMPLOYMENT

Customer Service Representative 1998–2003
American Life Insurance Company
Montpelier, Vermont

Salesperson 1996–1998
Beller's Department Store
New Haven, Connecticut

The **targeted format** clearly identifies what you can do in relation to a particular position. It also documents past achievements to support your claims and includes at the end a brief list of employment history and education (Jackson & Jackson, 1996). Designed to be highly specific, the major disadvantage is its limitation to just one position. If this is the job you want, the targeted resume is the best choice because it focuses on your directly related assets. See Figure 4.5 for a sample targeted resume. You can also find numerous resume samples in books (see Recommended Reading at the end of the book and Web sites listed at the end of this chapter).

No matter which format you choose, in order to be impressive and competitive today, you will also develop a resume to be used electronically. Obvious advantages are the speed by which you can respond to a job opportunity and the technological expertise that you are demonstrating. Online interactions between job seekers and potential employers are steadily increasing. The number of employers who use the Internet for recruiting is over 80 percent (Whitcomb & Kendall, 2002). You do not want to miss out on this interesting opportunity.

A scannable resume, defined earlier, is a necessity if you apply to a company that uses scanning technology. This type must be computer/scanner "friendly" so that it will be selected out of a database. In order for this to happen, it must contain **key words**—terms, words, phrases, and acronyms that relate to the position. These words are nouns, not the verbs or action words recommended for traditional resumes. For example, for a sales position, some possible words are sales representative, accounts, marketing, profits, quotas, and increase. During your employer research, an important question to ask is whether resumes are scanned. If so, yours must include the expected key words, or it will not be retrieved. If a job description is available, be sure your resume contains several of the nouns used in it. Books that focus on Internet job seeking such as *Jobsearch.net* (Straub, 1998) list several key words used in specific fields. Others, *Electronic Resumes & Online Networking* (Smith, 2002) and *eResumes* (Whitcomb & Kendall, 2002) direct you in developing your own key word list. Another good source of key words is the most recent edition of *Occupational Outlook Handbook* or online at www.bls.gov/oco/home.htm. Each key word your resume contains increases the likelihood that it will be sent on to a hiring authority. Unless you know for sure that the employer does not scan resumes, always send both a traditional formatted version and a scannable one, indicating which one is electronic. When mailing a resume that will be scanned, do not fold; send it in a large envelope with a scannable cover letter that follows the same guidelines as the electronic resume. Unless you are requested to do so, don't send a scannable resume by fax. If you do, also mail a high-quality copy.

Sample targeted format.

FIGURE 4.5

ROBERT WONG
2466 North 92nd Street
Lincoln, Nebraska 68520

(402) 477-6898 rwong@aol.com

JOB TARGET: **EMERGENCY ROOM STAFF NURSE**

EDUCATION:
Associate of Applied Science Degree in Nursing,
Southeast Community College, Lincoln, Nebraska
C.E.R.N., 2003
Active license as a registered nurse (RN) in Nebraska

CAPABILITIES:
Emergency medical treatment
Patient assessment
Successful patient rapport
Staff supervision
Training and development
Ability to think quickly and withstand pressure

ACHIEVEMENTS:
Performed all emergency room functions in a 12-bed emergency facility.
Assessed patient trauma in cardiac, respiratory, and psychiatric cases.
Supervised five emergency room staff members.
Provided continuing education to new personnel.
Treated serious injuries as a member of first-response ambulance team.

WORK HISTORY:
September 2003–present
Staff R.N., Emergency Room
Bryan LGH Medical Center, Lincoln, Nebraska
March 1996–September 2003
Emergency Medical Technician
Foster Ambulance Service, Lincoln, Nebraska

An electronic resume is scannable and is used in electronic transmissions (see Figure 4.7, later in this chapter). Following are steps to take to create an electronic resume:

1. Develop the traditional formatted resume using suggestions offered in this chapter.
2. Copy this resume into its own file. If not included before, add as many key words as you can and, if you choose, include a key word summary.
3. Create a plain-text (ASCII) version of the resume. Directions can be found in several books and on Web sites. The book *Resume Power* (Washington, 2003) offers very clear and easy-to-follow steps for converting into plain text.

Rather than converting a resume, you may prefer to create your own electronic one. If you do, make it plain and do the following.

- Use sans serif fonts such as Arial or Helvetica, which are clear with no extra strokes as part of the letters. The preferred font size is 12.
- Limit your lines. Recommendations vary from 65 to 75 characters. In most cases, set your left margin to 1.0 and the right margin to 1.25.
- Have all lines start at the left margin. Use separate lines for your name, phone number(s), and e-mail address.
- Do not use underlining, boldface, italics, bullets, vertical lines, or shading. As a highlight, you may use all capital letters to capture attention. Hyphens may be used.
- Use standard spacing between letters and lines. Do not use tabs.
- Use white 8½-by-11-inch non-textured paper with black ink. Use only one side.
- Print on a high-quality laser printer.

Besides mailing, your resume will now be ready for electronic transmissions.

Jot down key words that would apply to a position in your chosen field.

DECISIONS AND STEPS IN RESUME WRITING

After deciding about types and format, you will be faced with still more choices. This section presents questions and information to guide you in your answers. In some cases, a definite recommendation is given; however, you are free to choose what you think is best for you. A chapter-end activity offers questions and suggestions. After you make the decisions, take action. Assembling information, making a draft or what is more likely, several drafts, and then refining the information into a perfect piece will take plenty of time and energy, all of which can be one of the best investments you will ever make. Seriously consider the following questions and recommendations for resumes that are to be read—the traditional formatted type—and note the specific tips for a scannable version.

How Will I Head the Resume?

Every resume must have your name, address, and telephone number on it. You may also include a second telephone, fax number, and e-mail address. Your name should stand out. Centering it and using all capital letters and a slightly larger and bolder font is one possibility. Another is to leave a space between each letter so that instead of:

Janet R. Sterling

it is:

J A N E T R. S T E R L I N G

Many computer programs offer interesting heading formats.

That is a very creative resume.
What else do you have to offer our company?

Recommendation: Do not use "Resume" in your heading. Clearly the reader will know what this is! Be sure your name is the most obvious part of the heading; however, don't make it so much larger than the rest of the information that it looks "overdone." If possible, use computer technology to create an impressive heading. Definitely consider the impression your e-mail address conveys. For example, sexystud@hotmail.com is obviously a poor choice!

Do I Use a Career or Job Objective?

Not everyone agrees about this. Many career development experts recommend an objective in order to let a potential employer know what you want and to appear focused. Yet, some employers say to eliminate it. "An objective wastes space that could be better used for other information," says Ed Rasgorshek, a vice president in the agricultural credit industry. "A candidate is better off stating an objective in the cover letter rather than the resume and using one that specifically focuses on his or her unique strengths for the targeted position.

It's important that it not sound as if it were copied from a book," says Marcia Phelps, an associate director of career services at a university. Ted Milner, who owns his own executive temporary-help agency, puts it bluntly: "Objectives aren't impressive."

A disadvantage of an objective is that it can limit your resume, and if almost no information is conveyed, an objective doesn't help. Little is gained by writing, "To pursue a career in advertising utilizing my skills as an artist."

Recommendation: If you believe an objective in the resume will save the reader time or help you get the interview, write one that is clear and original. Otherwise, use a cover letter to define relevant goals.

What Comes After the Heading?

You may begin with one of the main categories or an eye-catching brief summary of your qualifications and skills. For a scannable resume, this section incorporates those recognizable key words and acronyms such as CPA. Use common industry-specific terms and jargon that describe your credentials. Regardless of format, a short, readable section describing what you have to offer calls attention to your assets immediately and saves time for the reader. Because of its position on the page, a summary has to be exceptionally well done. See the resume samples for recommended language and layout.

Recommendation: Write an easy-to-read, concise section that immediately lets the reader know what you can do for his or her business.

Do I Begin with Work History or Education?

The answer to this question is a quick, "That depends." A common mistake is to simply follow a format from a resume sample. That might not be your best choice. Remembering that a resume is supposed to impress an employer, describe your strongest area first. In some cases, strength is determined by which one is more recent. In the following scenarios, see if you can decide whether the applicants would be wise to begin with work experience or education.

> *Kelly has been in the workplace for seven years after earning a degree in psychology. For the past five years she has counseled in a hospital drug-rehabilitation program. She is seeking a similar position in a private clinic.*

In Kelly's case both her education and work experience are relevant. However, because she has had a position similar to the one she is applying for and her degree was earned seven years ago, work experience would be described ahead of education.

Alberto will graduate soon with a degree in economics and wants a position as a financial analyst. During college he worked in retail sales in a large department store.

Because Alberto has not had a job in his career field and his education is so recent, he would first cover education.

Tina has just earned an Associate of Applied Science degree in Fire Protection Technology. She seeks a firefighting position in a metropolitan fire department. For the past year she was an assistant in the state fire marshal's office and a member of a volunteer fire department.

This one is not as clear because both her education and her experiences are relevant and timely. In this case, as part of her research, Tina should find out which is more important to the fire department. If that doesn't give her an answer, it comes down to which, in her opinion, is her stronger asset. Because she is strong in both, it probably will not make a major difference.

Which is your greater strength—work experience or education?

Recommendation: Consider this carefully and don't just follow someone else's format. If your work experience and education are similar, find out which will be more impressive to a potential employer.

Is There a Certain Type of Wording to Use?

Most experts say to avoid the word "I." Rather than writing in complete sentences, the use of **telegraphic phrases** is highly recommended in a conventional formatted resume. These phrases begin with an action word such as *designed, sold,* or *instructed* and leave out unnecessary words such as *the, a,* and *also.* The phrases sound crisp and leave the distinct impression that you have been active. Select action words carefully (see Figure 4.6 for examples). A thesaurus can be an excellent resource. Marcia Phelps, Ph.D., a director of career development services at a university who has had several years of experience in human resources, says, "Employers today are most interested in what skills you can bring to the position. The most effective resumes are skills based rather than experience based."

If a resume will be scanned, the language is somewhat different. Most systems key in on nouns, and the words and acronyms you use must be the ones an employer has identified as desired qualifications.

FIGURE 4.6 Action words.

achieved	consulted	identified	reported
acquired	coordinated	increased	researched
acted as	created	informed	reviewed
addressed	delegated	inspected	revised
administered	designed	installed	saved
advanced	developed	interacted	scheduled
advised	devised	invented	selected
analyzed	diagnosed	maintained	sold
answered	directed	managed	solved
arbitrated	edited	marketed	sorted
assigned	employed	mediated	studied
assisted	engineered	monitored	summarized
balanced	estimated	negotiated	supervised
budgeted	evaluated	operated	taught
built	filed	ordered	tested
communicated	formulated	organized	trained
composed	gathered	recorded	updated
computed	generated	redesigned	utilized
constructed	hired	reorganized	wrote

Recommendation: Avoid "I" and complete sentences. For a read-only resume, use telegraphic phrases with specific action words. Anyone can use general words such as *worked, served as,* or *participated*. It's better to write specifically what you did. Another way to be specific is to include figures that favor you. Instead of "Serviced customer accounts," it is more impressive to write, "Serviced 165 customer accounts." Avoid "responsible for" as a lead-in because it does not describe action. Strive for consistency in verb usage rather than switching from past tense ("wrote articles") to present tense ("instruct students") when describing the same position.

Instead of abbreviating, write the word completely unless you are absolutely sure the reader will know what you mean, as in the case of college degrees. Even though postal abbreviations for states are commonly used, the more professional approach is to write the entire word. Any complete word will eliminate confusion and show that you can spell. If your resume will be scanned, include key words and acronyms such as *RN* along with "registered nurse."

What Is to Be Included in the Education Category?

If you are using the chronological format, the year or years will be included and are usually placed in the left margin next to the relevant information. Because the potential employer is most interested in your level of education, follow this order.

Degree or diploma

Major field of study

Name and location of educational institution

Generally, you can abbreviate the degree, as most people are familiar with the common ones such as B.A., B.S., M.A., M.S., and Ph.D. If your degree is not a familiar one, write it out completely.

Even if you have not completed the requirements for a degree or diploma, write: "Completed ____ hours in (course of study)," or you can write: "Will receive B.A. in May 2008." Listing a high school diploma isn't necessary because employers know a college student has completed high school. The exception is if you are a recent high school graduate with an excellent record either in academics, leadership activities, or both.

Most experts recommend that you include your GPA if it is high enough (3.0 or higher on a 4.0 scale) plus any recognition or honors related to academic achievement. Another possibility is to include relevant course work especially if education is your strongest asset or if the course focused on necessary or desired skills. For example, naming specific software courses and an interpersonal relations class lets employers know of valuable training and will likely make a difference.

Think of all relevant educational experience you would include.

Recommendation: Begin with your highest degree. Include any educational experiences that are assets, and almost all are. If your GPA is high and you have course work that is especially relevant, mention these. The simple heading of *Education* set off in capital letters and bold font is recommended in a formatted resume.

Interview Selection (Thomas et al., 1999)

Many interviewers gave the listing of relevant coursework as the reason for selection of interview candidates, and resumes listing GPAs of 3.0 are more likely to be selected than those with no GPA, according to research.

What Is to Be Included in the Employment Section?

Job or position title, duties and responsibilities, results, accomplishments, and former employers are featured here. If you are using the chronological or combination format, it also tells when and how long you have been employed. You may use years employed or months and years. A key point is that in the chronological format, you begin with your present or most recent position and describe your jobs in reverse order.

When you arrange the information, consider what the reader will most want to know. Of more interest usually is what you have done rather than for whom you have worked. The descriptions of job duties and responsibilities are where the reader will concentrate to see what you have actually done (duties) and the employer's level of trust and expectations (responsibilities). Resumes that are quickly readable are impressive. Scanning down a list is easier than reading left to right. Note the difference in the following descriptions.

> *Have taught courses in English and speech, developed new writing projects, and advised students; worked on a special team to improve teaching methods; and provided expertise to a student debate team.*

versus

- *Taught English and speech to diverse groups of students.*
- *Developed four innovative writing projects.*
- *Advised 50 students each semester regarding course schedules.*
- *Contributed creative ideas to a team designed to improve teaching methods.*
- *Led and provided expertise to a student debate team.*

The second one is easier to read and uses specific numbers. For a scannable resume, do not use bullets; however, you may use hyphens to set off your duties.

A scannable resume will use more nouns than verbs. For example, a job title or position such as "office management" is a better choice than "managed an office." On any type of resume, leadership or supervisory experiences and any advancement in responsibilities and positions are to be emphasized.

Recommendation: Emphasize your job title by putting it first, followed by employer name and location (exact address isn't necessary). Do an excellent job of describing duties and responsibilities by using specific action words and telegraphic phrases for a conventional resume. Arrange and set off the phrases so they are easy to read. For electronic resumes, use key noun words. On all resumes, include any evidence of leadership and advancement. If you use months, write out the word. If you list years only, be prepared to be more specific in an interview.

Possibilities for a heading are *Employment, Employment History, Employment Experience, Work Experience, Professional Experience,* and *Experience.*

How Can I Highlight the Education and Employment Categories?

Highlight or emphasize information by listing the most relevant information first. Use capital letters and, in the case of a traditional formatted resume, different font styles (bold or italics) to emphasize essential information such as job title. Place bullets in front of each telegraphic phrase to catch a reader's eye. Substitute hyphens or asterisks for bullets in a scannable resume.

Recommendation: Because an employer will most want to know your level of education and job positions, place them at the beginning of the descriptions and highlight them in some way. See the resume samples for possible ideas.

Besides Education and Employment, What Else Can Be Included?

Membership in professional associations related to your career can be included under such headings as *Professional Affiliations, Affiliations, Professional Memberships,* or *Memberships.* Most employers are impressed with volunteer activities. They are also looking for indications of teamwork and leadership in college and community activities. Unless they are specifically job related, don't use any that indicate religious, political, ethnic, or social affiliations or others that might concern a potential employer. Listing social fraternities or sororities is not advisable unless you believe this is necessary to show strong leadership.

What organizations can you include? Consider joining one or more that would add to your credentials.

Honors that indicate special expertise or leadership are quite important. This type of information can go in a separate section called *Relevant Experiences, Relevant Activities, Activities, Awards, Noteworthy Accomplishments, Accomplishments, Honors,* or *Activities and Honors.* Keep in mind that a potential employer is interested only in the ones that are assets for this position. If you were Girl Scout of the Year when you were in grade school, be proud of that; however, do not include it! Because so many candidates have similar educational and work backgrounds, supplementary information such as volunteer work, athletic pursuits, and elected offices can set you apart.

Licenses or certifications are assets, as well, and could be included under one of the categories mentioned earlier, if appropriate, or under a separate heading of *Licenses* or *Certifications.* If you have written articles or books that have been published, most employers will be impressed. In certain fields such as education, being published is a definite asset. These can be listed in a section called *Publications.* A thesis or dissertation can be placed in the education category. Special skills such as a second language or training in transferable areas such as interpersonal communication could make the difference in your getting an interview. You can indicate willingness to relocate or, preferably, write this in a cover letter.

Recommendation: Check your list of assets and include as many as possible. Know what the position requires and definitely include any experience that would document important characteristics and skills. Remember that a resume is a promotional piece that stresses what you have to offer this employer.

What About References?

This is an area of mixed opinions. Often, resumes end with the statement: *References Furnished Upon Request.* Because this is so common and is virtually useless at this point in the job search, you can, instead, include your references on a separate sheet headed *References.* This page is not a part of the resume. Consider the following reasons.

- Your references may help at this stage. For example, one day I received a telephone call from a man I knew from a volunteer organization. He owned his own printing company. He said, "I don't usually call references at this point. However, I saw your name and because I know you, decided to get your opinion right away." My positive comments about the candidate led to an interview that may not have occurred otherwise.
- Networking may pay off. If a name is recognizable and also credible. It can be particularly beneficial. When reading a list of references, I saw the name of a prominent citizen who was a top professional in the same career field as the applicant. This led me to be more interested in the resume than I might have been.
- Including references makes the potential employer's job easier. Instead of having to contact you and get your references, the list is right there. Incidentally, most employers don't bother to get an applicant's references unless he or she is one of the final candidates. Your impressive list of references may help you reach the final stage, if you include it at the outset.

If you have even the tiniest concern about a reference, you would be foolish to present this name. Otherwise, do all you can to see that your references are likely to be used.

You may want to vary the names depending upon the company and the actual position you are seeking. Following is a recommended way to list a reference. As a professional courtesy, do not use a home telephone number unless you have permission of the person.

Angelo Edwards, District Supervisor
United Industrial Products, Inc.
924 South 28th Street
Anchorage, Alaska 99502
(907) 486-2715
aedwards@uip.com

Recommendation: Selection of references was covered in Chapter 3. Include three to five references with your resume on a separate page headed *References.* Mention their inclusion in the cover letter. Use only professional references and include name, title, business address, telephone number, and e-mail address if possible. Be sure you have their permission.

Should I Include Personal Data Such as Age?

Most experts strongly advise not to do so. Besides age, personal data include marital status; children; religion; vital statistics such as height, weight, race, and sex; and condition of health. Ask yourself, "How will this information help me?" Any piece of personal information is just as likely to be considered a liability as an asset. Even though health is an asset, most employers know that nobody is likely to admit to less than excellent health. Your space is best used in other ways.

A most significant reason to avoid personal data is to show awareness of the law. If you include age or marital status, an employer is apt to wonder where you have been in recent years. This type of information is, in most cases, illegal for an employer to ask or to consider as criteria. Also, any candidate who would try to get hired on the basis of personal data is probably not the best applicant.

Recommendation: Do not include any personal data.

What Else Is to Be Avoided?

The following are on the list of "to be left out."

- Salary history or expectations
- Reasons for leaving past job
- Photograph (could be part of a portfolio for a modeling or acting position, but not on a resume)

- Hobbies and leisure time activities unless these are definite assets (if so, could be included when listing skills or accomplishments)
- Social Security number

Recommendation: Remember that the prime purpose of a resume is to convince the potential employer to give you an interview, and you have a limited amount of space. Not only does the information on the "leave out" list take up valuable space, it could actually be detrimental.

Guidelines for Inclusion of Information

- Will this create a positive impression of me?
- Will it enhance my employment chances?

How Can My Resume Have the Best Possible Appearance?

For a final copy, use a computer, a word processor, or a quality typewriter. If you don't have access to any of these, you will need to find someone or a company that can provide the service, or you can rent computer time. A quality printer such as a laser or ink-jet is necessary. Again, if you don't have one, find someone who does.

White space makes a resume more appealing. The page is to have at least one-inch margins on all four sides and adequate spacing between sections. A page completely full of print will turn off most readers. Accent lines and page borders can enhance the look of a traditional formatted resume. If you don't have software that can transform a plain typed page into an attractive piece, have it done for you. Businesses that provide layout and copying service typically charge a one-time fee for layout with small charges for future modifications.

After you have a "camera ready" copy, you have choices to make. One is selection of a reputable business firm that provides quality photocopying. Prices can vary considerably. While you are unwise to base your decision on which is the cheapest, there is no reason to pay a much higher price to a company that does not offer any higher quality than a less expensive one.

Another decision has to do with paper. Even though some people want to show creativity in a resume by producing a cleverly done brochure, a wiser choice is to stick with standard size paper. Choose a heavier-weight stock from the company's selection of professional resume papers. These are available in a variety of colors. Avoid anything other than light, conservative hues of white, ivory, gray, or beige. A potential employer is likely to make copies of your resume, so white or very light colors are much better. Avoid parchment papers; a textured or linen weave is acceptable. A wise idea is to purchase extra sheets for your cover letters and other correspondence. For scannable resumes, use white paper with black ink and have it copied on a high-quality laser printer.

Recommendation: Your resume is usually a potential employer's first impression of you. Consider what degree of quality you want to present. Follow the suggestions about producing the highest-quality resume. This is no time to be frugal if spending a little more will buy you a highly professional resume.

How Many Copies of the Resume Should I Order?

There is no absolute answer. Ask yourself how many copies of the resume you plan to use within a short period of time. If you plan to send out 50 resumes, get 55 copies so you have a few extra. It's foolish to order too many more than you will use right away. You can always get additional copies as you need them. Consider the case of Karla. "Out of excitement I had 150 copies made. I mailed out 25 the first week then got word from the telephone company that our number would be changed within a month!" If any information on your resume changes, you will want to create a new one.

Recommendation: Order only the number of resumes you plan to use within a few weeks.

What Else Is Important in a Resume?

Fine organization is a major plus in a resume. Readers want to recognize a logical sequence. What is called parallel structure is worth checking. For each job description, are you providing information in the same order? Are you consistent in verb tense unless there's a reason to switch?

What Can I Do with an Electronic Resume?

As mentioned earlier, the job of resume writing has become more involved in recent years. **Electronic resumes** are those that are needed for electronic transmission. Generally, the only people seeking jobs who won't need this type of resume are those who plan to work for an employer who doesn't have a computer (Whitcomb & Kendall, 2002).

One of the fastest ways to contact a potential employer and to reply to an advertisement is through electronic mail (e-mail), and you may be required to

WHAT DO YOU LIKE OR NOT LIKE ON A RESUME?

Key Advice

Architecture and Drafting: *"The format must permit a quick review. Don't get too cute or too artsy because this can cause difficulty in reading and be detrimental." —Lynn Jones, Chairman, Davis Design*

Drafting: *"Direct it toward the job you are applying for; don't be too generic. Make it clear that you have goals and have participated in school and community activities." —Mike Petersen, Supervisor of Drafting Services, Lincoln Electric System*

Machine Tool: *"Don't get any past employment dates mixed up, and be 'to the point' in describing your experiences. I definitely like to see references included." —John Buse, President, Precision Machine Co., Inc.*

Firefighting: *"I like to see evidence of experiences that contributed to positive character development such as worthwhile activities and organizations." —Darrell Eastin, Beatrice, Nebraska, Fire Department Chief*

"Put your personality into the resume. I want to know you, not a professional resume designer." —Mark Munger, Lincoln, Nebraska, Fire Department Captain

Communications: *"I prefer a short one-page resume with bulleted points that make for easy reading." —Doc Chaves, Marketing Communications Manager, Li-Cor, Inc.*

Automotive Technology: *"Previous employers and length of employment, driving record, certifications, and grades both in the classroom and in the shop." —Doyle Helmink, Owner/Manager, A & D Auto-Truck Service*

Child Care: *"Make it brief and include only current information." —Sue Collins, Director, KinderCare Learning Center*

Lending and Banking: *"I like to see a very organized and concise resume that has dates. Unexplained gaps in work history concern me." —Ed Rasgorshek, Vice President–Credit, United Agri Products*

Health Care: *"Resumes of length get lost in the shuffle. Details and listing every seminar you've ever attended are unnecessary." —Nancy Brown, R. N., Program Manager, State of Nebraska Health and Human Services*

Human Resources and Development: *"I want an easy-to-read and well-organized resume that has a neat and clean appearance. I don't need to know about hobbies and definitely don't need to see personal data." —Jody Horwitz, Vice President of Human Resources, The WB Television Network*

Law: *"Limit accomplishments to the most significant. Don't include every detail. Leave 'white space.'" —Jeanne Salerno, Director, Professional Development, Kutak Rock Law Firm* respond this way. The employer may tell you what and how to send; if not, send a plain-text (ASCII) resume to the employer's e-mail address along with a cover letter (discussed later). A good idea is to send a copy to yourself so you can see how it looks. It's advisable to also send a hard copy by regular mail unless you are told to not do so. Electronic resumes should be formatted according to the directions given earlier in this chapter (see Figure 4.7). Ideally, they are in plain text and contain key words that will show up in a scanning system.

What About Posting Your Resume Online?

The answer is a definite yes with a cautionary "however." First, definitely do not rely upon the Internet as your only avenue of delivering your resume. Then, don't expect an easy path to success. While online resumes do succeed in getting jobs, in many cases, they don't. As mentioned in Chapter 3, one estimate is that if the job isn't computer related, about 2 percent of resumes result in a job; if computer related, the success rate is about 45 percent (Bolles, 2001). Why? Though the number of employers using online job postings is increasing, the number of resumes posted is significantly higher than the jobs that are listed. In fact, an estimate is that there are 13.5 million resumes on the Internet (Nemnich & Jandt, 2001). The odds of your resume being selected from large resume banks are low. If you are aware of a particular opening or wish to be considered by a certain company or organization that has an Internet presence, go to the employer's Web site and follow the directions for electronic transmission.

Check First! (Smith, 2002)

Don't assume and don't guess. Always consult the source where you want to submit a resume. Then modify your electronic resume based on the specific requirements.

Although you may not land a job via the Internet, as a job seeker in the twenty-first century, you are remiss if you don't use it as one of your job-seeking methods. If you have any concerns about security, it would be a good idea not to include online your address or the addresses of other people such as references (Bolles, 2001). When posting a resume on a Web site such as Monster.com, you will be asked to register, then you will complete an e-form or resume template by typing text into specified fields. An employer's Web site usually has forms and specific directions about submitting your resume. Since technology changes so fast, your best approach is to stay abreast of current ways of building and posting a resume. For example, Rebecca Smith's eResumes & Resources (www.eresumes.com) helps in resume preparation, explains resume posting, and guides you in deciding where to post. The numerous

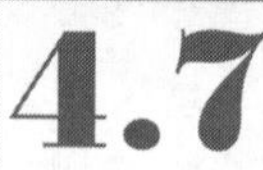

FIGURE 4.7 Plain-text resume (suitable for scanning and/or electronic transmission).

Kelly L. Hall
2226 Parham Place
Ann Arbor, Michigan 48104
(734) 770-5546
klhall@yahoo.com

OBJECTIVE Youth Counselor position that requires expertise in understanding and helping young people achieve psychological well-being.

QUALIFICATIONS
- BA in Psychology
- Youth counseling certification (CYC)
- Counselor to children aged 6-17
- Desire to continue to expand current level of skills

EXPERIENCE
2003-present
Counselor of Youth Services
Larchmount Clinic
Ann Arbor, Michigan
- Counselor to 16-20 children a week.
- Trainer of two new counselors.

1999-2003
Teacher Aide
Early Childhood Education Center
Columbia, Missouri

- Developmental guide for young children.
- Instructor of art therapy.

EDUCATION
2003
B.A., Psychology
University of Missouri, Columbia, Missouri
GPA: 3.98, graduated with high distinction

2001
Research assistant in study of teenage drug abuse
University of Missouri, Columbia, Missouri

AFFILIATIONS
- American Psychological Association (APA)
(Student Affiliate)
- Psi Chi Honorary Society
- Student Senate President

books devoted to electronic resumes contain detailed instructions and ideas of numerous ways to use them. These are found in Recommended Reading section at the end of the book. Web sites are provided in Online Resources at the end of this chapter. Whether you are new to or experienced with the Internet, look upon this as an opportunity to learn and perhaps land a job at the same time.

"Get rid of the idea that there is absolutely one right way to develop a resume. The 'right' way for you is the way that most effectively presents your skills and qualifications relative to the type of job you are seeking."

MARCIA PHELPS, Ph.D., Director, Career Development Services, University of West Florida, Pensacola, Florida

If you are ready to throw up your arms in despair because you don't think you can write an excellent resume, consider asking a friend or family member with more expertise to do much of it for you, or look into using a professional resume-writing service. A disadvantage of the latter is that these are often easily spotted by people who receive many resumes; in order to make yours unique, be the major consultant on the resume-writing project.

A computer is a valuable tool in drafting a resume.

If you opt to use a service, be sure to get references from others and shop around for a fair price as well as quality service. Most will offer a free consultation session. Above all, make sure you are satisfied with the writing style and the way in which you are presented to a potential employer. You can also go online for resume assistance on formatted, scannable, and electronic resumes. See the list at the end of this chapter.

When your traditional formatted resume has been written, proofread, printed, and copied, you are ready to mail it. Use a typewriter or printer to address the envelope and be sure to include a return address. The employer's address will look exactly like the cover letter's inside address, which usually requires four lines. A question is whether to fold a resume to mail. To present a neater appearance, use a larger envelope and an unfolded resume. If the resume will be scanned, definitely don't fold it. What is not open to question is a hard-and-fast rule: Do not send a resume without a cover letter. This leads to the next critical aspect of presenting yourself in writing.

Writing a Cover Letter

As difficult as you may think it is to develop a resume, writing an excellent cover letter can be even more challenging. And, even more than a resume, it may determine whether or not you get an interview. Why? Each cover letter is a creative endeavor. You may use the same resume for several positions while a cover letter is customized to the particular potential employer. A good way to destroy your chances for an interview is the obvious mass production of a cover letter. That is one reason Sue Collins, director of a KinderCare Learning Center, said she isn't interested in the cover letter. "They seem to all come from the same book." Obviously, you will want yours to be uniquely your own—and one that will arouse interest.

Another reason for a letter's importance is that employers realize that your resume could be the product of a professional resume-writing service. However, in most cases, applicants write their own cover letters. Because the cover letter is usually read before a resume, it becomes the first impression.

WHAT IS A COVER LETTER?

One day in class after I had been talking about the importance of a cover letter, a student asked, "This may be a dumb question, but what is a cover letter?" As an educator who doesn't believe that any question is dumb, I was happy that he asked! Specifically, a **cover letter** is a letter that accompanies a resume. Its purposes are:

- To introduce the writer and the resume
- To indicate a knowledge of and an interest in the particular employer and a desire for a position
- To explain briefly what you have to offer
- To request an interview

Your cover letter may be exploratory in nature, often called unsolicited, or may be solicited, such as in response to an advertisement. You could be writing because of one of your networking contacts. If this is the case, be sure you mention the person in your initial paragraph. See the examples in Figures 4.8 and 4.9.

GUIDELINES FOR COVER LETTERS

While each letter is written individually in one's own style, there are general guidelines. Unless it is absolutely impossible, the most important requirement is to send the letter to a specific person; in other words, use a name. Not doing so will most likely place your letter and resume behind the other candidates who did. Even if an advertisement directed you to send a resume to a search committee, find out the name of the head of the committee and give yourself an advantage. How do you find names? If you don't know who these people are, call and get the names and the correct spelling. If it's impossible to find out the name of the person who is hiring, the next best choice is to send your cover letter and resume to the human resources director. Again, use a specific name unless impossible. Be sure to spell all names correctly.

The letter, like the resume, is to be typed or printed from a computer. Using one half to three fourths of the page is preferable; this letter should not be more than a page long. If you are sending it electronically, follow the guidelines for either converting or creating it in plain text. Regardless of which way it is sent, perfection is again the key, so be sure you have no misspellings, grammatical or punctuation errors, or incomplete sentences. It's best to have someone else read the letter, as well, to check for errors and to see if the content is clear. Margins are to be at least one inch on each side, and there should be plenty of white space. One recommended format is to use single spacing with each line starting at the left margin. Double space between the paragraphs and don't use any indentations. Check to find out which form of a business letter is currently most preferred. In the case of a cover letter mailed with a scannable resume, convert it to plain text (ASCII format) as explained earlier. You will also use this cover letter version for e-mail transmissions.

CONTENTS OF A COVER LETTER

If you look at different samples, you will see various ways of heading and ending cover letters. A professional touch can be achieved in a traditional formatted letter by having your name, address, and phone number printed in a personal letterhead at the top. You can create your own letterhead on a computer. Other possibilities are to type your address and date at the top, or to begin with only the current date and at the end type your address under your name.

After the date, there is a quadruple space (four line spaces) then the inside address. The first line of this address will preferably be a person's name followed by a title. The next three lines contain the name of the company, street address, and city, state, and zip code. For the greeting you may use a title before the last name such as: *Dear Chairperson Steinberg, Director Carlson,* or *President Bowen,* or the customary *Mr. Thomas* or *Ms. Herrara*. At this stage of the search, using a first name is not recommended. What can you do if you are responding to a blind ad or have tried and been unsuccessful at getting a name? You may use either: *Dear Hiring Authority* or *Dear Human Resources Director.* **Never use:** *To Whom It May Concern, Dear Sir,* or *Gentlemen,* which implies that only men are in positions of power, or *Dear Madam.* End with a professional closing phrase such as *Sincerely* or *Respectfully* and four spaces below that, your full name. Use a colon (:) after the greeting and a comma after the closing phrase.

WHAT ARE YOUR RECOMMENDATIONS ABOUT COVER LETTERS? Key Advice

Communications: *"Send a 'killer' cover letter. This can be more important than the resume."* —Doc Chaves, Marketing Communications Manager, Li-Cor, Inc.

Architecture and Drafting: *"Address it to the proper individual. The personal touch helps. Be very careful about grammar and spelling as this is your opportunity to make a good first impression."* —Lynn Jones, Chairman, Davis Design

Drafting: *"Know who you are writing to and show that you know what product or service the company provides."* —Mike Petersen, Supervisor of Drafting Services, Lincoln Electric System

Automotive Technology: *"Introduce yourself, refer to the job you are seeking, ask that you be considered, and request an interview at the convenience of the employer. This should not be a long and involved letter, and I don't feel that salary requirements should be mentioned."* —Bob Batt, former owner, Auto Tek Service Center, Inc.

Health Care: *"A cover letter reveals a person's ability to write clearly and accurately. Writing skills are very important."* —Nancy Brown, R. N., Program Manager, State of Nebraska Health and Human Services

Machine Tool: *"Don't over-use the word 'I.' Other people helped you get where you are now."* —John Buse, President, Precision Machine Co., Inc.

Law: *"Make it short with no errors. Do not describe in the letter what is presented on the resume. Be sure to save information for the interview."* —Jeanne Salerno, Director, Professional Development, Kutak Rock Law Firm

Human Resources and Development: *"A cover letter is very important. I want to know immediately how and why this resume is coming to me. Is it a referral? What is the person looking for? Be sure you have names and titles correct and no misspellings."* —Jody Horwitz, Vice President of Human Resources, The WB Television Network.

If you aren't using personal letterhead paper, typing your address and telephone number under your name makes it easily accessible to the reader. Two spaces below that, type the word *Enclosure*, which indicates that a resume is enclosed. The samples shown in Figures 4.8 and 4.9 give you an idea of how this looks.

FIGURE 4.8

Sample cover letter (response to advertisement).

September 22, 20XX

Marcella A. Butler, Director
Early Childhood Learning Center
787 Prescott Road
Freeport, IL 61032

Dear Ms. Butler:

Your advertisement in the *Freeport Journal-Standard* attracted my attention. Because my career objective is to contribute to a child's optimum development and your center is considered one of the finest in this area, I would like to talk with you about the teaching position.

The job description intrigues me as the four-year-old age group is my favorite. During my graduate work at Oklahoma State University, I taught in the child center and researched language development. Evaluations from professors indicate that the children and I easily developed rapport and document my successes in encouraging and guiding their progress.

I would like an opportunity to meet with you and discuss what I can offer to your already outstanding center. Since my current job necessitates a great deal of travel and you may not be able to reach me, I will telephone you during the week of September 29, 20XX, to see that you received my resume and the other enclosed materials and discuss the next step. Your time and attention are appreciated.

Sincerely,

Elizabeth L. Neale
2822 N. Harrison
Freeport, IL 61032
(815) 232-8999
eneale@aol.com

Enclosures

FIGURE 4.9 Sample cover letter (exploratory).

4420 Hawthorne Lane
Springfield, Massachusetts 49015
April 25, 20XX

Ted Bowers, Senior Manager
Hallstead Accounting Firm
9046 Rayburn Place
Redondo Beach, California 90278

Dear Mr. Bowers:

Your accounting firm is held in high esteem by Nathan Goodwin, my uncle. Immediately after my graduation from the University of Massachusetts on May 10, 20XX, I am moving to the Los Angeles area and am eager to explore the possibility of making a contribution to your company.

Having paid for my tuition through scholarships and employment during the past four years, I look forward to beginning my career. The enclosed resume briefly explains what I have to offer. A few of my accomplishments are:

- 3.8/4.0 GPA while working 20 hours a week.
- Vice president of Delta Theta Pi Business Fraternity.
- Big Brother program working with disadvantaged youth.

I will be in Los Angeles on May 12, 20XX, and will contact you. If you would like any more information, you may reach me through e-mail or by telephoning me collect. I look forward to meeting you.

Respectfully,

Terry R. Mack
(413) 289-6447
trmack@yahoo.com

Enclosure

The main contents of a cover letter will vary somewhat depending upon whether you are responding to an advertisement or taking the initiative. In both the solicited and the unsolicited situations, the conventional letter has three sections; each is usually one paragraph long. The purpose of each section follows.

Introduction. Attracts the reader's interest and makes clear why you are interested and why you would be an asset. Your research should be evident; preferably, you express positive information about the business. The samples indicate some ways to do this. If your resume doesn't have an objective, be sure to include this. It will be clear to the reader why you are writing.

Body. Documents your assets; makes a strong connection between what you have to offer and what the business needs or what the position demands; calls attention to your resume. If you are responding to an advertisement, this section will convince the reader that you can handle the job. If you are initiating a search, it will point out why the employer would want to hire you. This part creates a desire to learn more about you.

Closing. Restates your keen interest in and regard for the specific business; requests a meeting at the employer's convenience; provides a way of contacting you; tells what you will do as a follow-up. If you are are responding to an advertisement, a comment about following up may not be appropriate; instead, you can acknowledge agreement with the described procedure. While many experts suggest that you write, "I will call to arrange an interview," You might consider a slightly different, and less direct, statement such as, "I will call to discuss setting up an interview." See the samples for other ideas. This last part requests action and shows without a doubt that you intend to play an active role in securing employment.

If you are responding to an advertisement, provide all requested information. Responding to "salary desired or expected" or a salary history request can be disconcerting. If the employer wants a full salary history, you may submit a separate sheet with an appropriate heading. Otherwise, you can include information about desired or expected salary in your letter. Ideally, your research will give you an idea of the exact wage or range for the position, or you can find lists of average starting salaries in various publications. If you don't have this information, decide what range is acceptable to you, such as "$35,000 to $40,000 a year," or use a general amount, such as "upper $30s a year." Do not offer any salary information unless it is specifically requested.

Of extreme importance is to sound enthusiastic and sincere. "An excellent cover letter conveys confidence and enthusiasm in its wording," says Tony Reimer, Claims Superintendent, State Farm Insurance, Rocky Mount, North Carolina.

Writing a rough draft as if you were talking directly to a person is a good way to start. Once something is on paper, you can polish the contents. Employers usually do not like letters that are filled with well-worn phrases and sound like everyone else's. Neither is it desirable to be overly clever such as: "How would you like to hire the best employee anywhere in the world? You have that opportunity if you choose yours truly!" Only a few would find this amusing and want to meet the writer.

"Don't just re-state what is in your resume. The phrase, 'As you can see by my resume,' is a turn-off. Tell me something I don't know."

MARCIA PHELPS, Ph.D., Director, Career Development Services, University of West Florida, Pensacola, Florida

You can also overdo a cover letter by writing too much. Just as a movie review is written to arouse interest in a film and not tell the whole story, you only want to motivate the reader to read the resume. "Tooting your own horn" too much will likely achieve the opposite effect. Your letter will create a positive impression if it's brief, readable, and error-free, and if it sounds like you—the "best of you in writing."

The cover letter and resume are always mailed together. A mistake that some job seekers make is to send this material with insufficient postage. Imagine what chance you will have if the employer is asked to pay for additional postage! If that doesn't happen, the mailing will be returned to you, and both time and money are lost. Take each mailing to be weighed for sufficient postage. You can use certified or registered mail although this could add up if you are sending several. Use the examples of cover letters for ideas, remembering not to end up with a letter that sounds like everyone else's.

Writing Other Letters

The cover letter is undoubtedly most important because it either "gets your foot in the door" or it doesn't. Other pieces of correspondence also play a valuable role in the job search.

FOLLOW-UP LETTERS

Potentially, the most effective letter is written following an interview. You can even consider sending one after a telephone conversation. Called a follow-up or thank-you letter, its main purpose is to show professional appreciation and, practically speaking, to place your name in front of a potential employer one more time. See Figure 4.10 for a sample.

The same guidelines, related to the inside address, greeting, and signature at the end, apply. One difference is that this letter typically is shorter. Similar to a cover letter, the follow-up has three parts.

Several drafts are necessary in order to produce a perfect letter.

1. *Introduction:* Whether the follow-up is after a telephone conversation or an interview, this short paragraph thanks the interviewer for her or his time and attention. This is stated simply and sincerely; gushiness is to be avoided.
2. *Body:* This part reinforces your interest in the position, shows any positive impression of the employer, and briefly calls attention to what you have to offer. Again, the emphasis is on what you can do for the company; as a result of your research or the interview, you probably know precisely what is needed.
3. *Closing:* At the end, either in a separate paragraph or in one sentence at the end of the body of the letter, the closing indicates the next step either on your part or the employer's.

A key point is to mail the follow-up letter the day after you speak with the person. The same day may give an impression of desperation. Follow-up letters are not written by all job seekers and if yours is impressive, it could make a definite difference. Use the sample in this section for ideas.

AFTER-REJECTION LETTERS

As strange as it may seem, writing a letter after you have not been offered a position can be quite advantageous. The overt purpose is to thank the employer for being considered; however, demonstrating an out-of-the-ordinary professional courtesy will leave a positive impression. Depending on the circumstances, you may also ask for another possible job source. See Figure 4.11 for a sample.

FIGURE 4.10 Sample of a follow-up letter.

October 24, 20XX

Marcella A. Butler, Director
Early Childhood Learning Center
787 Prescott Road
Freeport, IL 61032

Dear Ms. Butler:

After our interview yesterday, I was even more impressed with the Early Childhood Learning Center. I appreciated the opportunity to discuss the position of teacher for your four-year-old group. The tour and the positive experience of talking with several of your teachers were most beneficial.

The children were delightful, and I am very interested in and enthusiastic about being a part of their growth and development. They seem especially well suited for the language empowerment program in which I have had extensive experience. Since you indicated that this was a part of your future plans, I am confident I can provide quality instruction in this endeavor.

The Early Childhood Learning Center and you surpassed my expectations, and I would be pleased to contribute to its fine reputation. I look forward to hearing from you within a week.

Sincerely,

Elizabeth Neale
2822 N. Harrison
Freeport, IL 61032
(815) 232-8999
eneale@aol.com

Examples of all types of letters can be found in this section and in several of the books listed in Recommended Reading at the end of the book. Again, online help is also available (see end of this chapter). Critical in any type of written communication are accuracy, neatness, clarity, honesty, and sincerity. If a letter is error-free, readable, and genuinely represents you, it will enhance your chances of being interviewed and, ultimately, hired.

Sample letter in response to a rejection.

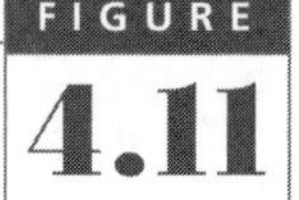

4420 Hawthorne Lane
Springfield, Massachusetts 49015
May 30, 20XX

Ted Bowers, Senior Manager
Hallstead Accounting Firm
9046 Rayburn Place
Redondo Beach, California 90278

Dear Mr. Bowers:

Even though I was disappointed when I received your letter telling me that someone else was selected for the accounting position, I want you to know that the opportunity to interview was a valuable learning experience. I realize that competition in the Los Angeles area is keen, and being one of the final candidates was a confidence-booster for me.

If your busy schedule permits, I would appreciate any advice you could offer as well as names of other potential employers. My positive impression of your firm has motivated me to continue in my career search. I appreciate the opportunity you gave me.

Respectfully,

Terry R. Mack
(413) 289-6447
trmack@yahoo.com

Filling Out a Job Application

Years ago an application for a job was probably the only writing expected of an applicant. In today's world of work, many companies still rely on an **application** to get the information they want and to scrutinize you as a potential employee. In these cases, even though you submit a resume and cover letter, you will also complete an application. Your research should indicate exactly what is expected of you: a resume, an application, or both. If you are hired, the application usually becomes a part of your permanent file. Regardless of how it is used, if an application is required, take pride in yours and make it *perfect*.

An application differs from a resume in one primary way. The resume is created by you so it's your choice of what and how much to reveal. On an application, you have no choice; an employer has decided what you are to provide. Because an application will usually ask for more information, just having a copy of your resume isn't enough. Having more information is much preferable to not having enough. Being prepared is essential.

If you can get a copy or copies of the employer's application in advance, do so. You may be able to fill it out at home; if so, you will probably have a choice of whether to type it or fill it in by hand. Be sure to check the directions. Typing can be challenging. For example, you may have difficulty staying within the allotted space. If a final copy is done at home, you will either mail it or return it in person. An employer may require you to come in person to fill out an application; if so, it helps to have an already-completed application to use as a guide.

APPLICATION INFORMATION

In whatever form, it's a good idea to have in writing the following information:

- The desired position
- Relevant data (your complete address including zip code, home and work telephone numbers, e-mail address, and Social Security number)

  You may wonder about anyone who wouldn't remember this information. However, "horror stories" from applicants reveal how easily memory can slip at critical times. You may even be asked for addresses for the past five to ten years, and your Social Security card may need to be photocopied.
- Complete education record including name and address of each school plus dates of attendance and graduation

  Some potential employers may even ask about elementary school.
- Complete employment record including names, addresses, and telephone numbers of present and past employers, names of supervisors, dates started and dates left, hours worked per week, total time of employment, pay at start and at end, duties, and reasons for leaving

  As you can see, applications may ask for information that is inadvisable to put on a resume. Space is usually limited so you will need to be able to explain your duties briefly. Action words are best. You may also be asked about military and volunteer experiences. A challenging question is reason for leaving. Avoid anything that sounds negative such as "personality conflicts." If you were fired, it's best to be honest, and writing "terminated" or "laid off" sounds less negative. Give positive reasons for voluntarily leaving such as "wanted advancement opportunities," "desired more hours," "returned to school," or "better position offered."

"The most common mistakes applicants make are not reading instructions carefully and failing to fully complete the form. Providing complete information is crucial. Failure to do so diminishes the opportunity for the candidate to compete."

DONALD L. BYRNES, Vice President for Human Resources and Staff Development, Southeast Community College, Lincoln, Nebraska

What if you don't remember some of the called-for facts? The answer is simple: Do everything in your power to find out. As one employer bluntly put it, "When it seems as if the applicant is too lazy to find a telephone number of a former employer, his or her application isn't considered." You can call schools and past employers to retrieve any forgotten information. In fact, it makes sense to call just to check for accuracy. "One of the most critical aspects is accuracy. Many times we see incorrect information," said Mark Munger, a fire department captain.

You will probably also be asked about citizenship, a past conviction of a law violation other than a minor traffic violation, and, if driving is required as part of the job, your driving record. The key is to be honest. This type of information can be easily checked, and dishonesty will probably be considered worse than what an applicant is trying to conceal. You might consider typing a brief summary of the circumstances of a conviction, leaving the impression that you learned from the experience. Matt, a young man, asked me after class one day, "What do I do about a minor in possession charge? It happened six years ago, when I was 16, and the juvenile records are sealed. Yet the application asks whether I have ever been convicted." After conferring with several employers, my advice was to be totally honest, add a few lines about it as a learning experience, and emphasize a clean record since. Six months later Matt called to tell me he had been hired by an employer who told him he had been quite impressed with his candor. The person told him, "Before I was old enough to drink legally, I could have had one of those myself; I was just lucky."

Another difficult question asks salary expectations. If your research has revealed the salary figure or range, then your answer is easy—just write that figure or figures. If it hasn't, the best options are to write "within the salary range," "prevailing wage," or "open to negotiation." Remember that salary information is readily available on most Internet job-seeking sites.

Most applications will also ask for a list of references. If the type is not specified, use only professional references such as employers or instructors. Because some employers also want personal references, be ready with these, as well. Information needed includes name, title, business address and telephone number, and length of acquaintance. These references are most likely to be contacted, so be sure you have selected wisely and then asked for the person's permission in advance, as discussed in "Selecting References" in Chapter 3. Immediately after submitting an application, contact your references and give them specific information about this particular company and position. Then, their comments can be even more beneficial. If a reference is a present employer, you have a choice understood by future employers. You may ask that the person not be contacted until you give permission, which may be during the final stages of hiring or after you have given notice.

Other possible questions on applications have to do with skills, activities, memberships, honors, licenses or certifications, and available employment starting date. If you are currently employed, be sure to indicate you will give the employer adequate notice. One more application went into the "dead file" when my husband read that an applicant who was currently working for another company could start immediately.

Does this sound like a lot of preparation? Instead of bemoaning the fact that there is so much required information, look upon it as an opportunity to impress a potential employer.

GUIDELINES FOR APPLICATIONS

Besides the data itself, applications can reveal other information to a potential employer. Even though you have filled out countless numbers of applications, treat each one as the difference between being hired or not. Create a perfect application. Following are further guidelines.

Be prepared. If you go in person, dress as you would for an interview, as you will be creating a first impression on at least one person. Take your own quality pen, preferably an erasable one that writes in black. Blue ink may be acceptable; black always is. A good idea is to take two pens. Walking in and asking to borrow a pen gives an impression of being unprepared.

Read the entire application before you begin writing. This can help you avoid several problems. Have you ever almost completed an application, then discovered you were writing on an incorrect line? Pay close attention to what you are to write where. "Take your time at this stage," cautions Sue Collins, day-care director. "Sometimes even yes–no questions can trick you."

Follow directions exactly. Common mistakes are made in the following areas:

- Information in the wrong place or writing in areas where it says not to write
- Order of information such as first or last name and employment history
- Too much or too little information, especially about employment history, as the application may ask for the past 10 years (or more or less)
- Type of writing, so instead of printing, an applicant writes in cursive
- Color of ink or whether typing is permissible

Be complete. Anything left blank is open to suspicion and concerns such as:

- Didn't have the information
- Didn't know how to answer or what to write
- Just forgot or was careless
- Didn't want employer to know

Would any of these reasons impress a potential employer? Blanks on applications lead to blanks in the job search. How do you avoid a blank? In some cases, you write a simple answer such as "no" or "none." For example, if the section is about military experience that you don't have, indicate that with the word "none." Writing NA, which means "not applicable," is appropriate if the question truly does not apply. An example would be: "Have you ever been convicted of a crime other than a misdemeanor?" to which you answered, "no." If the next question asks for details about the conviction, the appropriate response is NA. Writing "See resume" is also not recommended, as it can indicate laziness or taking the easy way out. Additionally, it makes the job harder for the person who is reading the application.

Be honest and accurate. These two coincide because a potential employer won't know whether the reason for the incorrect information is dishonesty or inaccuracy. This guideline is significant as any falsification on the application is cause for dismissal even after employment.

Write legibly and neatly. Poor writing can be misread so wrong information can be conveyed. If the application is difficult to read, most employers will be annoyed. Neatness deserves attention for other reasons, as well. An employer said, "If your application looks sloppy, I'm guessing you will do sloppy work." Either neatly erase any mistake or start over so that the end result looks perfect. Similar to a resume and cover letter, an application creates an initial impression.

Show excellent writing skills. An advantage of being prepared with the written information you need is the opportunity to check for any writing errors. Poor grammar and misspellings can lead an employer to think that you don't care enough. As on resumes, try not to abbreviate unless space demands it, and you are sure the reader will know what you mean. For example, NE as an abbreviation for Nebraska is fine if you don't have the space for the entire word. However, A.A.S. for the degree Associate of Applied Science may not be understood.

Recognize illegal questions and know how to respond. As a result of federal legislation, certain information is not to be considered as grounds for employment. Questions in any of the following areas are off-limits, and you have the right not to answer them.

- Age
- Sex
- Race, ethnicity, national origin
- Religion
- Physical or mental conditions unrelated to the job
- Marital or family status

Figure 4.12 provides a list of legal (on-target) and illegal (off-target) questions. Laws can change, so it is recommended that you check the most recent regulations with an agency such as the Commission on Human Rights or a government office.

If an application contains an illegal question, what can you do? Some applicants, who are willing to reveal this information, think their chances might be diminished by not answering, so they do. However, another course of action may be better. Instead of leaving a blank, you can write NA, or more clearly, "not relevant" or "unrelated to job qualifications." Or, you can write "see attached," and include a brief, tactful paragraph pointing out that this is an inappropriate question. An employer may be unaware of certain illegalities and even be impressed by your knowledge. If you are concerned that you might sacrifice your chances by pointing this out, consider whether you want to work for employers who might discriminate or who do not want mistakes called to their attention.

The final step in filling out the application is to sign your name. You will usually date the application, too. Amazingly, candidates do forget this all-important part of the process.

FIGURE 4.12

Solving the puzzle of on-target, legal questions.

Content Area	On Target	Off Target
Name	■ To ask whether an applicant's work records are under another name, for purposes of access to these records.	■ To ask the ethnic origin of an applicant's name. ■ To ask if a woman is a Miss, Mrs., or Ms. ■ To request applicant to provide maiden name.
Address/ Housing	■ To ask for applicant's address, phone number, and/or how he or she can be reached.	■ To request place and length of current and previous addresses.
Age	■ After hiring: to require proof of age by birth certificate. ■ To indicate minimum legal age for specific type of employment.	■ To ask age or age group of applicant. ■ Before hiring: to request birth certificate or baptismal record.
Race/Color/ National Origin	■ To indicate that the institution is an equal opportunity employer. ■ After hiring: to ask race and/or national origin for Affirmative Action plan statistics.	■ To make any inquiry that would indicate race, color, or national origin.
Gender	■ To indicate that the institution is an equal opportunity employer. ■ After hiring: to ask gender for Affirmative Action plan statistics.	■ To make an inquiry that would indicate gender unless job related. (Such jobs require written state government approval.)
Religion/ Creed		■ To ask an applicant's religion or religious customs and holidays. ■ To request recommendations from church officials.
Sexual Orientation		■ To inquire about sexual preference.
Citizenship	■ To ask whether ALL applicants are legally authorized to work in the United States.	■ To ask for date of citizenship or whether applicant is native-born or naturalized citizen. ■ To ask whether parents or spouse are native-born or naturalized. ■ Before hiring: to require proof of citizenship.
Marital/ Parental/ Family Status	■ After hiring: to ask marital and parental status for tax purposes. ■ After hiring: to ask name, relationship, and address of person to be notified in case of emergency.	■ Before hiring: to ask marital status. ■ To ask the number and/or age of children, who cares for them, and if applicant plans to have more children.

(continued)

Adapted with permission of Equity, Access & Diversity Programs, University of Nebraska, Lincoln, Nebraska

FIGURE 4.12 Solving the puzzle of on-target, legal questions (continued).

Content Area	On Target	Off Target
Military Service	■ To inquire into service in the U.S. armed forces. ■ To ask about branch of service, rank attained, and any job-related experience.	■ To request military service records. ■ To ask about military service in armed service of any other country. ■ To ask about type of discharge.
Education	■ To ask whether the applicant has the academic, professional, or vocational training required for the job, and to ask which institution provided it. ■ To ask about language skills such as reading and writing foreign languages, if job related.	■ To ask the racial or religious affiliation of schools attended. ■ To ask how foreign language was acquired.
Criminal Record	■ To inquire about convictions if the reason for the inquiry is a business necessity.	■ To inquire about arrests.
References	■ To request general and work references not relating to race, color, religion, sex, national or ethnic origin, age, disability, or marital status.	■ To request references specifically from clergy or any other persons who might reflect race, color, religion, sex, national or ethnic origin, age, disability, or marital status.
Organizations	■ To inquire about professional organizations, union memberships, and any offices held.	■ To request listing of all clubs to which applicant belongs or has belonged.
Photographs	■ After hiring: to require photographs for identification purposes.	■ Before hiring: to request photographs.
Work Schedule	■ To ask about willingness to work the required work schedule. ■ To ask if applicant has military reservist obligations.	■ To ask about willingness to work any particular religious holiday.
Physical Data	■ To require proof of ability to do manual labor, lifting, and other written physical requirements if necessary for the job.	■ To ask height and weight, impairment, or other non-performance-related physical data.
Disability	■ To ask whether the applicant is capable of performing the essential functions of the job with reasonable accommodation.	■ To exclude disabled applicants as a class on the basis of their type of disability. (Each case must be determined on an individual basis by law.)
Other Qualifications	■ To inquire about any area that has direct relevance to the job.	■ To inquire about political affiliation. ■ To make any inquiry not related to a bona fide requirement of the job that may present information permitting unlawful discrimination.

"Of 90 applicants for one position, 80 were 'weeded out' by minor writing errors on their applications. It was a quick, easy way to screen out those who really didn't seem to care."

DOC CHAVES, Marketing Communications Manager, Li-Cor, Inc., Lincoln, Nebraska

Too often, applicants do not take applications seriously. Individuals come in totally unprepared and then, in a lackadaisical manner, partially complete the form. They don't get the job. Instead of doing a less-than-excellent job, the successful applicant realizes that an application, because it's a company product, is to be taken seriously and is an integral part of pursuing a desired position. It is my hope that you will be like a former career development student who, after being hired at a major printing company, said, "One of the first questions I was asked in the interview was where I had learned to fill out an application. The person said 'It's the best application I've ever seen!' I think it had a lot to do with my getting this dream job."

Use the application example at the end of this chapter as a way of preparing for a basic part of the job search.

Writing skills matter a great deal during the job search and after you are hired. You will be expected to present yourself in writing in several ways. The inability to excel in these efforts will severely deter you in your career. To be successful, your written communication deserves the finest effort.

KEY POINTS

- How you present yourself in writing usually makes the difference between getting an interview or not.
- A resume is a short promotional piece highlighting an applicant's qualifications, educational and employment background, and accomplishments. It is designed to create interest in you as a potential employee.
- In today's world more than one type of resume is recommended. Any job seeker needs to be aware of resume types including formatted, plain text, scannable, and electronic.
- There is no one "right" resume; yet, certain guidelines are to be followed.
- Resume formats include chronological, functional, combination, and targeted.

- Being aware of decisions and steps to follow in developing an effective resume and reasons for differences will help you choose the best resume for you.
- A cover letter always accompanies a resume and is as important as the resume, if not more so, to most employers. If you send a resume electronically, the cover letter will need to be changed to match the text of the electronic resume.
- Other letters are indicators of your interest and professionalism, as well as your writing skills.
- Even though all employers don't require a written application, learning how to fill one out is necessary.
- Typically, an application will indicate your ability to follow directions and also provide information about you.
- In all forms of written communication, honesty, readability, neatness, and accuracy are essential.

ONLINE RESOURCES

Best College Resumes: www.collegegrad.com/book/3-0.shtml
Career Lab: www.careerlab.com/letters

JobSmart: www.jobsmart.org/tools/resume/index.htm

Quintessential Careers: www.quintcareers.com/resres.html and www.quintcareers.com/covres.html

Rebecca Smith's eResumes & Resources "eResumes 101": www.eresumes.com

The Riley Guide: www.rileyguide.com (link to resumes and cover letters)

WetFeet: www.wetfeet.com (link to resumes)

For posting resumes, see sites listed in Online Resources at the end of Chapter 3.

KEY STEPS

PUTTING YOUR WRITING SKILLS TO WORK

Your list of assets that you identified in a Chapter 1 activity contains essential information you can use for resumes, cover letters, and applications. After reading the material about resumes, answer the following questions. Then, show that you can impress a potential employer in writing by filling out the basic job application that follows this section.

- Do I understand the need for more than one type of resume and have I researched to find which ones I will need? If so, list those below.

  ____

  ____

  ____

- Regardless of the types I develop, what type of resume *format* will best serve me?

  ____

- Will I use an objective? (If yes, write a few possibilities.)

  ____

  ____

  ____

- What experiences, skills, and achievements would I list in a summary?

  ____

  ____

  ____

  ____

- Will my first category be education or employment?

  ____

- From Figure 4.6 in Chapter 4, which action words can I use in describing what I have done? (Write them below.)

  ____

  ____

- What key words can I use in an electronic resume? Write several below.

  ____

  ____

- How will I head the education category?

  ____

- What will I include in this category?

  ____

  ____

- How will I head the employment category?

  ____

- What will I include in this category?

  ____

  ____

- What will I include in the following areas?

  Memberships and affiliations:

  ____

  ____

  Volunteer work:

  ____

  ____

  Honors, activities:

  ____

  ____

  Certification, licensure:

  ____

  ____

- What else might I want to include?

  ____

  ____

  ____

Look at your list of assets from Chapter 1. How many have you emphasized?

Draft a cover letter following the suggestions in Chapter 4. Ask someone to proofread it and give you honest feedback.

APPLICATION FOR EMPLOYMENT
(*Type or print in black ink*)

Last name ______________________ First ______________ Middle ______________

Street address ____

City ______________________ State ______________ Zip Code ______________

Home telephone number Work telephone number

( ) ______________________ ( ) ______________________

E-mail address ____

Social Security number ______________ Are you age 18 or over? ❑ yes ❑ no

(used for computer retrieval only)

EDUCATION RECORD

Do you have a high school diploma or GED? ❑ yes ❑ no

Name and location of secondary school Highest grade completed

____

Name of college Location

____

Major field of study Degree Dates attended

____

Name of college Location

____

Major field of study Degree Dates attended

____

Other ____

____

____

____

EMPLOYMENT RECORD

Begin with current employer and list all employment for the past 10 years. Use other paper, if necessary.

Present or last employer ______________________________

Job title ______________ Name of supervisor ______________

Address ______________________________

City ______________ State ______________ Zip Code ______________

Total time employed ______________ Date started ______________ Date left ______________

Hours worked per week ______________ Pay at start ______________ Pay at end ______________

Describe duties: ______________________________

____

____

Reason for leaving or wanting to leave: ______________________________

May we contact? ❑ yes ❑ no Telephone (   ) ______________

Employer ______________________________

Job title ______________ Name of supervisor ______________

Address ______________________________

City ______________ State ______________ Zip Code ______________

Total time employed ______________ Date started ______________ Date left ______________

Hours worked per week ______________ Pay at start ______________ Pay at end ______________

Describe duties: ______________________________

____

____

Reason for leaving: __________

May we contact? ❑ yes ❑ no Telephone ( ) __________

Employer __________

Job title __________ Name of supervisor __________

Address __________

City __________ State __________ Zip Code __________

Total time employed __________ Date started __________ Date left __________

Hours worked per week __________ Pay at start __________ Pay at end __________

Describe duties: __________

____

____

Reason for leaving: __________

May we contact? ❑ yes ❑ no Telephone ( ) __________

MILITARY

Have you ever served on active duty in the U.S. Armed Forces? ❑ yes ❑ no Branch __________

Primary duties: __________

____

____

OTHER INFORMATION

Are you a U.S. citizen? ❑ yes ❑ no

If no, do you have the legal right to work in the United States? ❑ yes ❑ no

If no, please explain: ______________________________

____

Have you ever been convicted of any violation other than a minor traffic violation? ❑ yes ❑ no

If yes, please explain: ______________________________

Type of employment desired (check all that apply):

❑ Permanent ❑ Full-time ❑ Part-time ❑ Temporary Date available: __________

REFERENCES

Name ______________________ Title ______________________

Address ______________________________

City ______________ State ______________ Zip Code ______________

Telephone number(s) ______________ E-mail address ______________

____

Name ______________________ Title ______________________

Address ______________________________

City ______________ State ______________ Zip Code ______________

Telephone number(s) ______________ E-mail address ______________

____

Name ______________________ Title ______________________

Address ______________________________

City ______________ State ______________ Zip Code ______________

Telephone number(s) ______________ E-mail address ______________

____

APPLICANT'S SIGNATURE ______________________ DATE ______________

5

A successful interview is a springboard to a fulfilling career.

Interviewing with Confidence

For almost all career builders, a job interview is inevitable. Nearly 95 percent of all employers require them prior to hiring, and most consider an effective interview to be the most important hiring factor, more so than work experience, recommendations, and academic achievement (Krannich, 2000). If you have been asked to interview, congratulate yourself for reaching this stage and view it as a supreme opportunity. Also realize that an interview ranks among the highest anxiety-provoking life experiences and that impressions, once made, are hard to erase. You will want to manage the anxiety and make a positive impression. Being fully prepared for the interview can considerably lower your anxiety and set the stage for a successful outcome.

Preparing for an Interview

In actuality, the entire job search up to this point has been preparing you for interviews. Ideally, you have conducted several informational interviews and have amassed valuable knowledge while polishing your communication skills. Of utmost importance is to realize that your first conversation with a potential employer to arrange an interview is critical. Be open, adaptable, and positive!

Once a meeting is arranged, two invaluable pieces of information are the length and type of interview. One hour for an interview is typical, although this can vary. As to type, will you be talking to just one person, and if so, is this person in the human resources department, which would be a screening interview, or is it a supervisor of the position? This information will help you prepare in terms of what questions to expect and which ones to ask. You will also want to know, if possible, how many interviews will be required before a hiring decision is made.

Your interview may be conducted by a group. Not expecting this can create panic at the time of realization. In actuality, a group interview has its advantages. For example, if five people are on the team, you will need to impress only three of them. Additionally, eye contact may be easier because you aren't required to keep focused on just one person.

Most of the material in this chapter focuses on a face-to-face first interview. You may be interviewed on the telephone. If so, it's important to convey a positive, pleasant voice and to answer each question clearly and efficiently. Often, employers conduct second interviews that are almost always face-to-face. In this case, you know you are among the final applicants. Questions will probably be more specific and are often situational ones that are discussed later. All types of interviews are clearly described in *The Everything Job Interview Book* (Adams, 2001), and Web sites often have specific advice on second interviews (see end of chapter). Knowing what to expect and having the maximum amount of information increase your sense of control. The best advice is to practice. Employers, such as two in the firefighting field, concur.

> The most important piece of advice I can give is for a person to practice for an interview. Too often, individuals show up and have never considered how or what might be asked of them. That's the wrong way to go.
>
> *—Captain Mark Munger*

> Practice for an interview cannot be over-stressed.
>
> *—Fire Chief Darrell Eastin*

Ideally, you would go through a mock videotaped interview. The students in career development classes find that this experience, while a little frightening, is extremely valuable. "I didn't know I did that" was a comment about a specific gesture. "I liked the way I answered that question. I'm going to remember to use it" was another. Seeing yourself in action is a priceless picture. If videotaping isn't possible, you can still practice interviewing skills with someone else and learn a great deal from the frank appraisal of the mock interviewer or a person who acts as an observer. Ideally, being able to see yourself on videotape exactly as the interviewer sees you is the best learning experience of all.

PREPARING YOURSELF MENTALLY

Most candidates approach this stage of the process by thinking: "I want to impress the employer so he or she will offer me this position." Even though this is a worthy goal of a successful interview, a preferable attitude is: This interview is a mutual exchange of information during which I will decide if this position is right for me. Realistically, because the interviewer will be deciding if you are right for the position, being impressive is essential. Yet, placing yourself in the position of an equal partner in the interview can lower intense pressure, eliminate a feeling of desperation, and elevate your confidence. Thinking about this interaction as similar to any in which you want to let yourself

A practice videotaped interview even without professional attire is excellent preparation.

be known, get to know another person, and, hopefully, impress each other, will help you be more comfortable. Another thought that can provide a psychological boost is to realize that the interviewer wants to be impressed by you. Trying to find the right person for a job is difficult, and you are in a position to make this easier. In reality, the interviewer would like to hire you!

Determining a goal for the interview is a critical part of mental preparedness. Would a logical one be to receive a job offer at the end of the interview? Remember that any employer who would hire you "on the spot" may be too hasty in decision making (you may be fired just as quickly) or is desperate. Neither of these types would make a worthy employer! A more realistic goal is to impress the interviewer so that you are a top contender.

KNOWING WHAT EMPLOYERS WANT

What qualities do almost all employers seek? Two individuals, because they work closely with employers, know what is wanted. "Strong oral and written communication skills, interpersonal skills, responsibility shown in attendance records and quality of work, computer literacy, and, in several cases, a second language," says Marcia Phelps, director of career development services at a university. Jeanne Baer, a consultant to many employers, says: "Flexibility, being open to change, commitment, problem-solving abilities, and evidence of being a team player." According to Regina Pontow, who maintains an Internet site (www.provenresumes.com), communication and problem solving are two of the ten hottest skills desired by employers. Likewise, Lynn Willey, a placement specialist for a community college, says, "Employers who post positions with us list good communication skills, positive attitude, and ability to be a team player before they mention technical skills." As much as possible, these characteristics should be apparent or expressed during an interview. Read Key Advice for ideas from employers and college program chairs.

If what you have to offer matches with an employer in your career field, use the interview as an opportunity to convey this. Also enlightening is to know what keeps people from being hired. Check Key Info on page 192 for interviewee mistakes.

Importantly, review your assets with a specific focus on the particular position. "What does this company need that I have to offer?" "What can I bring to this position?" If your research has not been complete, these questions demand attention. Essentially, interviewers are much more interested in what *they* want than in what *you* want. Thus, a major interview goal is to directly address the employer's needs and convey how your skills and abilities match. Display the attitude that you have characteristics and skills that will be of great benefit to this business. Focus your attention on this employer's needs.

The most critical part of the preparation process is to learn how to interview. You may have exactly what the employer needs and still not be selected. The art of interviewing is just that—an art, and, as such, must be mastered if you are to be successful.

WHAT DO EMPLOYERS WANT? Key Advice

Enthusiasm, energy, loyalty, verbal skills, humor—Mark Munger, firefighting captain

Mechanical aptitude; formal education; physical endurance and agility; knowledge of fire prevention, rescue, and supervision practices; ability to establish and maintain effective working relationships—Darrell Eastin, firefighting chief

Enthusiasm, quiet confidence, ability to work with people and communicate, knowledge of job tasks, honesty, and ethics—Lynn Jones, architecture and drafting firm chairman

Desire to help the company, commitment, innovative ideas, initiative—David Hanna, insurance regional office manager

Willingness to learn and take on challenges, ability to start tasks with limited direction, flexibility so that you can work in a multi-project setting, punctuality, and the ability to work with others; a "people" person—Mike Petersen, drafting supervisor

A balanced ego so you believe in yourself but are not brash, basic communication skills, compassion about work, ability to interact with others, and taking what you do seriously but not taking yourself too seriously—Doc Chaves, marketing communications manager

Communication skills, maturity in judgment, commitment, efficiency, professional manner—Jeanne Salerno, law office development director

Dependability, meaning being at work every day and on time, dedication; enthusiasm; motivation to do the job right the first time; the drive to accept continuous training; ability to get along and have fun at the job; a neat, clean appearance as it has a direct influence on the business; and a college degree—Doyle Helmink, automotive repair business owner

Good attendance, positive attitude, ability to work safely—Jerry Baxter, manufacturing plant manager

Ability to perform the tasks, pride in what one does; being comfortable with change, self-motivated, quick to learn, strong "people" skills, ability to sell and attract clients—Lisa Patterson, accounting firm senior manager

Commitment to the job, loyalty to the company, reliability, integrity, honesty, team spirit, flexibility, adaptability, and an ability to think "outside the box" (i.e., creatively and innovatively)—Jody Horwitz, media and entertainment vice president of human resources

(continued)

WHAT DO EMPLOYERS WANT? Continued **Key Advice**

Self-motivation, organization, interpersonal skills, and ability to prioritize—Laura Mann, sales representative

Reliability, straightforwardness, organization skills—Ed Rasgorshek, agricultural credit vice president

Integrity, efficiency, dependability, professionalism, effective communication skills—Nancy Brown, state health and human services system program manager

Training and education, dependability, reliability, good communication skills, flexibility, appropriate motivation—Alicia Baillie, early childhood education program chairperson

Punctuality, ability to get along with other people, technical skills—Janis Bible, medical laboratory technology program chairperson

Professional attitude, willingness to learn new techniques, technical laboratory skills, responsibility—Don Mumm, laboratory science technology program chairperson

Positive attitude of being a team player, problem solver, desire to help the company be profitable and grow, good attendance, motivation to achieve academically—Millard Carnes, machine tool technology program chairperson

Technical skills, "people" skills, broad training background, flexibility—Linda Bettinger, computer technology program chairperson

Strong work ethic, commitment to the job and the profession, ability to get along, and positive attitude—Kathleen Uribe, surgical technology program chairperson

Self-confidence, preparation in the field, open-mindedness, good people skills—Jo Ann Frazell, office technology program chairperson

Positive attitude, ability to problem solve, communication and interpersonal skills, dependability—Virginia Hess, nursing program chairperson

Ability to use technology, creativity, problem-solving abilities—Dan Masters, drafting technology program chairperson

Respect for the chain of command, positive attitude, sound problem-solving skills, honesty, "people" skills, dependability—Sue Asher, dental assisting program chairperson

WHAT DO EMPLOYERS WANT? Continued **Key Advice**

Confidence, good hygiene, alertness, modest dress (with no tattoos, body piercing, or extreme hairstyle), ethical character, reliability; a happy person who is committed to lifelong learning; and willingness to work evenings, weekends, and holidays—Iris Winkelhake, practical nursing program chairperson

Employees who know the latest technology and stay informed on what is coming; currently, the biggest selling point is the ability to adjust and adapt to the people you work with and for—Sherry Kohout, radiologic technology program co-chairperson

Good attendance, following directions (both text and verbal), and decision-making skills that show a good use of logic—Ken Jefferson, automotive technology chairperson

Selling Yourself During the Interview

What will make a positive difference during an interview can be determined from a quick look at the four developmental areas of self—physical, mental, emotional, and social—followed by other success tips and ways to communicate. A survey of employers revealed the most sought-after skills (Shakoor, 2000).

- Interpersonal
- Teamwork
- Verbal communication
- Analytical
- Computer
- Written communication
- Leadership

Selling yourself involves knowing what employers want and letting them know that you possess these qualities.

PRESENTING YOUR BEST SELF

The whole self will come across in the interview as a "total package." Yet, you can use knowledge of the four developmental areas to bring the best "you" to this important interaction.

KEY INFO

Common Mistakes Made by Applicants (Adams, 2001; Madry, 1988)

1. Poor or too casual attire and appearance
2. Arriving late for the interview
3. Inability to express information clearly
4. Lack of interest and enthusiasm
5. Lack of planning for career; no purpose and no goals
6. Nervousness, lack of confidence and poise
7. Putting too much emphasis on money
8. Overaggressiveness
9. Tendency to make excuses
10. Lack of tact, courtesy, and maturity
11. Not knowing about the company or job
12. Condemnation of past employers
13. No genuine interest in job or company
14. Not enough eye contact
15. Sloppiness on application form
16. Little sense of humor
17. Speaking too much and speaking too quickly
18. Failure to express appreciation for interviewer's time
19. Failure to ask questions about the job
20. Giving vague responses to questions

Physical Self

Preferably, several weeks before a scheduled interview, you will make decisions and take action regarding your physical presence. How you appear to an employer is a vital part of first impression and reveals a great deal about pride in self. You want to emphasize your positive appearance points and de-emphasize the negative ones. Three key aspects of appearance are essential: neatness, cleanliness, and appropriateness.

Being appropriately dressed demands expenditure of time and probably money. Consider it one of the best investments you will ever make. "Appropriate" means suitable for the occasion. A job interview is a semiformal event, and in most cases, to be appropriate, you must look professional. Dressing too casually or showing a lack of professionalism will dim your chances. Conversely, overdressing is inappropriate. Just as a man would not think of wearing a tuxedo to a job interview, a woman does not want to look as if she is going to a formal affair. Wearing a quality outfit is advisable.

"It impresses me when it's obvious the applicant has tried to be impressive in appearance."

TED MILNER, President, Executive Temps, Burbank, California

A general "rule of thumb" is to dress one step above what you would wear to work. However, it could be two steps above. Research can help. During an informational interview, ask about interview attire, not just what you can get by with wearing but what will make the most positive impression. Unless one is applying for a manual labor or truck driving position, both men and women can safely dress in a business suit, and in most white-collar positions, this is expected. In some occupations, rather than a suit, a man could wear slacks and a dress shirt. Shiny shirts are not advised (Adams, 2001). An owner of a trucking company commented, "Even though I wear a suit, I might wonder about a person in a dressy suit applying for a truck driver position. He or she would need to be neat and clean, however."

Looking too casual isn't appropriate for an interview.

What about color? Gray, dark blue, or black is preferred, although other conservative colors are permissible. As long as it's not overly bright or flashy, if a certain color is especially complementary, that is a good choice.

Females should avoid low-neck blouses and very short skirts even if they are in style. One young female, after watching a videotape of a mock interview, commented, "Wow! I didn't realize how revealing that blouse is or how much of my legs would show. I'm glad I saw this here first!" Jewelry should be tasteful and not distracting. Also, a woman may want to consider taking an extra pair of hosiery along just in case there is a need for a change. For both sexes, shoes that go with the attire should be clean and polished and fingernails clean and trimmed. If you polish your nails, it's advisable to use a light, neutral color. You may love your bright purple nails yet be interviewed by someone who isn't impressed.

Keep comfort and confidence in mind. Wear an entire outfit before the interview so you can feel "at home" in it. If you've made a wise choice, your appearance should increase your confidence. Whatever you wear, interviewers will be impressed by a healthy, energetic look. Applicants who look tired, unhealthy, or apathetic have definite liabilities. Taking good care of yourself and aiming for wellness, getting a good night's sleep, then maintaining an alert, interested, and pleasant facial expression will go a long way in enhancing your physical appearance.

Ideally the applicant and interviewer will have similar attire.

An interviewer can be "turned off" for any number of other physical reasons. Tattoos and body piercings are relatively common, yet a wise job seeker realizes that the job could be put in jeopardy and makes sure they don't show during an interview. When two finalists are close, these seemingly simple fashion statements will likely make the difference. Years ago when men began piercing their ears, this was mentioned in a career development class. As one who didn't object to it, I added that a person might not want to work for an employer who was so against this particular "look." Keep in mind that you have a choice of what you want to do. Two other "turn-offs" have to do with scent. Consider these scenarios.

Emma looked the part of a career woman as she walked confidently in to be interviewed by Bridget, the department manager. Unfortunately, it was not only Emma's appearance that was noticed. The perfume that she had evidently doused herself with permeated the office. "The worst part about it," said Bridget to a co-worker, "is that it's a scent I really detest."

Emma undoubtedly didn't realize that it's possible to smell just one drop of perfume diffused throughout an entire small house!

Matt puffed nervously on his cigarette as he drove to his interview. After he left, the interviewer thought: "He smelled like he had been sitting in a smoky bar for hours before he came here. I wouldn't want to put up with that day in and day out."

One of the strongest odors is cigarette smoke, and it's sure to be annoying to a nonsmoker. If you smoke, be sure you don't do so before an interview.

Certain other habits are bound to interfere with your interviewing effectiveness. These include gum chewing, nail biting, hair flipping, and knuckle cracking. Anything that creates noise or is visually distracting is to be avoided.

The reality of life is that human beings are judged somewhat on physical appearance. You will not get a job solely because you look a certain way; however, you could end up not getting a job because of poor appearance or physical habits that send a negative message. Use the checklist at the end of this chapter before an interview.

What can you do to improve your physical appearance?

Mental Self

Depending upon the position, certain intellectual skills are necessary. Even though you may assume that the interviewer knows your capabilities, you are responsible for pointing out all desirable skills. If grade transcripts are required as part of your application materials and your grades are not high, be sure to address this during the interview. Probably more important than your grades is whether you were at a satisfactory level of achievement and if you worked up to your potential. If you earned high grades, make this known even if transcripts are not required.

Regardless of the job, potential employers want to know that you can think clearly and solve problems. Additionally, desire and willingness to learn are key transferable assets. Alicia Baillie, chairperson of a college early childhood education program, believes that mature judgment and decision-making skills are high on the list of employability factors. Similarly, Dan Masters, head of a college drafting technology program, says, "The industry wants creative drafters who are problem solvers."

"The ability to create and sustain a professional relationship with an employer along with a high level of integrity are definite assets."

SUSAN ASHER, Program Chair, Dental Assisting, Southeast Community College, Lincoln, Nebraska

A positive attitude is a "must." Whether or not this is discussed in an interview, your broad outlook on life will probably come across. Both verbally and nonverbally, we move through life as if we are carrying a lighted sign that flashes "positive" or "negative." Body language cues and comments can influence an interviewer. "The applicant slumped in his chair, said little, and had a disinterested look on his face. His whole demeanor was negative," said one business supervisor. Adverse comments about past employers, supervisors, or co-workers will dampen any enthusiasm for you. Likewise, not taking responsibility for your past experiences and blaming others for problems indicate negativism. Candidates who have a professional attitude demonstrated in their demeanor, a willingness to learn new techniques, and a respect for chain of command have an advantage.

Think of an experience in which you exhibited a positive attitude. In an interview this would be worth mentioning.

Emotional Self

Balance in emotionality is an asset. An interview is no place for total emotional expressiveness; however, the bland, seemingly unemotional individual is unlikely to be impressive. A proper balance is to appear relaxed and calm, yet enthusiastic and pleasant. Any feelings of frustration, dismay, anger, or unhappiness are to be concealed during a job interview. Picture the impression in the following.

Christine impatiently thumbed through a magazine waiting for an interview. She had been delayed in traffic, had worried about being late, and now was being kept waiting. She heaved a few sighs, and the receptionist looked at her with a quizzical look. When told to go in, Christine said, "It's about time." As she approached the owner's desk, her facial expression was one of annoyance.

Are you surprised that she wasn't among the final candidates?

A typical emotion associated with job interviews is anxiety. Most interviewers expect an applicant to be nervous. The key is to keep it enough under control in order to think and communicate positively. What might help is to realize that the interviewer is probably nervous as well. "As silly as it sounds, I'm always uptight at the beginning of an interview. I want the applicants to be impressed by me and my business, so I feel the pressure, too," was an interviewer's comment. Another way to relieve anxiety is to use cognitive techniques, discussed in Chapter 1. Thinking, "Just because I'm a little nervous doesn't mean I will do poorly in the interview," and "Even though this is a job interview, it isn't a 'life or death' matter. I'll just be myself." Right before the interview, a drink of water and the use of deep breathing are soothing strategies.

How well you handle stress and pressure will be of interest in most interviews. To be prepared, have a specific example to describe your success in coping with stress and pressure.

Answer this question: "How do you handle stress?"

Social Self

During an interview this aspect of self will be the most apparent. Both you and whoever conducts the interview will create social impressions during this brief interaction. Establishing rapport is necessary; if this doesn't happen, it is unlikely that you will advance to the final stage. Getting called for the interview means you have the basic requirements for the position. What will really separate you from the others are personality and your ability to connect with the interviewer or team of interviewers (Masikiewicz, 1999). According to a study (Caldwell & Burger, 1998), personality characteristics were significant factors in interviews, because they influenced candidates' degrees of preparedness and the impressions they made.

Each of our personalities is unique, and being yourself is imperative. Being hired on the basis of a "false front" is a disservice to both the employer and yourself. Generally, if you are friendly and pleasant and appear to be motivated and interested, most interviewers will be impressed. For some people, one of the hardest tasks is to smile during introductions and, when appropriate, during the interview. Yet, this cordial gesture is all-important. One of the reasons for this is that, above all else, you want to appear likable. If an interviewer thinks, "I like that person," you will likely be among the top candidates.

Because communicating and interacting with others are necessary career skills, the interviewer is likely to either directly ask or probe to determine your abilities. You may even be asked to take a personality inventory because certain characteristics can spell either success or failure for a particular type of job. Rather than be intimidated by an inventory, look upon it as a help for you as much as the employer. Remember job satisfaction? If your personality isn't suited for the duties, you won't be happy.

The social self affects all work relationships, and "people" skills are necessary for successful career development. Among the assets you will want to communicate verbally and nonverbally during an interview are your most positive personality traits and your ability to get along with others.

How would you answer if an interviewer asked about your "people" skills?

BEHAVING IN IMPRESSIVE WAYS

Certain behaviors deserve special attention. Professionalism means being where you are supposed to be with time to spare. Punctuality is an absolute requirement. Being late to a job interview is worse than being late to your own wedding. Guests may wait patiently and not interpret your behavior as rude; interviewers are not likely to be so understanding.

To ensure that you will be punctual, plan to arrive ahead of time. Some suggest as much as fifteen minutes. However, being in the office of the interviewer five minutes before your appointment is fine. Arriving at the site several minutes before that time gives you a chance to freshen up, check your appearance in a restroom, and take a few deep breaths. Don't forget to get rid of gum or any chewable item and turn off a cell phone. To relieve stress, get the following information when the interview is scheduled.

- *Know the day, date, and time of the interview.* Getting both the day and the date ensures that no mistake has been made.
- *Know the exact location.* Some companies occupy large buildings or portions of them, so ask for details such as floor and room number. For driving directions to the building, use a travel site such as www.expedia.com.
- *Ask about available parking.* You can ask either the interviewer or the receptionist about the best place to park; be sure to bring cash to pay for this, if necessary.
- *Find out the type of interview.* Will it be conducted by one person or a team?
- *Confirm the exact name or names of the interviewer(s).* You may have this information, yet it's wise to confirm it.

A good idea is to make a trial run before the interview. At least, drive to the location about the same time of day to see how long it takes. Harish reported feeling much more confident because a few days before his interview, he had actually gone to the door of the office. "I knew how long it took me to get there, and on the actual day I felt calmer because it was familiar."

Taking extra copies of your resume with you as well as other supporting documents such as grade transcripts and licenses is advisable. Whether to take anything else to an interview is optional. Obviously, you will not be taking another person! Having a professional-looking binder with a notepad and a pen is worth considering. You can use it to jot down the points you want to make, such as your assets, as well as a list of questions you wish to ask. Referring to these ensures you aren't forgetting anything. As long as you don't read from it or let it detract from the interview, such behavior typically looks professional. Also, interviewers tend to be impressed with applicants who take notes. Prepared written questions show organization skills and assertiveness. Your note taking should not interfere with good eye contact or be distracting. Be prepared, also, for the interviewer to take notes, as this is fairly typical.

In certain occupations, taking a **portfolio,** samples of your work, is highly recommended. This is especially appropriate in fields such as art, drafting, and design if your interview is with a person in that specific department or area.

Usually, the interviewer will ask to see whatever you have brought; however, if the interviewer doesn't mention it, be sure that you do. A word of caution is not to be like Antonio, who spent his entire interview discussing in detail all the finer points of his drawings. The interviewer was impressed with his work, yet didn't learn much more about Antonio.

What items would you take to an interview?

Once you are in the office, remember you are now making a first impression on everyone you see. Greet the receptionist by name (learned through your research, of course). Some nervous applicants make a mistake of continuing to chat, which will probably not be appreciated by a busy person. A better idea is to let the other person take the lead in developing conversation.

Whether to appear busy or simply wait while maintaining open, alert body language is up to you. If any company literature is available, definitely show an interest. You may also choose to review your resume or interviewing notes. Do appear calm and poised, not like the following.

Andrew looked well groomed. However, his nervous mannerisms in the reception office were being noticed. He chewed a fingernail, tapped his fingers on the arm of the chair, and swung his foot back and forth briskly. "I thought I might have to revive him at any minute," commented the receptionist.

In most companies, the opinions of a receptionist or other staff members do carry weight, and your goal is to impress everyone.

Finally, the time has come for you to meet the interviewer. Certain behaviors deserve attention, and practicing them prior to the interview bolsters confidence.

- Smile! Look directly at the person.
- Offer an appropriate greeting such as "Hello," "Good morning," or "Good afternoon," and use the person's last name preceded by Ms. or Mr. In some cases, a title works best, such as President Nielsen.
- Following the greeting, add: "I'm (your name), and I'm here to discuss the (title of job) position with you." This is a good idea in the unlikely event that the person needs a reminder of who you are.

During or shortly after the greetings, the interviewer may offer a handshake. As the applicant, it's better to let the interviewer take the lead. If a handshake is offered, you respond. Even though it seems so customary and simple, this behavior ranks high among interviewers. "I put a lot of stock in how the person shakes hands," said one employer. Even though you have probably heard it said many times, recommendations about handshakes bear repeating because the first impression is still being created. You can err at one extreme or the other. The overly firm handshake not only can hurt, but also can leave one with the impression that the "shaker" is aggressive and overbearing. "It seems as if the person was trying to prove something, and it wasn't positive," was how one interviewer described a handshake. The opposite—a limp, hardly noticeable handshake—leaves a distinctly negative impression.

In a career development class, students actually practice shaking hands. One young man said he thought it was silly until his less-than-positive handshake was noticed by another student. A stereotypic behavior was called to the group's attention. After a male student's handshake to a female came across as less than firm, he was asked if this was his typical handshake. He said, "It's how I shake hands with females." He was reminded that he didn't need to differentiate by sex; both males and females are capable and appreciative of assertive handshakes!

Practice shaking hands with several different people and ask them to honestly assess how yours feels.

The interviewer will probably indicate where you are to sit. Be sure you comfortably face the interviewer, then wait for that person to begin the interview. Some superficial conversation may transpire as the person tries to ease the tension of the initial meeting. Even though such chit-chat may feel comfortable, you don't want to be responsible for continuing it too long. Remember, you have a limited time to achieve your goal of giving and receiving valuable information and deciding whether this would be a good match. The most impressive behaviors convey friendliness, positiveness, interest in the position, and professionalism.

SELLING YOURSELF NONVERBALLY

Reviewing the communication suggestions offered in Chapter 2 will help you prepare for the interview. If you come across as an excellent listener, you are well on the way to being a top candidate for any position.

Each of the following behaviors will ensure a positive impression.

Maintain the best posture and body position. Your posture is an indicator of who you are. Being erect and alert while appearing relaxed is the best combination. Show interest by leaning slightly forward. Try to sit comfortably with your lower back against the chair back, shoulders back, feet on the floor, and your hands in your lap. Definitely do not cross your arms at any time during the

KEY INFO

How Can You Create a Positive First Impression?

- Appear poised and relaxed.
- Carry yourself professionally and confidently.
- Smile.
- Listen attentively and actively.

interview. Also, resist any temptation to place your arm on a desk or table in a leaning position.

Use direct eye contact. Even though steady eye contact is not the norm in all cultures, it is expected in the American society. This does not mean staring fixedly at the interviewer. When listening, about 75 percent of the time your eyes should be somewhere on the person's face, not necessarily looking directly into the eyes. While talking, the percentage of desired eye contact is somewhat less—at least half the time. If you catch yourself gazing away from the interviewer, just bring your eyes back. Along with the handshake, this is a major factor in the minds of interviewers. "If the applicant does not look at me, he or she will not get hired," was the blunt comment of one employer.

Change facial expression. In a job interview, as in personal conversation, a blank face implies disinterest. Being animated and providing appropriate expressions of interest, curiosity, excitement, pleasure, and even surprise add greatly to the exchange. Employers interpret a great deal from facial expression. "Your face will show whether you are confident and enthusiastic. Facial expression can reveal a sense of vitality, interest, and a high energy level," says Jeanne Baer, a career consultant and training specialist.

Even though it sounds strange, practice changing facial expressions in front of a mirror.

Nod affirmatively. A moderate number of affirming nods, when appropriate, indicate that you are listening and either agree with or like what you are hearing. Additionally, nods can energize and motivate the interviewer, so they are bound to be appreciated. You can overdo these, however. A student after viewing a videotape of a practice interview said it looked as if her head would fall off as she watched herself nod frequently and too vigorously.

The difference between impressing an interviewer—or not—can be a matter of body language.

Use gestures. Keeping hands in your lap or at your side during the entire interview makes you appear stiff, and your communication style will lack liveliness. Positive communicators utilize a proper number of gestures while resisting the tendency to "talk with their hands," which ends up being annoying. Also, you want to avoid certain gestures, such as pointing your finger at the interviewer. Gestures can emphasize and add meaning to verbal comments, and doing so brings life and color to the interview.

Avoid distracting behaviors. Certain habits or nervous behaviors fall into this category, such as tapping fingers on the desk, table, or arm of a chair and fiddling with one's hair or jewelry. Refrain from any movement that indicates undue nervousness or takes the attention of the interviewer away from what you are saying.

Tiffany came to the interview with her own notebook and pen. Unfortunately, her preparedness resulted in a problem. Throughout the interview she clicked the top of the pen to the annoyance of the marketing supervisor. "Almost all I remember about the interview is the noise of that pen," he said.

Respond with brief comments or questions. Remember that you can remain a listener and still make brief comments and ask encouraging questions. For example, after an interviewer describes certain job duties, a comment of, "That sounds interesting," or a question of, "What portion of the time would I spend at the computer?" are quite relevant and demonstrate positive listening.

SELLING YOURSELF VERBALLY

Even though listening skills are critical during an interview, what is said and how it is said separate successful applicants from the others. An effective interviewer will be sure that you do most of the talking. Occasionally, the meeting goes the other way. "I didn't have a chance to say much of anything," said an applicant after a job interview. "He spent the whole time telling me about the business." The results of these monologue interviews are lack of information about the applicant and, unfortunately, usually a poor impression of the job seeker as well. As the applicant, it's your responsibility to do all that is reasonable to convey what you can do for the employer. In the process, paralanguage, clarity, efficiency, and effective content are key elements.

Use effective paralanguage. Variations in the voice itself, called paralanguage, were covered in Chapter 2, and you are encouraged to review that section. During an interview you will want to pay special attention to how your voice sounds to the interviewer. Varying rhythm and inflection can clarify and add interest to what you say. You will want to use moderation in volume, pitch, and speed, and speak distinctly without overly enunciating. You want to be heard and interpreted correctly. Mumbling is bothersome and certainly not conductive to creating a clear message.

If possible, check your paralanguage with an audio or video recorder.

Be clear and concise. Clarity can be achieved by using accurate and specific descriptive words and sentences. Saying that you did a good job is a global comment and not precise; instead, describe exactly what you did that was good. The use of action words, a moderate amount of detail, and adjectives and adverbs to describe activities and behaviors creates clear, interesting messages. Sometimes a person will say one thing and indicate another with body language. If you state that you have a high level of interest in the position, be sure that your nonverbal behaviors don't show disinterest.

To speak efficiently, be concise and avoid distractors. "You know" repeated over and over will be a definite annoyance to an interviewer (unless you happen to find one who has the same poor habit). One interviewer said, "If I hear 'and stuff' or 'like' one more time, I may lose it." He may have been hearing something like this:

> *I really enjoy working with computers . . . and stuff. Like . . . uh . . . learning how to design houses on CAD . . . and stuff . . . has been fun. I also am . . . like . . . interested in mechanical drafting . . . and stuff. And . . . like . . . I took courses in sociology and psychology . . . and stuff.*

Do you see why the interviewer was ready to throw up her hands?

Efficiency is also saying what you want to say with just enough detail to be interesting. The most effective responses last less than two minutes. "One of the worst things an applicant can do is talk too much," said Marcia Phelps, Ph.D., a director of career development services at a large university.

"I detest rambling answers. Respond clearly and concisely."

ED RASGORSHEK, Vice President–Credit, United Agri Products, Omaha, Nebraska

Respond to questions in the most positive way. Most of the interview consists of answering questions posed by the interviewer. The way to verbalize in an interview is a little different from the open communication style suggested in Chapter 2. For many responses you will want to sound more sure of yourself than what the use of "I think" conveys. For example, saying, "I think I can offer you a high level of expertise" isn't nearly as powerful as "I'm sure (or confident) that I can." Use "I think" or "I believe" only if you are giving an opinion. Assertiveness is appreciated.

A verbalizing behavior to avoid is any tendency to qualify yourself. **Qualifying** means to use words that limit or discount your abilities. Notice the underlined qualifying words in Aaron's response to a question about his strengths.

> *I enjoy office work. I'm a <u>pretty</u> good typist. I <u>kind</u> of like to talk with people on the phone, and customers are <u>usually</u> satisfied with the way I handle complaints. I <u>only</u> have my associate's degree but hope to continue my education. During the past year my jobs were <u>just</u> in construction, but I proved I can work <u>fairly</u> hard.*

Eliminating the qualifying words creates a more assertive and impressive statement.

Definitely avoid any comment that can destroy your chances. Humorous, yet devastating, was a comment made by a candidate for a job in firefighting: "As a child I liked to start fires. I've always had a fascination with fire." Said Mark Munger, a fire department captain, "That's not something we like to hear from a prospective firefighting candidate." Charlotte Nedrow, a career development instructor, offers valuable advice: "Ask for the person to repeat a question if you are not sure of it, and also request and then take some time to think about a response if you need it. Above all else, sound enthusiastic. An employer told me, 'Applicants need to show me the spark in their hearts.'"

You can prepare by going over all possible questions ahead of time and practicing your responses. Excellent job seekers do not go into an interview "cold"; neither do their answers sound rehearsed. Instead, they are in familiar territory and talk about their assets in a confident manner. Following are typical and not-so-typical, yet possible, questions and recommended answers for your consideration and rehearsal.

SAMPLE QUESTIONS AND POSSIBLE RESPONSES

Before you read the recommended responses, decide how you would answer the following questions. After you read the suggestions, note any better ways to respond.

WHAT IS IMPORTANT IN AN INTERVIEW? Key Advice

Machine Tool: *"Wear clean clothes and have your hair combed. Be on time; otherwise, make a telephone call and explain."—John Buse, President, Precision Machine Co., Inc.*

Firefighting: *"Interviewees must be prepared to present what they want the interviewer to hear."—Darrell Eastin, Beatrice, Nebraska, Fire Department Chief*

"Individuals need to exhibit energy, enthusiasm, honesty, and a solid work ethic in just a few minutes. If they don't they'll be in the 'also ran' category."—Mark Munger, Lincoln, Nebraska, Fire Department Captain

Architecture and Drafting: *"It's better to be over-dressed than under-dressed while still being conservative in appearance."—Lynn Jones, Chairman, Davis Design*

Communication: *"My favorite question is: 'If I ran an ad for a position and you think that this is exactly the right job for you, what will the ad say?' I learn so much from the answer."—Doc Chaves, Marketing Communications Manager, Li-Cor, Inc.*

Banking: *"I can usually tell when people answer my questions the way they think they* ***should.*** *I'd prefer that they be themselves rather than 'on cue.' "—Ed Rasgorshek, Vice President–Credit, United Agri Products*

Human Resources and Development: *"Be prepared to talk honestly about yourself and let me know why you want to work for this company. A professional demeanor is very important."—Jody Horwitz, Vice President of Human Resources, The WB Television Network*

"Be candid and professional. Demonstrate an interest and knowledge in as many areas as possible."—Jeanne Salerno, Director, Professional Development, Kutak Rock Law Firm

Health and Human Services: *"Giving impressions of professionalism and confidence is important."—Nancy Brown, R. N., Program Manager, State of Nebraska Health and Human Services*

Automotive Technology: *"Eye contact, answering all questions honestly without going on and on about themselves, showing sincere interest in working for me specifically as opposed to just looking for a job, and dressing appropriately for the interview."—Doyle Helmink, Owner/Manager, A & D Auto-Truck Service*

Child Care and Early Childhood Education: *"A successful applicant will be upbeat, positive, and communicate well with good eye contact."—Sue Collins, Director, KinderCare Learning Center*

"Convey what will enable you to succeed with children—compassion, caring, and patience plus a sense of humor and sense of wonder that you can then instill in them."—Alicia Baillie, Program Chair, Early Childhood Education

Construction: *"Express yourself clearly and avoid the over-use of common words and slang. Convey a keen desire to be productive and contribute to the company."—Bob Dinkel, Owner, Accent Fence Company*

■ *Tell me about yourself.* This question is a common opener and one that interviewers may use either as a tension reliever or as a way to elicit information and see how you respond. If you are unprepared, this is a challenging and stressful question. Immediately, one thinks, "What does the person want to know?" Some applicants will even ask, which is not recommended. They usually are told, "Whatever you want to tell me."

The following are *not* desirable answers.

- Your life story
- Your weaknesses or liabilities
- Trivial or uninteresting, nonhelpful information
- Anything personal

The latter category can be illustrated by Abigail's answer. Would this impress the interviewer?

> *Uh . . . well, I can't really think of anything. Uh . . . I just got divorced, I have two kids, and I like to bowl. That's about it.*

Because she wasn't prepared, what finally came to Abigail's mind would do her no good and possibly some harm. Incidentally, whatever you say, do not end with "That's about it." This implies that you know little about yourself.

Instead of panicking and providing a poor answer, use this as an opportunity to present yourself positively. This is the time to verbalize the assets that are relevant to your interview goal. For a recommended response, select a top asset from each of the following categories and mention it briefly.

- Experience (either from paid work, volunteer work, or school)
- Education
- Personality characteristics, other transferable skills, and goals

Often, an interviewer wants to be told information that isn't in your resume, so definitely include information from the last category. However, don't hesitate to mention facts from your resume. Even though the interviewer has probably read it, your response can be an effective review, and it doesn't hurt to remind the interviewer of what you have to offer. Design your response so that you don't tell too much and, instead, leave the interviewer wanting to hear more. Read how Bryan answered the question.

> *For the past three years I've been employed at Raynor Marketing as a sales representative. This past year I was honored as the top salesperson in the firm. My college degree*

> *is in marketing. I've had specialized training in professional interactions and client relationships and consider myself to be a positive person who is highly motivated to succeed.*

Notice that he didn't begin with an "uh" or "well," neither of which is necessary. Bryan's response was descriptive, yet concise; it set the stage for additional questions. Most important, he ended on a very positive note.

- *Why did you choose this career field?* Resist a "cliche" or ordinary answer that interviewers hear all too often. For example, a teacher or child development applicant could reply, "I love children." Even though a love for children is certainly a requirement, this response is expected and will not set you apart from all other applicants. "Successful candidates need to convey an appropriate motivation for entering the field of child care. It must truly be for the purpose of helping children and families—not to meet their own needs," cautions Alicia Baillie, a program chair of a child development program. If possible, relay anything in your personal background or experience that is unique, such as Ryan's response.

> *When I was in sixth grade, my class visited the local fire station. Because I was so fascinated, I continued to stop there often. In fact, the firefighters considered me a mascot until I was in high school, when they decided I was too old to be one. My keen interest plus my desire to help people motivated me to pursue a degree in fire protection technology, and I'm more interested and enthusiastic than ever. I do, however, realize that this career field is much more comprehensive than my sixth-grade mind realized.*

Ryan also helped himself by showing a reasonable understanding of career realities. Professional truck-driving students, for example, know that their occupation is much more than jumping behind the wheel of an 18-wheeler and driving off into the sunset! If you have chosen a career field wisely, this question is best answered by explaining your decision.

- *What are your career goals? Where do you want to be in five or ten years?* If the question is phrased as the latter one, don't worry about the specific five- or ten-year period. Most interviewers just use this as a way to focus on goals. Having some clearly defined goals and being able to articulate these are pluses in your favor. Research about this particular employer will provide insight into its policies and goals, and you want to make your objectives sound compatible. For example, if advancement at a company is rare, a goal of "quickly moving up the ladder" is not in your best interest.

It may even be necessary to conceal some of your goals. If a company intends to invest time, effort, and money into hiring and training you, the following is a response to avoid: "I want to work for a good company for a few years and then start my own business." If you feel compelled to mention wanting your own business, phrase it as a tentative long-term goal: "I do have aspirations of perhaps owning my own business in the future." Sounding as if you would be there only for the "short term" or being more focused on "your own thing" than on what the employer needs will diminish your chances for employment.

■ *Why do you want this job?* You will answer this question easily if you have a clear idea of how the job requirements and your abilities and interests match. It's imperative that you make a clear connection between what is needed in the position and your capabilities. Don't be vague or general and respond with, "It sounds like a good job," or "I think I can do a good job for you." State specifically what is good about the job, about yourself, and how the two are linked.

■ *Why do you want to work for this company (or us)?* This is a little different from the previous question, although your research will again provide the answer. This is the time to relay positive information about this particular employer. After you have demonstrated admiration for the company, the rest of the response reveals how you can contribute to its positive image. The following is how one applicant fielded this question.

> *This company is a respected leader in the field of architectural design. I'm familiar with past and present projects, and I see why you have earned such an excellent reputation. Because I have developed innovative projects in my present position and strive for excellence in all I do, I'm confident that I could make a significant contribution to your design team.*

Incidentally, if this question isn't asked, be sure that you let the interviewer know that you want to work for this employer. Because this seems so obvious (why else would I be interviewing here?), most applicants don't specifically state this. After I was hired, a member of the interviewing committee said, "A strong point in your favor was that you were the only one among the five finalists who said that you wanted to teach at this college."

■ *Why are you leaving your present position? or Why did you leave your last job?* Ideally, the reason is a positive one or you can make it sound as such. Indicating a desire for more opportunity or even more compensation is a suitable response. You may have not liked some aspect of the job. Without sounding negative or critical of a past employer, you can offer a brief reason for dissatisfaction. If you were laid off or terminated and there's any possibility that this can be discovered (and there usually is), state this. Then, tell what you learned from the experience.

■ *Tell me about your education, or How did your education prepare you for this position? or Did you get out of your education what you expected? or Do your grades reflect your best efforts and your true capabilities?* Questions about your educational background are designed to find out how you feel about education, in general, and to see if you understand the relevancy of your training. Think about how your education has benefited you and be prepared to discuss this asset.

■ *What experiences have you had that qualify you for this position?* Listen carefully to how this question is phrased. If asked about experiences in general, as in the question here, you can use work, volunteer, and educational experiences to support your qualifications. One or more from each category could make an excellent response. However, you may be asked just about work experiences. Well-qualified candidates have blundered by only responding, "None," or "I haven't had any." Instead, you can answer, "Even though I haven't had paid work experience, I consider my experiences in college (or in a volunteer position) to be valuable work." Then, describe how those experiences have contributed to your ability to perform the job duties.

A mistake is to avoid mentioning unrelated work experiences. Unless you did poorly in a job, all work experiences demonstrate transferable skills as well as your employability. Likewise, volunteer work, course projects, and activities usually will show leadership, teamwork, ability to get along with others, and dedication, among other assets. On the other hand, few interviewers appreciate applicants who inflate the value of their experiences. Sally had conducted a small research study for a sociology course. Her version of what she had done sounded as if she were ready to move into a researcher's position with no further experience or training. The interviewer was not fooled and certainly was not impressed.

If you have done your research, you will know the required skills for the specific position and will relate those to yourself. A candidate for a counseling position responded to the question by saying, "I qualify for this position because I have excellent skills in active listening, establishing rapport, problem solving, and assertive communication." All of the ones she mentioned were listed in the position description. She went on to describe when and where she had demonstrated those skills.

■ *What past job did you like best and why?* This is a golden opportunity to demonstrate enthusiasm. Ideally, the past job and the applied-for position are similar, and your response will emphasize these comparable aspects.

■ *What past job did you like least and why?* If you have not disliked any past job, state this, then briefly describe one that you least enjoyed. Employers understand that most people experience dissatisfaction at least once during their career. If you let the person know that you learned from a less-than-favorable experience, the question is of benefit to you. A cautionary note is not to sound negative about a job or some aspect of it that is similar to the applied-for position.

- *How would you handle this situation? What would you do under these circumstances? (followed by a scenario)* Situational questions can be quite challenging. Bluffing or acting as if you can do something you aren't capable of is foolish. Admitting that you may need to ask for guidance is much preferred to acting as if you know it all. If you have been trained or had work experience, the best answer is to describe how you would currently deal with the matter. In some situations, there may not be a right or wrong way; instead, the person may be simply interested in your thought process. If the question is related to specific company policy, a good idea is to say that you would follow what is expected.

Situational questions are commonly asked during a second interview and in certain fields such as education. Here's how an early childhood education graduate named Mark responded when asked what he would do if three-year-old Stephanie had bitten another child, Joshua.

> *First, I would check to see if Joshua was hurt and tend to him. Then I would take Stephanie aside. We'd both sit so we were at the same eye level, and I'd talk with her. What I would say would depend upon history. Is this the first time, or does she have a habit of biting? If this was the first time, my message would be that biting is not allowed and suggest some other behaviors to work off frustration or anger. If this had happened before and if a consequence had been established according to the center's policy, I would explain what would happen now. In the past this has worked with other children under my supervision.*

Showing knowledge in the subject area required is obviously your best response, and being candid is essential. John learned this the hard way when he tried to bluff his way through a question about overhauling a transmission and was told that he needed to get more training before he would ever be considered. The repair shop didn't want a person to muddle through a job and create more problems along the way!

- *How well do you get along with people?* You may be tempted to give a to-the-point answer of "Fine." Instead, use **documenting**—giving specific instances to support your response. "Answer with examples of what you have done," advises Tony Reimer, Claims Superintendent for State Farm Insurance in Rocky Mount, North Carolina. Note the following.

I get along with people very well. In my last position I worked successfully with several diverse individuals. On evaluations I consistently was given the top rating on ability to get along. I enjoy all types of people.

If you didn't get along with everyone, it's better not to sound as if you did. Most people don't have unblemished records; yet, you don't want to call attention to this or belabor the point.

- *How did you get along with your past employer?* Hopefully, your answer can be a positive one. If so, provide brief information describing your rapport. If you did not get along, it's best to be honest because this could be revealed by that past employer. Avoid phrases like "personality conflicts," and indicate that you wish the relationship had been better. A cardinal point is to not degrade a former employer, and you certainly don't want to sound as if you are blaming all the problems on someone else. When an applicant told Bob Dinkel that three of his past employers were impossible to work for and unlikable people, there was no doubt that Bob didn't want to take a chance of being the fourth! A simple, "To be honest, we had some difficulty working together. I wish it would have been different; however, I did learn from the experience." If this is the only time you have had problems with an employer, you can state that, as well.

- *Describe an ideal job or describe an ideal supervisor.* If asked the first question, the best answer is to describe the tasks and responsibilities of the position you are discussing. Even though it may not be ideal, if you are spending your time in an interview, it's one you think you would enjoy. Use the research about this position as your guide. The second question is best answered honestly. If the supervisor is totally opposite of the one you would consider ideal, it's better to know this now, as you undoubtedly would be unhappy in this position.

- *How would a good friend describe you?* This is a slightly different way of asking you to describe yourself. A key tip is to use words that would be considered assets for this position. For example, a good friend may say you are "fun, caring, and happy-go-lucky," yet these descriptors aren't necessarily what will most impress a potential employer.

You may also be asked more specific questions about yourself such as how you handle criticism, make decisions, work under pressure, and follow directions, as well as ones that relate to interactions and people you find difficult. Some employers are interested in what you consider to be your greatest achievement and disappointment thus far. Again, if you have a solid understanding of yourself and think about your responses ahead of time, you can handle these questions with ease.

■ *What did you like about your past job?* This question is usually an easy one to answer as long as you enjoyed your work. If possible, indicate satisfaction with responsibilities and tasks similar to the job for which you are applying. If you didn't like your past job, explain briefly the reasons without being critical. "I found I didn't enjoy routine work" is much preferable to "The job was boring" or "The boss never gave me anything interesting to do."

■ *What didn't you like about your past job?* This can be difficult unless the past job and the position under discussion are very different from each other. Again, don't sound like a complainer. Instead, explain the mismatch between the required tasks and your personality preferences or a lack of challenge and stimulation. Employers realize that dissatisfaction is certainly possible. Keep your answer brief.

■ *What are your strengths?* Assets, assets, assets—having developed a list will solve any question of how to respond. Select your top five or six in the various areas of importance and practice a response that is no longer than a few minutes. Even though your resume contains the same information or you have already mentioned an asset, repetition of your top strong points is fine. Again, be sure that these assets are needed for this particular position.

■ *What are your weaknesses? or In what ways would you like to improve yourself?* One of the worst answers is to say that you don't have any weaknesses. Nobody is perfect, and we can all improve in some way. When a student was asked to list his liabilities (weaknesses), he couldn't think of any. One was suggested: inability to recognize any weaknesses!

Preferably, you will mention a weakness that you are either in the process of strengthening or one that is easily changed. Strengthen your answer by telling what you are doing to change this liability. Avoid naming any that will destroy your chances such as: "I have a drinking problem," "I can't control my temper," or "I have a hard time relating to people." Notice how positive this response sounds.

> *Being a perfectionist, I've found, isn't necessarily in my best interest. I've read some materials about it and have now developed realistic goals. Instead of perfection, I strive for excellence and find that my efforts produce much better results.*

An interviewer may ask about strengths and weaknesses in the same question. If so, it's better to first touch on a weakness then end with a longer discussion of your strengths.

What if the interviewer doesn't actually ask you about weaknesses? Usually you will also avoid the subject. However, if the weakness is an obvious one that might stand in your way, you are probably wise to bring it up. For example, if you are an older applicant, at some point you might say, "Even though I may be older than the other applicants, I see this as an advantage to an employer. I'm mature, dependable, have a great deal of job experience, and a strong work ethic." If you think you might be perceived as too young, mention energy, ambition, flexibility, and willingness to learn. Anticipating what the interviewer might consider a weakness can enable you to discuss it positively.

- *What would satisfy you in a job?* Knowing yourself well will help you answer this question as well as impress an interviewer. If you have thought about job satisfaction, as covered in Chapter 3, this question will not be a problem. Ideally, your answer will reflect the requirements of the applied-for position. Definitely don't describe factors that aren't possible with this employer.

- *What motivates you?* Candidates decrease their chances by naming only external motivators such as pay and other inducements. Most employers want to hear that applicants are self-motivated by challenge and a desire for excellence. Mentioning that you like to be appreciated for your efforts is fine as well. A high degree of motivation is a true asset, and if you can document instances of high-quality performance as a result of your self-motivation, the response can be of major benefit.

- *It seems that you are overqualified for this position. What do you think?* If your experiences or education or both are perceived as more than the position demands, you will probably be asked this question. You might anticipate that this is in the interviewer's mind and broach the issue, as discussed under the question about weaknesses. It's beneficial to let the person know that you have thought about this and still want the position for what it offers. Mentioning that job satisfaction is more important to you than titles or compensation could turn this potential liability into a definite asset.

- *What magazines do you read regularly? or Tell me about a book you have read in the past year.* These are not common questions and are more typical of a second interview. Not thinking about them ahead of time could lead to an embarrassed silence or a poor answer. Ideally, you could offer something related to your career field; publications that indicate a well-rounded personality are also good to mention. Employers usually don't want candidates to be 100 percent career oriented. "An outstanding interviewee demonstrates interest and knowledge in several areas. Being informed about other things in the world, as well as the company and the position, is most impressive," says Jeanne Salerno, a director of professional development for a law firm.

- *What salary do you expect?* Not doing your homework may cost you money if you cite a lower amount of pay or could cost you the job if your figure is too high. This one question may be one of the best reasons to conduct prior research. Knowing the typical salary or range of pay for the position makes this formidable question an easy one. Several Internet sites can provide this information. See recommendations at the end of Chapter 3. If you do not have this information, you can say that the figure would depend upon a full understanding of the position and other benefits. Also, you can ask, "What is the range of pay for this position?" or state that you are open to a discussion of what would be fair compensation for a person with your background. If a question about salary and benefits is not asked, do not bring up the subject.

■ *If hired, how long can we expect you to remain with this company?* This is a "loaded" question, and a recommendation is to refrain from giving any certain length of time. While an employer would doubt that you will remain with the company your entire career life, that employer does want a sense of stability and commitment. Lyn's response is impressive.

> *Stability and security are goals of mine. I want an interesting and satisfying position that I will be committed to for many years, and your company has several such positions.*

■ *How do you plan to stay up to date in this field?* Keeping abreast of new developments and updating your skills are essential, and you will want to mention several possibilities including further technical training or coursework, reading, and learning from others. Don't make the mistake of just mentioning employer-sponsored training activities. You want to give the impression that you will continue to learn and grow even if you do it at your own expense and on your own time. An interview suggestion from John Buse, president of Precision Machine Co., Inc., is: "Don't say you've done everything and give the impression that there's nothing to learn."

■ *We are committed to diversity. Describe any experiences you have had with diverse groups of people.* Ideally, you have interacted with people of all types at work, at school, and in your personal life. Even if your exposure to different racial groups has been limited, you can describe experiences with various ages and social classes. If you haven't had certain experiences, be honest and then indicate an attitude of acceptance. If you've had coursework in diversity, this is an excellent time to communicate about it.

■ *Why should we hire you?* This is likely to be the most critical question of all and is commonly reserved for the end of the interview. However, be prepared for it at any time, even as a lead-in question. The wording may be slightly different; in any case, this is the time to communicate what you can do for the employer. If the wording of the question includes "over the other applicants," simply disregard that part. Starting out with "Well, I'm not sure I have more to offer than the others" is a poor beginning. Explaining briefly your top several assets *as they pertain to this position* is the key to your response. Draw from the areas of (1) experience, (2) job-related skills and abilities, (3) education, (4) transferable assets including personality traits, and (5) interests and motivation. Practicing ahead of time is highly recommended, although you don't want to sound stilted. Consider this polished response.

> *My work experience has increased the technical skills I learned while earning my business administration degree and given me an opportunity to use many "people" skills. I have demonstrated that I can increase office efficiency and consistently turn out high-quality work. I am dependable, positive, friendly, enthusiastic about my career, and very interested in this particular position. I'm confident that I can make a significant contribution.*

If this question is asked toward the end of the interview, you have probably already mentioned some of the assets. That doesn't mean you would want to leave those out. Instead, regard this as a summary of your strengths and repeat the most positive ones. Your prime purpose is to draw a mental picture of how you can benefit the employer. As one business owner put it, "An interviewee should let me know how he or she can solve my problems."

Responding to Illegal Questions

What to do if you are asked an illegal or questionable question is, in itself, a challenging question. Just as there are inappropriate application questions that could lead to discrimination, several interview inquiries fall into the same category. Generally, if information being sought is not related to the job, the question is inappropriate, if not illegal. These inquiries were covered in the job applications section of Chapter 4; be sure to review those before going to an interview.

Even though most interviewers are well versed on the legality of questions, some are not. Often, employers don't use the information to discriminate; they are just unaware of the laws. You certainly may ignore the illegality and provide the information. However, because of the nature of the information, this could become an obstacle as in the response: "Yes, I have three children under the age of ten." The interviewer is thinking, "Good chance that this applicant will take plenty of sick leave. That's a definite drawback." Answering could also indicate to a potential employer that you aren't aware of illegalities and will offer anything to get the job.

What is a suitable response to a questionable question? If you think the interviewer is inclined to discriminate, an especially assertive response is appropriate. "I don't see the relevance to the position," or even, "I prefer not to answer questions such as that unless they are specifically related to the position." If you consider it an innocent query, you can ask, "I'm not necessarily opposed to telling you. However, I wonder if it is related to the job duties and responsibilities?" Generally, an interviewer will recognize a mistake and retract the question. Otherwise, the reply will be a clue as to your next step. If relevancy to the position is explained, an excellent reply is, "I appreciate your explaining that to me. I have no physical disabilities that would prevent me from doing those tasks." The book *101 Great Answers to the Toughest Interview Questions* (Fry, 2000) offers suggested responses to many questionable questions.

If an interviewer persists in asking personal or other illegal questions or does not react well to your reluctance to respond, you probably won't be hired. Yet, would you want to work for someone who doesn't abide by fairness and the law? There are far more employers who are objective in their interviewing and hiring methods. You deserve to work for one of those!

Asking Impressive Questions

An interview can be ruined if you answer "no" when asked, "Do you have any questions?" A cardinal rule of positive interviewing is to have several questions to ask. Not asking anything could suggest disinterest, laziness, or inability to formulate questions. None of these will get you hired. No questions could also indicate nonassertiveness and a lack of curiosity, which are both undesirable qualities.

A business owner stated, "I learn more about the applicant from the questions asked than the answers given." Is there any doubt how crucial your questions will be? Questions, if they reflect a sincere interest in the employer and the position and a desire to contribute, will serve as invaluable assets.

Even though you have done adequate research, there are still questions to ask or information to verify. In fact, the actual research often opens up further possibilities for inquiries. Obviously, if the interviewer has already adequately covered the subject, you could appear to be a poor listener by posing a question. Yet, if you want more clarification, be sure to ask. Very important is to not ask questions that indicate a definite lack of research on your part. "What do you guys do?" is not only poorly worded but also shows that the applicant has not bothered to find out. Following is a list of reasonable topics to explore if they have not been addressed. Because the time for your questions may be limited, a good idea is to prioritize your list and ask in the range of two to four questions.

- Duties and responsibilities of the position
- Hours, work schedule, typical day experiences, overtime expectations, if any
- Skills and qualities most desired
- Specific needs of the employer (i.e., "What can I do to benefit you?")
- How employee performance is measured

- Advancement possibilities
- Opportunities for continued learning, training
- Major strengths and growth potential of the company
- Present and future company projects, if appropriate
- Chain of command, organizational chart
- Work environment, equipment, tools
- Degree of rapport among personnel
- Wellness philosophy and how physical and mental health are encouraged
- Materials furnished by the company (if appropriate)
- Next step in the hiring process including the time frame for a decision

After hearing about the desired skills and qualities plus the needs of the employer, ideally you can attest to being the best candidate. For example, "I'm glad to hear that, because I am a creative person, I have excellent writing skills, and I pride myself on meeting deadlines."

Think of at least three questions you would want to ask at most interviews.

Complimenting the employer in your question is impressive. For example, Ryan said, "I realize that your company was ranked among the top ten national leaders this past year. In what ways do you encourage this degree of excellence?" Ming showed knowledge and offered praise when she stated, "I'm pleased that you strongly encourage wellness. What specific employee programs do you have?"

You may have noticed that salary and benefits are missing from the list of question topics. Heed the advice of countless experts and do not ask about salary at this time. First, if you have done your research, you will already know either an exact or approximate figure, so there is no reason to ask. Even if you don't know, consider when it would be to your advantage to discuss the subject. At what point would you be in the strongest position to receive the highest offer? Would it be during an initial interview, before the employer even knows if you are the first choice? Obviously, your advantage comes after the employer has decided on you. If you like to fish, you probably know that setting the hook comes after the fish has taken the bait! After an employer has said that you are wanted or, better yet, needed, you are in the best position to negotiate salary. As one employer said, "I hadn't even decided that I was interested in him, and he was asking how much he would get paid. Because of that, he will never get paid by me." Most people recommend that applicants never ask salary questions.

> *"Until I'm ready to offer you the job, I don't want to be asked about benefits. When I decide to hire you, then it's my turn to impress you."*

DOC CHAVES, Marketing Communications Manager, Li-Cor, Inc., Lincoln, Nebraska

Waiting to discuss salary after an offer has been made "puts you in the driver's seat." Above all else, you don't want to sound desperate or as if your interest lies only in what's in this for you. Applicants who give these impressions are usually unsuccessful. Salary negotiation is covered in Chapter 6.

Often, the interviewer mentions benefits when describing the job and the company. If not, after the interview you can make a simple request for written or verbal information about benefits. Chapter 6 discusses benefits.

What you don't say or ask is just as important as what you do. Use the "Preparing for an Interview" at the end of the chapter to help ensure a successful interview. Thoughtful preparation can turn a harrowing interview experience into a pleasant one.

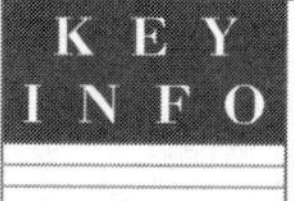

Preparation for an interview is essential. You can then afford to relax, and, most important, be yourself.

ENDING THE INTERVIEW

Determining the end of the interview is a responsibility of the interviewer. As the applicant, you want to be careful that you don't take the lead and, perhaps, end the discussion before you have achieved your goal. A career development student emerged from a mock job interview after only about five minutes. He had a big smile on his face. "That was quick," he said. "There was a pause so I thanked him for his time and left." The smile left his face when he was told that extremely short interviews usually aren't the most successful ones. "I was just glad to get it over with," he admitted. Be sure you aren't thinking in this way.

On the other extreme, you don't want to continue the interview past an appropriate end. If you know the allotted interview time and are aware of the interviewer's cues, you can be ready for the closing; usually, at the end you will be asking questions. If in doubt, ask if there is time for another one.

If the person does not explain the next step in the process, you are advised to ask. A most stressful situation is waiting for an unknown period of time for word from the employer. "When can I expect to hear from you?" is a polite request for valuable information. You may also ask about calling if you have more questions. Expressing thanks for the time and opportunity and a genuine interest in the position are positive closing remarks.

Evaluating Yourself

Spending time soon after the interview to assess how well you did is time well spent. The following questions draw on evaluative material provided to interviewers.

- Did I listen and respond directly to all questions? If I didn't, which questions were troublesome and need more thought and practice?
- Did I probe for clarification, if necessary?
- Did I turn negative information into positive?
- Was the atmosphere relaxed? Did we experience rapport?
- How did I appear nonverbally?
- Did I overwhelm or underwhelm the interviewer? (Incidentally, neither extreme is desirable.)
- Did I demonstrate that I was well informed about the employer and the position?
- Did I use understandable, appropriate language?
- Did I ask appropriate questions that didn't sound rehearsed?
- How do I feel emotionally about the interview?

Review what employers want, presented earlier in this chapter, and ask yourself whether these qualities were evident in what you said and did. Also, check Key Info "Common Mistakes Made by Applicants" and score yourself in "How Well Did I Do?" at the chapter's end.

Following Up

Either the same day or the one following, effective job hunters write a letter to the interviewer. Its purpose is to express appreciation for the opportunity to discuss the position and to reiterate what your strengths are in relationship to the opening. You can mention significant points from the interview itself, keeping in mind that you are responsible for matching yourself with the position.

A thank-you note to the receptionist or others who assisted you in some way is also recommended. These written communications show that you are courteous and have a keen interest in the job. A distinct advantage is to get your name registered one more time in the mind of the potential employer. Another possibility is to telephone with additional information; however, this could be an interruption in a busy person's schedule and is recommended only if the employer's hiring schedule does not allow time for you to write a letter. Even though many job seekers are told to follow up, most do not, so this is another chance to set yourself apart in a positive way.

Keep in mind that the ultimate purpose of an interview is to set yourself apart from all other applicants. By thoroughly preparing yourself physically and mentally, rehearsing the questions that may be asked, and then, if possible, going through a practice or mock videotaped interview, you will have done all you can to ensure that you make a positive and memorable impression.

What if you did the best you could do and didn't receive a job offer? Obviously, a decision was made that another candidate would be a better "fit" for the employer. Review the section about handling rejection at the end of Chapter 3. Also helpful is to know the findings of a survey reported in *Hispanic Times Magazine* (2002) indicating that a person's chances of being hired after an interview are just one in five. Take advantage of the advice in this book and the others listed in Recommended Reading at the end of the book. Maintain a positive attitude knowing that eventually you will be the one who gets the position!

KEY POINTS

- The interview is the final stage in securing a position.
- Candidates are advised to mentally prepare and know what employers want with the idea that they need to sell themselves physically, mentally, emotionally, and socially. Knowing what is impressive in these areas and what is not is critical.
- Heading the list of impressive behaviors are dependability, ability to get along with others, and professionalism.
- Much of the impression you make is based on nonverbal behaviors.
- An interview is designed to glean information; your ability to sell yourself verbally is essential. Knowing whether you will be interviewed by one person or a group and recognizing the unique aspects of telephone interviewing and a second interview are essential.
- Thinking about and practicing answers to the multitude of possible questions increases your confidence.

- An interviewer may ask an illegal question, and it's wise to plan a response ahead of time.
- Asking appropriate questions is just as important as responding and will enhance your chances.
- After an interview an honest evaluation and a follow-up with the interviewer are highly recommended.

ONLINE RESOURCES

Job-Interview: www.job-interview.net

National Organization on Disability (interviewing tips): www.nod.org

Public Service Employees Network: www.pse-net.com/interview/interview.htm

Quintessential Careers, Types of Job Interviews: www.quintcareers.com/job_interviews.html

KEY STEPS

INTERVIEW CHECKLIST

Use this checklist to be thoroughly prepared for an interview.

______ Do I know exactly where I am to go? Where to park?

______ Have I made a "trial run" so I know how long it will take me to get there?

______ Can I pronounce the name of the interviewer?

______ Do I know exactly what I plan to say as a greeting?

______ Do I know the exact job position?

______ Have I rehearsed all the typical interview questions?

______ Do I have information about the employer?

______ Do I have at least four good questions to ask? (Write these.)

______ Do I have the items I want to take?

______ Do I have in writing anything I might forget? (questions to ask, assets, etc.)

______ Do I look clean? (Check fingernails, hair, teeth, etc.)

______ Do I look neat? (Check hair, lint on clothes, etc.)

______ Do I look professional?

______ Am I dressed comfortably?

______ Am I wearing any jewelry or cologne that could be distracting or bothersome?

______ What could possibly go wrong, and am I prepared for what I can be prepared for? (extra pair of hosiery for women, etc.)

______ Have I done all I can do to calm myself?

______ Am I remembering that an interview is a "two-way street" and that my evaluation of the employer is equally important?

______ Do I have clearly in mind what I have to offer that this employer wants?

______ Do I know why this employer would want to hire me for the position?

PREPARING FOR AN INTERVIEW

Write an effective answer to each of the following questions.

- Tell me about yourself.

- Why did you choose this career field?

- What are your career goals?

- How well do you get along with other people?

- What are your strengths?

- What are your weaknesses?

- What would satisfy you in a job?

- What motivates you?

- Why should I hire you?

Read the recommendations in Chapter 5 and compare your responses to them. Are you emphasizing your assets? Now select any other question from Chapter 5 that might be troublesome and write a response. Verbally practice all responses.

HOW WELL DID I DO?

On the following scale, rate your interview.

5 = Perfect 4 = Very good 3 = Average 2 = Not very good 1 = Unsatisfactory

_______ 1. Did I arrive at least five minutes ahead of time and feel little or no time pressure?

_______ 2. Was my appearance neat, clean, and professional?

_______ 3. Did I feel relatively calm?

_______ 4. How was my first impression, including smile, greeting, and handshake?

_______ 5. Did I use the interviewer's name?

_______ 6. Was my body language open and positive?

_______ 7. Did I listen?

_______ 8. Did I appear to be listening?

_______ 9. How were my answers (content)?

_______ 10. How were my answers (verbalizing style including paralanguage)?

_______ 11. How were my questions?

_______ 12. Did I appear interested and enthusiastic?

_______ 13. Did I thank the interviewer for the opportunity?

_______ 14. Do I know the next step in the process?

_______ 15. Have I written a follow-up letter?

Total your points. A perfect score is 75. While it isn't necessary to score that high, you want a high score. Write below how you can improve next time.

____

____

____

____

____

____

____

Successful career design charts a path to self-fulfillment.

Developing Your Career

The career path begins when a person decides to pursue a certain field of study. Depending upon whether you have been rejected for a particular position, decided not to accept a job, or received an offer, your path has taken various turns. Even though there is a tendency to think of choices as either right or wrong, realize that a decision simply means following a different path. As long as you keep your direction focused on your career goals, you can achieve them via a number of ways.

Negotiating and Accepting an Offer

Doing research before applying or at least before an offer is the key to successful salary negotiation. The primary source of information is the potential employer; ideally, a salary range is provided in a job description. Another source is a competitor. The Internet has several sites that provide salary information (see Online Resources at the end of Chapter 3). Besides the expected salary, three other areas of information are vital. First, and covered in the next section, are benefits. The second area covers cost-of-living pay increases as well as the basis and timetable for salary increases. Opportunity for promotion is third.

UNDERSTANDING BENEFITS

Research definitely involves benefits. Preferably, this information would be in writing. Conceivably, benefits can add 30 to 40 percent to one's salary with 36 percent most typical, according to Cindy Siddons, Benefits Director, E! Networks, Los Angeles. As such, they should be considered as part of the total package. As one employer remarked, "We pay a slightly lower starting wage, but when you consider our benefits package, we offer an employee much more." The common benefits are listed in Key Info.

Prioritize the benefits. Which are most important to you?

Becoming much more common are "paid time off" days. These can be used for any reason, and they replace the traditional sick leave. About two-thirds of employers in the United States now offer them (Wessel, 2003). Benefits may be open to negotiation. For example, some employers don't pay for missed work. You might be able to negotiate so many days with pay. Getting an employer to provide uniforms or pay for cleaning could make a difference in how much money you have available. In large companies, benefits aren't usually negotiable; yet, they may be. "Some companies give higher-level candidates additional benefits such as stock options as part of the hiring negotiation," according to Cindy Siddons. Besides monetary pluses, benefits can make a difference in morale. Wellness programs and company-sponsored functions have physical, social, and emotional value, as well.

NEGOTIATING SALARY

The other source of valuable salary information is you. In addition to knowing what the offer is likely to be, you also must know what salary you need. If the job involves relocation, be sure to take that into consideration and know the geographical differences in cost of living. Going online can provide you with valuable information.

KEY INFO

Possible Employment Benefits

Those marked with * are most likely to be offered.

- vacation and holiday leave*
- sick leave*
- personal leave*
- education and training opportunities*
- tuition reimbursement*
- wellness programs*
- bereavement leave*
- health insurance*
- life insurance*
- employee assistance programs*
- accidental death and dismemberment insurance*
- disability pay*
- retirement and pension plans*
- pretax deduction plans and flexible spending accounts*
- savings plans, stock options, profit sharing programs
- professional leave
- moving expenses
- paid parking
- child care
- company car or transportation considerations
- uniforms and tools
- health club memberships
- recreational programs
- outplacement and severance counseling
- flexible hours
- telecommuting

Several Web sites offer salary calculations including www.salary.com. Check the end of this chapter and Chapter 3 for sites. Generally, you provide your present salary and city of residence plus the desired living location and find out how much salary would be needed to maintain your present living standard. The bottom line is: If you don't have information about salary, you are in no position to negotiate, and you are at a distinct disadvantage.

Timing in negotiation is critical. Negotiating after an employer has selected you is best. At this point, you have more power than you may ever have. A typical initial reaction to an offer is a feeling of euphoria that can be followed by a quick, "Yes, I'll take it." Enjoy the emotional high while resisting the impulse to accept. Instead, express appreciation, continued genuine interest, and a desire for further discussion. You now have an advantage, and in these cases, it isn't unusual for an offer to be increased. It also shows that you take time to consider important decisions, which is a positive characteristic.

Negotiation is best done in person; in cases of long distance hiring, the telephone will be necessary. The psychological advantage is in favor of the one sought after—in this case, you! Use this to bolster your confidence while not allowing it to make you appear superior. Keep in mind that offers can be withdrawn. A major problem in negotiation is that the candidate assumes a nonassertive position; this is especially true for women. Only 7 percent of female graduates negotiate for a higher salary compared to 57 percent of men. Not surprisingly, starting salaries for males are more than 7 percent higher than for females (Babcock & Laschever, 2003).

While assertiveness is key, your role in the negotiation process is to wait and let the potential employer mention a figure. Generally, the one who mentions a dollar amount first loses the most in the end. What if the other person asks about your expectations or requirements? A recommended response is, "I have thought about compensation and have confidence that you will be fair. I'd like to hear what you have in mind." At this point your research will pay off. If the person names the position's maximum amount, and it is near the top of the range, the next step is easy. If the figure is in the middle or lower, you can use your knowledge and leverage to an advantage in your response.

> *I understand how important it is to keep costs low in order to make a profit, and I'm confident that I will help the company do just that. Because of this and the other assets I bring to this position, I believe a salary of $______ is justified.*

Your figure will be at the top of the range. Be ready to document specific ways you can save and make money for the company so the person can see why you are worth the higher salary. Keep in mind that $2,000 a year difference over several years becomes a significant amount and that most raises are figured on a percentage of the current wage. In fact, $1 an hour difference over a year's time equates to $1,920. Over a 40-year average work life, you would experience a net gain of $76,800. The next step after your request is up to the employer.

What is the minimum salary you would accept right now?

Other questions to have answered during this deliberation process have to do with probationary periods, if any, and the all-important salary reviews. If the company has a probationary period, find out its length and purpose. Regarding salary reviews, timing makes a difference. Whether the initial adjustment to salary will be made within 90 days or one year makes a definite difference. Is the raise automatic or based on merit? In some occupations, you will receive an increase regardless of your performance; in others, it's dependent on you. Also, you will want to know the typical increase. It may be set or negotiable.

Take careful notes during the discussion. Before you accept an offer, review all aspects of the job. Because this is a critical decision, you owe it to yourself and the employer to take all the time you need. The exercise "Knowing What You Want" at the end of the chapter can help prepare you for the negotiation process.

KEY INFO

What Else Is There to Know Before Accepting?

- bonuses
- work schedule and hours
- at-home work
- relocation possibilities and help
- social expectations/obligations
- community involvement expectations
- training programs
- advancement opportunities
- travel expectations/compensation
- company expense allowance
- uniform expectations/expense

ACCEPTING A POSITION

After a verbal agreement, if you are not offered the terms in writing, request this. Again, you are demonstrating that you have a "good head on your shoulders," and neither of you will end up surprised or disappointed. You may prefer to write a letter of acceptance. This letter expresses appreciation for the offer and enthusiasm about the position. In it, you convey your understanding of the terms of the offer including the starting employment date.

During this stage of the process, you will also want to prepare yourself for the first workday. If you don't already know, ask about orientation activities, dress code, parking, food availability, appropriate ways to address supervisors and other employees, and company policies.

Rejecting an Offer

As an applicant, you may be forced to accept and deal with rejection. But what if the reverse occurs? After going through the job-search process, you may find yourself not wanting the position. This presents a challenge because you want to leave a positive impression.

If an offer is given verbally either in person or by telephone, you can respond immediately or tell the person you would like time to consider. If you delay, your response can be either verbal or in writing, and it is appropriate to express appreciation for the offer. Following is a possible verbal rejection.

I appreciate your offer and have given it serious consideration. Even though my regard for your company is high, I've decided that the particular position is not what I want. Thank you for your time and interest.

A letter of rejection is brief, sincere, and positive. The beginning paragraph expresses appreciation for the offer and contains a statement declining the position. Giving the precise reason or explaining your immediate plans is optional. In another paragraph write positively about the employer, interviewer, or offer and repeat your appreciation for the time and efforts.

Beginning Your New Job

The initial days on the job can be exciting, challenging, overwhelming, and frightening, and these feelings can last for some time. Many businesses offer a formal orientation to new employees; however, some just expect you to jump right in!

"A challenging aspect of employment for me was the confusion and overwhelming feeling of the first several months. I think it's important that new employees realize that this is normal."

LYN PATTERSON, Staffing Coordinator, The Eastridge Group, San Diego, California

Thinking of the entire first year as separate from the rest of the career ladder is a good way to help the work world make sense. You're no longer a student, yet not really a professional either. Think of this time as a transition stage. Laura Mann, a sales representative for Prentice Hall, sums it up nicely.

There is a learning curve with every new job. It seems like the first year you work nonstop and wonder why you ever agreed to take this position. In the second year, things get a lot easier, and you start to enjoy the job more. By the third year, you really start feeling good about your skills and achievements.

You will be making several first impressions that you will want to be positive. Your appearance is important. The same interview guidelines of appropriateness, cleanliness, and neatness prevail. Part of your preparation for the first day would include finding out what manner of dress is expected. What might have been acceptable elsewhere may not set well with this employer. For example, professors at some universities may be allowed to wear jeans or shorts, while other institutions frown upon this. As a new employee, dressing according to the norm or slightly better is advisable. Looking professional in a business setting certainly will be to your advantage.

Communication plays a major role in all aspects of life and takes on even greater dimensions when you are newly hired. Listening intently and reinforcing what you hear by taking notes are highly recommended. You will be receiving so much information, and even with the best memory, you won't have total recall. When you're introduced to someone, write the name along with the title and make a concerted effort to remember the person. Writing directions and explanations will help you and is usually interpreted positively as well.

Another necessary communication behavior is asking questions. If you have concerns about not knowing, realize that lack of knowledge is expected. Not asking any questions can be risky. In fact, you can make a positive impression by acknowledging how much you don't know and asking. Almost everyone is flattered by being considered a knowledgeable person. When you seek information from a supervisor, co-worker, or secretary, you are, in a sense, elevating that person.

Every company has its own communication system, which you should learn as soon as possible. Individual offices will often have established procedures for answering telephones and taking messages for one another. You may have your own individual telephone and voice mail. When you use the telephone, be sure to sound professional and friendly. You may have available a fax machine and e-mail as well. Be cautious about your use of the various modes of communication. For example, many employers do not want work time used to send personal messages, including non-work-related e-mails. Find out the acceptable procedures and policies. Also, learn e-mail etiquette and practice it.

A task that you may not like, yet one that is decidedly beneficial, is reading the company manual or policies. If a manual is not offered, ask about its availability. You may be expected to read it outside of work hours. Again, ask questions if certain policies are not clear.

For many new employees, setting up a working space is a major early task. Your goal is to create an efficient area. Even though individuals differ in the degree of neatness they maintain, new employees help themselves by being neat and organized. In most work areas you will have room for some personal

Being oriented to a new position relieves some of the overwhelming feelings.

touches such as photographs. Avoid any display that is negative, insensitive, or offensive. If you are sharing space with others, be considerate.

Interpersonal relations skills are regarded as essential throughout one's career. When you are new, a demonstration of friendliness and congeniality will be well received. Logically, other employees would introduce themselves to you. Yet, because long-term employees don't always know how new you are, they may hesitate to extend an introduction. For example, José commented, "I introduced myself to a person I thought was a new employee and was quite embarrassed when he said he had worked here for two years!" If you have a list of employees, you can mark off the name of each one you meet as another way of remembering individuals. Building relationships in the workplace is an ongoing process and is thoroughly covered in Chapter 7.

How much of a friend do you become? Do you socialize outside of work? Are such relationships encouraged? This is a learning experience as companies vary in what is appropriate. Generally, it's best to maintain a balance between your personal and professional life, and in the beginning, to move gradually into work relationships. An open communication style, along with an avoidance of profanity and slang, is appreciated. Sometimes a problem for new employees is being drawn into petty conflicts or gossip. Even though you may feel that this is a sign of being accepted, it's better to avoid getting involved. Develop professional maturity, which means using good judgment and trying to build positive relationships with everyone you meet.

Learning the "culture of the company" is a good idea, according to Susan Brown, an advertising director. A company's unique personality and culture translate into unique sets of **norms,** expected ways of behaving. Knowing the mission and philosophy of the business and paying attention to the ways things are done will make a positive difference. You want to "fit in" before you demonstrate your unique qualities. A new employee may face some teasing. One new firefighter reported that he went through a few weeks of good-natured, "new person on the block" bantering. "I just laughed and went along with it, and after a few weeks, it was over," he said. "It's a tradition at this station so I knew what to expect."

While enthusiasm is welcomed in most jobs, proceeding with some caution is advisable. Sometimes a person "plunges in" with too much zeal and, in the process, either makes unnecessary errors or gives the impression of wanting to take over. Whatever changes you desire, it is more to your advantage to move gradually. Some new graduates act as if they know everything, which is a good way to create animosity. You will fare better by seeking advice and acknowledging that you have much to learn. Most people are flattered to be perceived as experts. An exception is making unnecessary inquiries without attempting to discover an answer through personal effort, such as reading directions. An instructor of a career development course, Charlotte Nedrow, agrees. "Continue your research and don't mention changing anything. Start building credibility. Don't expect or demand it; start earning it."

Making some mistakes at first is not unusual. When you do, your best course of action is to correct the problem and, when appropriate, take responsibility for the error. Trying to cover up a problem often makes it worse. Jessica forgot to give her supervisor a message from a client. Instead of admitting it, she said there had been no message. A confrontation ensued that adversely affected customer relations. In order to avoid losing the client, she finally told the true story. Earning back her employer's trust was challenging, and she learned a valuable lesson about honesty and taking responsibility.

An immediate supervisor is the most important person to a new employee, especially during the first year. Suggestions for making this as positive as possible follow.

- Be loyal. No matter how tempted you are, refrain from doing anything that seems disloyal. This includes keeping any negative comments to yourself. Use a personal relationship to vent, not a professional one.
- Learn what is expected of you.
- Be supportive. This includes doing what is asked of you as well as offering more when needed.
- Provide solutions, not problems.
- Do everything you can to help your supervisor perform her or his job well and look good.
- Take responsibility for yourself. Excuse-making or trying to blame the supervisor or a co-worker for a poor performance or a mistake only makes it worse.

In a sense, a relationship with a supervisor is akin to a parent–child one, and you are the child. If you want to succeed in this position, you may have to take more or put up with more than you would from another person. It may seem terribly unfair, yet the reality is that this single person has more control over your future career than anyone else, except you. Building a positive working relationship is definitely in your best interest.

In the beginning your willingness to put in extra time in order to learn a new job will be impressive. Even if you don't receive extra compensation, consider it time well spent. Also, you may be asked to do some things that you didn't expect. "In the beginning if I was asked to run get a cup of coffee for my supervisor, I did it," said Matt about his work in a television studio. You will show a keen interest in the work and a desire to learn, and the additional effort will undoubtedly make your job easier in the long run. "During the first years you do what it takes to learn and grow," says Lisa Patterson, senior manager in an accounting firm.

Maintaining Balance

As much as it's worthwhile to work hard and demonstrate your capabilities and enthusiasm, it's important to be realistic. Like a candle burning at both ends, you can lose the ability to be effective. Most new employees become aware that as long as they are willing to take on all tasks, more will be assigned. At some point you will reach a saturation point. After a few years, Susan became keenly aware of an imbalance. "If you're doing your job as well as you can, and you still feel completely overwhelmed, it's time to let that be known. Otherwise, what can happen is a continual buildup of tasks."

To maintain balance, you can realistically set parameters or boundaries for work. How much is too much needs to be clearly established and then modified. A good supervisor wants you to perform effectively and will be receptive to knowing when you have more than you can handle. A way to proceed is to request a time to discuss the issue. Then, using the open communication style, you can document your task overload and request what seems realistic. Often, some minor changes can make a major difference. For example, Stephanie was expected to enter data into the computer and keep employment records updated. Because her desk was in a reception area, she was asked questions by people who walked in and often spent a great deal of time either helping them or answering the telephone. After she discussed the problem with her employer, she was given permission to use a small, remote office area. Her productivity increased significantly.

Effective time management can reduce pressure. You may find that coming in early on occasion when things are quiet is a good idea. You may choose to shorten your telephone calls. For example, some systems allow you to leave voice mail even when the person is there. While this may seem silly, you might find that it's in your best interest to leave a short, effective message rather than engage

DILBERT reprinted by permission of United Feature Syndicate, Inc.

in a longer, unnecessary conversation. Time management is covered in more detail in Chapter 8.

Balance also means maintaining a personal life. Getting away will usually make a person much more productive at work. Even though it's common for employees to put in longer than a 40-hour week, you are wise in saving adequate time for pleasure and relaxation. Personal time can serve as a valuable replenisher so, in the long run, your career will benefit.

Keeping Personal Records

Throughout your career, maintaining a personal career file is one of the most practical and worthwhile things you can do. Reasons include a need for documentation as well as preparation for a change of jobs. Well-organized records make life less stressful. The following should be included in a career file.

- All data for an application including job records
- Current resume
- Education record including grade transcripts
- Degrees, diplomas, and certificates
- Current and past job descriptions
- Salary records
- Summary of achievements and honors
- Any news clippings or articles about your career, job, or yourself
- Your publications and a portfolio of your work

- Letters of recommendation from past employers, educators, clients, and others
- Names, addresses, and numbers of contacts and past and present references
- All job evaluations and performance reviews
- Brochures about seminars and workshops you've attended

When you consider that there's a good chance you will change jobs up to 12 times during your lifetime (Shakoor, 2000), keeping a well-organized career file makes sense. Having this information up to date and readily available will make the next job search much easier. Sometimes being prepared makes a major difference. Just one day before applications closed, David heard of a dream position. Because he kept a current employment file, he was able to deliver a polished resume in due time.

Making Contacts

Networking, which is important in a job search, is essential throughout your career. Positive relationships help to create a satisfying professional life. Much of our learning and professional development are dependent upon others. Imagine having to figure out everything by yourself! Instead, from the first day at work, you will undoubtedly ask questions and seek advice, and people will voluntarily offer suggestions and show you how to perform certain tasks. You may even have a **mentor,** a specific person who serves as a guide and role model—who may "take you under his or her wing" and offer to provide help and advice. This may come from an assignment; more often, it just evolves. Effective career designers have several mentors. Cultivating multiple and diverse developmental relationships in order to build a "personal board of directors" is recommended by Harvard Business School professor Linda A. Hill (1994). Successful mentoring is usually reciprocal; your willingness to provide help and advice in return solidifies the relationship.

Think of someone you admire. For what reasons do you admire that person? In what way could this individual serve as a mentor?

Contacts are especially helpful as you advance. Having a number of people who know and appreciate your contributions and who will vouch for your abilities can spell the difference between being promoted or not. If you decide to change jobs, references will be needed; you will be in an enviable position if you can draw from a respected group of people. You can also find job leads and receive advice from your networking circle.

List all the members of your current networking circle.

You are wise to collect business cards and keep them in a special file. Additionally, you can make file cards with name, title, address, and telephone number plus the circumstances under which you met or by what means you know the person. If the person helps you in any way, be sure to show your appreciation. People with whom you connect fall into three general categories (Latas, 1993).

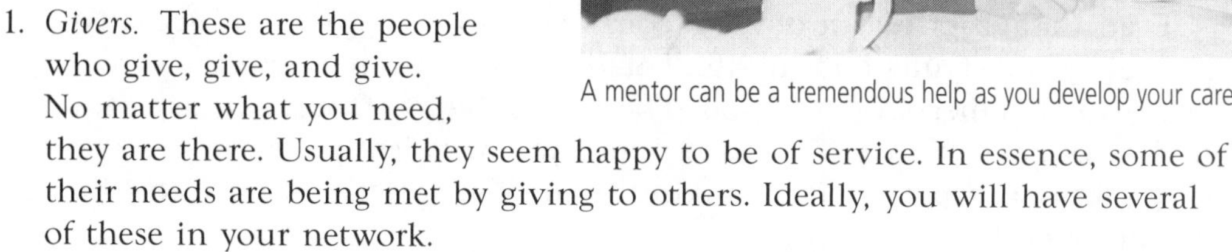
A mentor can be a tremendous help as you develop your career.

1. *Givers.* These are the people who give, give, and give. No matter what you need, they are there. Usually, they seem happy to be of service. In essence, some of their needs are being met by giving to others. Ideally, you will have several of these in your network.
2. *Traders.* As long as they get something in return, they are willing to be of service. You may need to show them how they can benefit. Know that they do "keep track," and if you "owe them," they will expect a return favor.
3. *Takers.* Because they are completely preoccupied with getting, these people are of no use to you. Invariably, you will be disappointed if you do ask, so build your network from the other two groups. It's good to realize that even though some of these people may be family members or friends, you'll profit more from a stranger who is a giver or a trader.

One recommended way to build contacts is to serve on committees or teams. In recent years employers have been encouraged to use teams, so you will probably have opportunities to be a contributor to a group effort. Involvement in company-sponsored activities is another excellent way to make contacts. Many employers encourage participation in volunteer activities. For example, many companies encourage employees to take part in fund-raisers and community service projects. "These activities give people a chance to get to know each other, to learn to work cooperatively toward a mutual goal, while fostering a tremendous feeling that they have contributed," says Lyn Patterson, who has coordinated many such projects.

People really do need people! Your contacts will provide advice, support, and actual help throughout your career. A priority of a successful career person is to develop and maintain the most valuable resource of all—a wide network of people.

Handling Performance Reviews

A performance review or evaluation is likely to be scheduled on a regular basis. The initial one can occur anytime within the first year; typically, you will have at least one review every year. The most positive attitude is to view this as an opportunity to learn about your performance so that you can continue what is effective and make improvements, if necessary. You may also be encouraged to share your ideas and, in a sense, evaluate the employer. Try to find out ahead of time exactly what is involved in the discussion.

Even though criticism often is considered to be negative, it actually refers to judging both faults and merits. Thus, in essence, a **performance review** is a time for a supervisor to discuss both positive and negative aspects of an employee's performance. In this chapter, you will learn how to receive unfavorable criticism positively. Thinking about your reactions ahead of time can be quite useful.

PREPARING YOURSELF FOR CRITICISM

You may be especially sensitive and have a difficult time being criticized. Several emotions are possible. After being told how performance could be improved,

Christopher experienced a feeling of hurt,
Jody felt defensive and angry,
Jack became depressed.

If you know you are apt to react with an unpleasant emotion, take steps to diminish its impact.

What emotion do you typically experience when you are criticized? How do you react?

To develop a positive way of responding to any criticism, mental preparation or mental realignment is necessary. Rather than seeing a performance review as an assault on your abilities, view it as an opportunity to improve. Even though we have heard over and over not to take criticism personally, most of us will. However, *how* you take it personally will make a difference.

"We've been conditioned to regard criticism as bad, and we need to learn that it's not the end of the world. A response can be as simple as, 'Thanks. I appreciate knowing that.'"

DOC CHAVES, Marketing Communications Manager, Li-Cor, Inc., Lincoln, Nebraska

You can challenge any irrational belief that comes to mind. Think about the thoughts that triggered the hurt, defensiveness, anger, and depression experienced by the three individuals mentioned previously.

> CHRISTOPHER: *The supervisor must not like me as much as she does the others. That's terrible.*
>
> JODY: *I can't believe he would think I can do any better. He's the one who needs to improve!*
>
> JACK: *I'm just worthless. I'll probably get fired.*

The use of cognitive restructuring would help in all of these cases. Instead of the thoughts they had, a more constructive and realistic one is:

> *Just because the supervisor is pointing out some ways I can improve doesn't mean I haven't done a good job. I know I have, and this will help me do even better.*

The ability to change your thoughts allows you to reframe the entire situation and calm yourself. Taking a deep breath and either counting slowly to 10 or just remaining silent for several seconds can also help you calm yourself. This will keep you from overreacting.

AVOIDING NEGATIVE RESPONSES TO CRITICISM

Eliminating ineffective or negative responses can clear the way for ones that work on your behalf. A primary personal purpose of any exchange is to avoid making things worse for yourself, and, if possible, to make them better.

In general, people respond to criticism either aggressively or passively, or a combination of the two. An aggressive method is one of counterattack. Because a person feels wronged, justifiably or not, that individual lashes out. In the workplace this will probably get you fired. Passive responses, either verbal or nonverbal, are ones that apologize, acquiesce, or agree. Silence can be perceived as surrender, apathy, or hostility. Some people respond passively while they harbor resentment and then try to get back at the critic later.

A most annoying response is one that denies responsibility. Excuse-making is a far-too-common reaction and seldom achieves positive results. "Yes, but" or "I know I can do better, but" is an irritating response. You are well advised to leave the word *but* out of the statement. Putting the blame on others or on external circumstances only makes a person appear immature and irresponsible.

RESPONDING POSITIVELY TO CRITICISM

If you want to maintain or increase your self-esteem, preserve or improve the relationship, and make the situation better for yourself, positive responses to criticism are the key. Remember "I" statements? Be sure to review this type of assertive language as well as paralanguage and body language. Positive responses use "I" statements. Likewise, your tone of voice and the message transmitted by your body position and movements are to be positive and open.

Using a sequence of steps can turn a difficult situation into a positive one. What you say depends upon the extent of your agreement with the criticism.

Agreeing with the criticism. Even if the criticism is justified, you may feel defensive and hurt and respond in a way that will make the situation worse for you. Instead, follow these steps using "I" statements.

1. Agree with and acknowledge the criticism using such phrases as "I agree," "I realize," "I know," or "I understand."
2. An optional step (you may not want to tell why) is to state the reason briefly, being sure you are giving a reason, not an excuse. Do not begin with *but.*
3. State what you plan to do to prevent future occurrences or tell what you think will solve the problem.

Pretend you have been told that one of your weaknesses is punctuality. Instead of making excuses or trying to blame others or circumstances such as traffic, use the following refreshing response that is likely to produce a positive outcome.

1. I know I've been late several times, and I can understand your concern.
2. (optional) I've had several problems with my car.
3. I'm having my car fixed, and I will be punctual in the future. I realize how important it is.

Dramatically promising that you will *always* be on time is unwise because you might be late in the future.

You can also agree with part of the criticism. The person's interpretation might be all that needs clarifying. For example, if the supervisor says, "You seem to have lost interest in doing a good job," you can respond, "I can see why you would think that because I have been late several times recently. I want to assure you that I haven't lost interest. My being late is due to other factors that I will correct. I realize how important it is." Incidentally, be sure that you know the supervisor's remark is due to your lack of punctuality; otherwise, you may be revealing something the person didn't know!

Not understanding the criticism. Frequently, criticism is vague, and you honestly don't know what the person means. Emotionally, this is difficult to handle because it seems so unfair. A temptation is to defend even if you don't know the person's reason. Resist this temptation and use the following approach.

1. State your lack of understanding or confusion with phrases such as "I don't understand why you think that," "I'm confused as to why you think that," or "I don't know why you have that impression."
2. Tell the person what you need to increase your level of understanding with such phrases as "I'd like for you to explain to me why you think that way," "I'd appreciate your telling me what I've done or not done to lead you to think this," or "I would like to have some clarification about this."

Pretend you have been told, "You don't seem to be committed to teamwork," and you don't understand the reason for the comment. You can respond as follows.

1. I don't know why you think I'm not a team player.
2. I'd appreciate your telling me what has caused you to think so.

Notice that you don't explain how you have been a team player. This can be used later, if necessary. At this point, because you don't understand, what is needed is more information. Using "I" statements, you have been open, honest, and polite in letting the person know of your confusion and desire to be enlightened. The critic is now in the responding position. The answer, hopefully, will enable you to respond specifically because you are dealing with concrete, descriptive data.

If the person seems unable to provide you with specific information, you can still guide the conversation in a positive direction. You can do this with polite questions such as: "Can you give me some examples?" "Exactly what has happened?" "Can you describe what I have done?" If you have any idea regarding the reason, you can probe with such questions as: "Is it because I missed the last meeting?" "Are you basing this on my disagreement with the team at our last meeting?" Be careful about this, however, as you may be telling something the person doesn't know and "adding fuel to the fire."

If the person still doesn't provide you with the needed data, the best you can do is express continued confusion and lack of agreement with the interpretation by saying, "I am committed to working with the team and still would like to understand why you think I'm not. If there is something I can change, I'm willing to do it. However, without specifics, there's very little I can do." See if you can respond positively by completing the Key Steps activity at the end of the chapter.

Not agreeing with the criticism. Emotionally, the most difficult situation is one in which you disagree with the criticism. You know what led to the person's interpretation, yet you don't agree with it. A positive response is still in your best interest. Give yourself a few seconds to compose yourself, then use the following steps.

1. State your disagreement politely, yet firmly. Avoid a quick "I disagree." Instead in a calm, modulated voice, say, "I don't see it the way you do," or "I don't agree," or "It seems we don't agree."
2. If appropriate, use precise descriptive language to tell what happened and what you experienced that would lead to a different interpretation. Another option is simply to state your disagreement and wait for the other person to speak. A future discussion is a possibility to suggest, or you can acknowledge that two people can disagree, and move on.

Pretend that your supervisor is talking with you about concerns regarding your interactions with a co-worker.

SUPERVISOR: There have been two incidents between you and Michelle in which you seemed to lose your patience. The first occurred two weeks ago when you were showing her how to use the new word processing program. Then yesterday I overheard her say to you, "I wish you would give me more of your time because I don't understand it yet," and you replied, "I think I've given you plenty of my time."

YOUR RESPONSE: I don't think I have been impatient with Michelle, and I'd like to explain to you what happened both times. After you asked me to demonstrate the new software, I did so. Then I spent a couple of hours during work time and an hour after work guiding her through the basics. I suggested that she read the manual and continue to practice on her own. I don't think she did that because yesterday she asked me several basic questions which I had already covered that are also in the first chapter of the manual. What you heard was a request for help after I had already answered questions three different times. By that time I may have sounded frustrated; however, I think I have shown a great deal of patience. I would be glad to discuss this further with both you and Michelle in order to clarify the situation.

This type of response takes longer and requires more effort than a quick denial of the supervisor's version of the situation. Yet, just responding that you have been patient or, even worse, lashing out at Michelle would likely make the situation worse. If you are caught completely off guard by criticism that seems unfair, especially if your feeling is one of anger, it's best to delay a response. You can simply state your surprise and confusion, then be sure that you understand the criticism, and state, "I would like to think about this and then discuss it with you." Waiting for a while to compose yourself rather than quickly reacting allows for far more constructive responses.

You might receive both a verbal and a written performance review. You then may have an opportunity to respond in writing to the evaluation and can express agreement, lack of understanding, or disagreement. Be sure that your written words show the same openness and positiveness as your spoken ones!

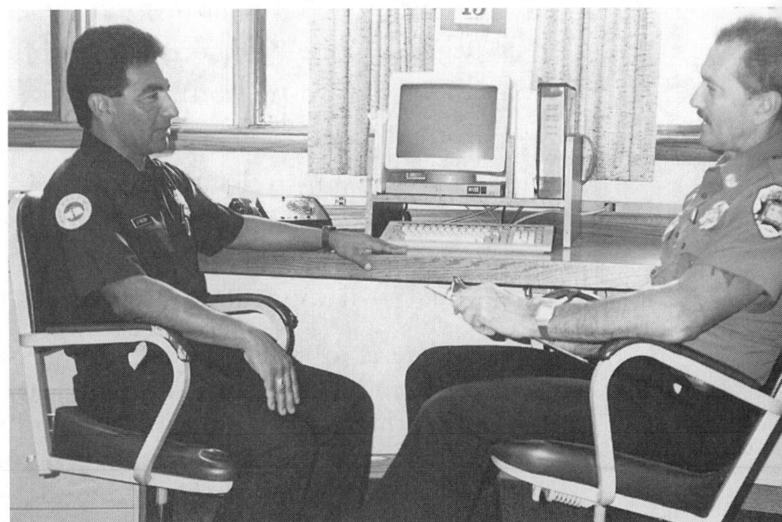

When two people can positively give and receive criticism both they and their employer benefit.

Positive responses to criticism are built on honesty and sensibility and aren't difficult to learn. They lead to enhanced self-esteem and a feeling of being in control. A formal review is quite likely to include some criticism, and a good idea is to plan your reaction. During a workday, criticism is also going to occur. You can expect it from co-workers, subordinates, and customers or clients. Remaining in charge of your emotions, being able to exhibit a calm exterior, and using positive responses will move relationships in positive directions.

DISCUSSING SALARY INCREASES

A formal review could include an increase in salary. If no set amount has been established, you will want to have salary information and an idea of what you think is fair. This depends upon the range of salary for employees of your same tenure either in the same company or in others. Have documentation of reasons why an increase is justified.

Perhaps you will work for an employer where formal reviews are not given and salary increase times are not established. It may or may not come as a surprise that some employers will avoid giving salary raises as long as they can. Then it's up to you. If six months have passed and a salary increase has never been addressed, you are justified in initiating a discussion about this. Of course you may wait longer if you want. Bringing up an increase before six months has passed isn't advisable.

Asking for a raise isn't easy. It has been described as more traumatic than wearing a bathing suit to the beach after a long winter of hot fudge sundaes! Following are several good pieces of advice (Mackay, 1993).

- Pick the most opportune time in terms of your performance, the economic condition of the company, and the employer's state of being.
- Request a raise based on your performance, not on a personal crisis or need.
- Know what you're worth and what is possible.
- Don't threaten to leave; this is a sign of weakness.
- Be prepared with documentation of your fine work.
- After clearly defining what you have done for the employer, tell what you intend to do in the future. A good idea is to present your goals in writing.
- Know what you will do if no raise is forthcoming.

If there is to be no increase, the reasons should be explained, and you can benefit from hearing what they are. If the employer contends that lack of profit doesn't permit a raise, you can suggest other benefits in lieu of money. For example, Jason was given three days of vacation with pay when a salary increase was delayed. You can be assertive and ask for reasons and ways to justify an increase in the future. You and the employer are involved in a give-and-take proposition, and you are entitled to a fair wage in return for your contributions. Always be sure that you are giving as much as you are taking.

What to Do with a Raise (Switzer, 1996)

Strongly consider investing in your future and start as early as possible. A 25-year-old who sets aside $2,000 each year for 10 years will have more assets at age 55 than someone who starts at age 35 and invests $2,000 for 20 years.

Regardless of whether you receive a raise or not, if your company offers a tax-deferred investment program, especially if your contribution is matched by the employer, you are fortunate. Otherwise, find other sound ways to ensure a financially sound future for yourself.

What, if anything, are you doing to invest in your financial future? What can you do?

Continuing to Learn

A common assumption is that after graduation from college and entry into the career field, formal learning is over. Most people realize that they will learn on the job yet often fail to recognize the need for other learning experiences.

Do you recall that a common interview question has to do with how you plan to keep abreast of changes in your field? Anyone committed to "staying current" will need to seek information actively and then cultivate new skills. Ideally, your employer will be committed to helping in this endeavor, and education and training will be among your benefits. Often, employees are encouraged to attend conferences, workshops, and other training sessions by receiving paid leave and, in some cases, even having registrations and other expenses paid by the employer. This still can mean some hardship on your part as you put in extra time preparing to be gone and then play "catch-up" when you return. Yet, taking advantage of these experiences is highly advisable.

What if the employer doesn't provide or pay for learning and training opportunities? The clear answer is to learn and train on your own time at your own expense. You can read professional and trade publications as well as take classes and attend conferences and training sessions, even if it takes personal time, effort, and money. Similar to your efforts in getting a job, you can research and even visit other employers in your career field. To motivate yourself, complete "Progressing in your Career" at the end of the chapter.

The benefits of continued learning are many. Primarily, you develop into a more valuable employee by acquiring new information, upgrading skills, strengthening self-esteem, and increasing self-efficacy. Learning experiences are usually rejuvenating. You can also make contacts and keep informed about other employers. Juan attended a regional conference and later reported, "I didn't learn as much as I had hoped, yet I met several interesting people. In fact, I just called one of them as we have decided to relocate to his area. He gave me several job leads!"

According to Dave Sonenberg, director of student services and financial aid at Southeast Community College, anyone who wants to advance keeps an eye on the future and does whatever is needed to become more marketable. He says, "Just knowing that improvement is important gives you an edge. People throughout their career life who increase and enhance their skills become winners."

A definite quality that separates those who succeed from those who don't is commitment to continued learning and training. Count yourself fortunate if your employer encourages and supports such efforts. If this isn't the case, your taking the initiative to fulfill your potential will be rewarded in a variety of ways. Lifelong learners are invariably the career winners.

WHAT WILL MAXIMIZE CAREER SUCCESS? Key Advice

Medical Laboratory Technology: *"Take advantage of every opportunity to learn." —Janis Bible, program chairperson*

Laboratory Science Technology: *"Continuing education, perhaps working toward a higher degree, helps one advance." —Don Mumm, program chairperson*

Microcomputer Technology: *"After entering into a microcomputer career, a person must be constantly reading and learning to remain current in an ever-changing field." —Linda Bettinger, program chairperson*

Early Childhood Education: *"Continued professional growth is a necessity." —Alicia Baillie, program chairperson*

Nursing: *"Professional growth, dependability, and legal and ethical accountability." —Virginia Hess, program chairperson*

Office Technology: *"Keep up to date in your field; continue your education formally and informally." —Jo Ann Frazell, program chairperson*

Machine Tool Technology: *"In this profession we are in a continuous explosion of new technology, which mandates retraining to remain technically competent. Additional education also opens the door to new opportunities." —Millard Carnes, program chairperson*

Drafting Technology: *"Continuing education is becoming more and more essential with technological advances. More education and training can open new doors of career opportunity." —Dan Masters, program chairperson*

Automotive Technology: *"Pay attention to detail. Use your time effectively." —Ken Jefferson, program chairperson*

Surgical Technology: *"Be committed to the job and the profession, continue your education with the belief that education and learning don't stop with graduation, be willing to go beyond average employer expectations, be a team player, view negative experiences as learning, and practice leadership behaviors instead of falling victim to mediocre 'followership.'" —Kathy Uribe, program chairperson*

Practical Nursing: *"Continue your education and licensing requirements after graduation. Develop a reputation for being reliable, honest, and ethical as well as a person who values teamwork. It's important to be flexible as health care facilities are often operated 24 hours a day, 7 days a week, and nursing service is required on all shifts." —Iris Winkelhake, program chairperson*

Advancing in Your Career

Do your career goals include promotions and advancement? Most people possess the American dream of upward mobility. Yet, advancement isn't for everyone. Some individuals don't possess the particular skills required for higher-level positions. Others would not be happy in those jobs. I remember discussing with the division dean whether to apply for his position when he retired because it was the next step on the ladder for me. He said, "I think you could do a very good job, but I don't think you'd like it. You love teaching, and that's not what I do." After a discussion of exactly what he did, which was certainly not to my liking, the decision was made.

Some companies will expect you to be promotable. In these cases, those incapable of advancing will be the first to be let go. Also, you may have to accept a promotion into a position you don't want in order to get where you do want to be. Other times you may move into a **lateral position,** one that is at the same level as your present job. What is necessary is to determine your final goal and then decide if an advancement is a step in that direction.

Personal success and satisfaction need to be defined by you. Moving up might not mean continuing on a forward track. For example, you may need to get different types of experience in order to be promotable. Ed Rasgorshek, a corporate executive, left a company for a few years in order to get direct lending experience in a bank. "I needed a diverse background to get where I wanted to be. I went to a new employer for a few years to get different experiences, then returned."

Are you interested in advancement? To what level?

TAKING ACTION

If you want to advance, planning becomes significant. You start by choosing employment where promotional opportunities exist. Then, certain behaviors enhance your chances.

- Perform as well as you can in your present position.
- Do more than what is expected of you whether this means additional time spent, more work completed, or greater displays of effort.
- Document your accomplishments.
- Display professionalism in your everyday actions and by becoming involved in career organizations. In all circumstances, demonstrate a high degree of ethics.

- Keep your resume and other records updated.
- Observe those above you. If possible, use job shadowing to see what the jobs entail.
- Research as carefully as you did when you chose this career field. Learn as much as you can about all aspects of the company and the upper positions. For example, for what reasons are people promoted?
- Prepare yourself to initiate a discussion of advancement possibilities if the company has no set timetable and if promotions haven't been mentioned.

"A promotable employee has demonstrated a history of performance, a positive attitude, the willingness to 'go the extra mile' without complaining, and does more thinking about the 'good of the group' rather than of him- or herself."

DAVID R. HANNA, Assistant Vice President (retired), New York Life Insurance Company, Cleveland, Ohio

In all situations, the use of open, positive communication skills is likely to produce the best results. Jerry Baxter, Lejeune Steel Company, Minneapolis, credits dependability and "people" skills for his amazing advancement from an hourly welding job to plant manager of a large company. "I've always believed that problems are nothing but a wake-up call for creativity," he said.

MAKING RELOCATION DECISIONS

Even though you could be asked to relocate without a promotion, the two usually go hand in hand. Perhaps one option clarifies the other as you could be offered a higher-level position you don't especially want, yet be moved to the perfect geographic location.

For some people, relocation isn't really a choice. "I knew that in order to move 'up the ladder,' I would have to move geographically, as well, and accepted that as part of life," said my brother Dave. He and his family relocated six times in 16 years as he moved up the ranks to become one of five regional managers and an assistant vice president for New York Life Insurance Company. "The last tenure was the longest. The 13 years before I retired I spent in one location," he recalled.

In most instances, the decision is somewhat complicated. Along with several other career decisions, whether to relocate requires a thoughtful process. A major obstacle is fear of the unknown that leads a person to immediately turn down a relocation opportunity. As one who has lived in four different parts of the country and moved numerous times, I'm amazed by the reluctance of individuals to even consider living elsewhere. While some areas are less than desirable, almost all sites have unique advantages, so try not to limit yourself because of fear.

You can gather helpful information about the new location from a chamber of commerce or a special office that provides material to potential citizens and from other company employees who live there, especially those who have relocated. States and cities have Web sites, and career information sites also provide relocation information. Most employers will provide you with a firsthand look at the new location, and if you have a significant other, he or she is usually included in the visit, too. You will want to know the anticipated length of your tenure there and whether or not you could expect to return to your present location. If expenses are higher in the new location, will the company pay a cost-of-living differential, or will the salary be higher enough to compensate? Any decision carries with it a concern about whether it's "right" or "wrong." A good idea is to challenge the concept of rightness or wrongness. In all probability, if you relocate, you will have wonderful and not-so-wonderful experiences just as you would have if you didn't move. One definite benefit of relocation is the opportunity to experience newness and to broaden your life experiences.

FOSTERING LEADERSHIP SKILLS

Advancement usually means becoming a leader. Generally, **leadership** means taking responsibility and being in a position to direct, guide, and influence others. Depending upon the specific leadership position, an individual may be expected to perform different roles.

Types of leadership roles. Think of an example of a leader of any group of which you have been a part. Did the person emphasize completion of tasks—getting things done? If so, that person would be considered an **instrumental leader.** This type of leader concentrates on performance and would be apt to reward or punish employees based on how much they accomplish and the quality of their performance. You may prefer this role both as a follower and as a leader. The instrumental leader would probably have a personality type on the Myers–Briggs Type Indicator that prefers facts, takes care of details, and likes efficient standard operating procedures (sensing); chooses to analyze the facts and apply logic to decision making (thinking); and likes to bring about closure in an orderly, organized way (judging).

Advantages of this personality type include the ability to be productive, meet deadlines, be objective, and complete tasks in an organized fashion. As a leader, you would likely earn respect from others, yet be considered distant from them. Instrumental leaders expect others to complete tasks efficiently. Some pitfalls of instrumental leadership are being perceived as cold and unfeeling and ignoring people's concerns because of the focus on task completion.

The other type is the **expressive leader,** who emphasizes collective well-being. Tasks are considered less important than getting along with people, being supportive, and maintaining harmony. The personality preferences usually found in expressive leaders are intuition (a capacity for visualizing many ideas and preferring flexible policies and different ways of doing things), feeling (considering personal feelings and values in decision making), and perceiving (being open, tentative, and spontaneous).

If you favor this type, others will probably feel warm and affectionate toward you as long as you maintain fairness. This is sometimes hard for expressive leaders to do even though they want to be fair. Ideas are welcomed by an expressive leader, and the environment is likely to be friendly and personal. A disadvantage is that expressive leaders can have difficulty getting tasks accomplished. Productivity may be slowed in the interest of harmony and the desire to listen to everyone's ideas.

Perhaps the ideal type would be a blend of the two, drawing on an instrumental or expressive style depending upon the circumstances. For example, the president of a manufacturing firm hosted a breakfast for his supervisors, at which time he solicited ideas for an upcoming project. He praised their cooperative efforts. At the end of the meeting he announced the project schedule, made sure everyone understood the assignments, and told them the completion date. He said, "I sincerely appreciate your efforts so far, and I expect the same caliber of work from you. The success of this venture depends upon all of us."

Which leadership style do you favor?

Characteristics of effective leaders. Being an effective leader goes far beyond successful job performance. An effective leader has to excel in all interpersonal skills including, but not limited to, understanding people and their interactions, demonstrating assertiveness, being optimistic, using humor effectively, and dealing with conflict. Emotional intelligence, discussed in Chapter 1, accounts for about 90 percent of what distinguishes outstanding leaders from those judged as average (Kemper, 1999).

An outstanding leader is an excellent communicator. Being able to give clear instructions is primary. The use of the open style of verbalizing encourages exchange and creates a positive communication climate. In today's work

Being an Effective Leader (Covey, 1999)

- Anticipate problems; don't just react.
- Continually sharpen your skills; don't be completely satisfied with the way you do something now.
- Have a vision so you know what needs to be accomplished to get to where you want to be.
- Manage your time well so your life is well managed.
- Work well with others and draw on their energies.
- Seek first to understand, then to be understood.

environment, e-mail and voice mail are efficient ways of communicating; however, face-to-face contact, what is called a "human moment," is still essential (Hallowell, 1999). Listening demands equal attention. Most executives spend a larger portion of their workdays listening rather than talking or writing. Unfortunately, listening is often a neglected tool. Active listening, discussed in Chapter 2, helps a leader develop a full understanding of another person's situation, concern, or point of view. As you manage others and deal with customer or client concerns, you will want to listen closely as a means of solving problems and building rapport.

For a leader, planning and organizational skills are needed in contrast to the lower levels where the "doing" part of work is instrumental. In most businesses time equates to money made or lost. Poor planners or those who are disorganized waste precious time and end up losing money. Perhaps more challenging is what Doc Chaves, a marketing communications manager, calls the vision issue. "A leader has to be able to assess the task at hand while seeing the total picture; she or he has to always be looking for better ways to accomplish what is to be done."

"Above all, a leader needs to provide vision–the ability to scan the horizon, envision what is over the next hill, and translate the vision into an imagined reality for those one is leading."

PATRICIA K. KNAUB, PH.D., Dean, College of Human Environmental Sciences, Oklahoma State University, Stillwater, Oklahoma

Perhaps one of the most difficult functions of a leader is in delegation of responsibilities and tasks. To **delegate** means to commit powers or functions to another. "If you don't delegate, you won't have the time to do your job. Delegation means to give clear directions to others, then let them 'run with the ball.' Also important is to know when to check how they are doing and make adjustments, if necessary," explains Lisa Patterson, a senior manager at a major accounting firm.

A leader determines who can best do the job or who is available and then makes assignments. For most people, the most difficult aspect of delegating is to let go. "I have a hard time thinking that anyone can do it as well as I can with all my experience, so I tend to step in and either do the job or at least help a lot," said Phuoc, a restaurant owner. According to Susan Brown, an advertising director, "An excellent supervisor is available for help yet gives you autonomy. Not being able to delegate means spending too much time and energy involved in the business of those at a lower level."

A major benefit of delegating is that you are setting the stage for your own further advancement while you help others. Grooming subordinates and allowing them to learn and grow teaches them to do your job so it is easier for you to progress.

What if tasks aren't completed or someone does the job poorly? Then another invaluable skill is needed. Anyone placed in a leadership position must be able to give criticism. This can be extremely difficult for certain personality types. "They put me into a supervisor role because I was good at my job. It was a horrible experience because when people didn't perform, I just couldn't tell them," said Sharon, an individual who scored a very strong feeling preference on the Myers–Briggs Type Indicator. In spite of your personality type, you can learn effective ways to deliver criticism.

Delivering criticism in a positive way is an art. An effective beginning is a positive comment about the person. Then, with the use of "I" statements, specifically describe undesirable behaviors or practices. Beginning a sentence with the word *you* is definitely to be avoided. Note the following.

> *James, I'm impressed with your creative ideas, and I'm eager to put them into practice. I do have a concern about your ability to meet a deadline. The report you were assigned to write was due yesterday, and I still don't have it. I'd like to know the reason.*

This method of openly verbalizing the concern or displeasure is likely to elicit a desired response. Practice your delivery by using the suggested scenario exercise in Key Steps at the end of the chapter.

As necessary as giving criticism and advice is the habit of praising. If you want an emotionally healthy and productive workplace, appreciation and recognition of employees and their accomplishments are vital. Yet, on many occasions, employees doubt that their work is being recognized. You have probably heard the advice, "Catch them doing something good." Praise and recognition are powerful motivators (Wiscombe, 2002).

If you have supervised, can you recall praising an employee? In the workplace, when was the last time you were recognized?

Leaders are expected to get along with everyone and to meet the challenge of building teamwork and positive relationships among their subordinates. The information in Chapter 7 about personality temperament types at work can reveal how to deal with differences in a positive way. As a leader, you can use this knowledge to assign tasks and to help your subordinates develop an appreciation of one another's strengths.

Outstanding leaders possess empowering beliefs, and they teach others to tap their full capabilities. Becoming an effective leader at work requires more than you might have anticipated. Even though advancement has many benefits, you will also need to work hard, keep abreast of advances related to the career field, and continually strive to develop and improve your leadership style. Assess your leadership capabilities by answering the questions at the end of this chapter.

What leadership characteristics do you possess? If you are lacking, it's possible to develop most of them.

Changing Careers and Jobs

While you may feel as if you're the only one contemplating or making a career change, you're definitely not alone. Career transitions are common. The average person can expect to change careers 5 to 7 times and jobs up to 12 times (Shakoor, 2000). Years ago an individual most likely started with and stayed with not only the same career but also the same employer. The career world is simply not like that anymore.

Dissatisfaction stemming from a poor choice is a common reason for a career change. As Marci explained, "For years I didn't understand why I hated to go to work. After attending a conference, I realized that my personality type and the career field were completely incompatible." At earlier stages of life, most people aren't aware of what they really want out of life. Betty Knapp of Lakeville, Minnesota, had a nursing career, then changed to real estate. Today she is a multi-million-dollar sales producer in the Twin Cities area. "I decided I wanted to make more money so I found a career that I enjoy where higher incomes are possible." The opposite course could be taken. Connie Hanna Gengenbach, who was a marketing merchandising manager for a large home-building corporation in San Jose, California, returned to teaching. She explained, "Even though the marketing position had satisfying elements and the pay was lucrative, I missed the deep feeling of satisfaction from challenging the minds of children and being a positive influence in their lives."

Most of us experience a change in needs over time. You may be familiar with the **hierarchy of needs** (Maslow, 1968). The theory is that human beings are motivated to satisfy their needs on one of five levels: (1) physiological, (2) safety, (3) love and belongingness, (4) self-esteem, and (5) self-actualization. Conceivably, as lower needs are met, higher ones become dominant, and a present career or position may not offer what is needed. To reach self-actualization, the highest level, human beings work to achieve their full potential and make a meaningful contribution to the world. Self-actualizers desire more meaning from life, which could demand a change in career or position.

Whatever the reason for a change, you will again want to do thorough research on yourself and your career possibilities. Earlier chapters plus other books can be quite helpful. You will want to include an assessment of what areas were unsatisfying so that you choose differently the next time.

More commonly, people change jobs as a result of what can be called "pushes" or "pulls." When dissatisfied with a present position, a person feels pushed to look elsewhere. Individuals who were asked why they opted to change their career or their job within a field responded as follows.

- "I wasn't challenged."
- "Whatever I did went seemingly unnoticed."
- "I found out that it just wasn't 'me.'"
- "I was burned out. The stress was unbelievable."
- "My supervisor was overly demanding, and it didn't look as if things would change in the near future."
- "It was a dead-end job."
- "At first I was willing to work for less than I deserved. However, that got old after some time."
- "There wasn't flexibility or support for family time."
- "Earning money wasn't enough. I wanted to make more of a difference."

As you can see, some of these situations would not have developed if the person had been knowledgeable before accepting a job.

If you have been dissatisfied with a job, do you know why?

While it's always a good idea to be open for better opportunities, you will want to carefully examine the reasons for your dissatisfaction. Is it just a temporary problem? What would it take to make the job satisfying and is this feasible? The best course of action is to have a frank discussion with your supervisor about your concerns. Too many job changes can become a liability, and you could leave one job only to find the same hardships in another. Nevertheless, if you truly decide that the current situation is unacceptable and not likely to change, a search is advisable, preferably while you still hold a job.

In this job search, a few things will be different from the job-search strategies discussed earlier. Depending upon the demands of your present job, it may be best to use an employment agency. When interviewing, it is imperative to remain professional and positive when discussing why you are leaving your present job, and unless you have informed the current employer of your intentions, be sure to ask potential ones not to contact anyone in your workplace at this time.

A change of jobs could be precipitated by a "pull," an attractive offer. You may be satisfied and be contacted either directly by another employer or by search firms, commonly called **headhunters.** This is flattering, yet you don't want to be led into making an unwise decision. Careful research, logical decision making, and honesty with the person who has contacted you are of utmost importance. Because you may want a future contact with this person, sound advice is to "burn no bridges."

Another "pull" is a desire to live in a new place. Government offices and chambers of commerce will have data showing unemployment rates and types of employment available. Also make use of Internet sites that allow you to find out where the jobs are and to calculate salary needs in a certain desired location (see Online Resources at the end of this chapter). You could be like one young woman who said, "I've always wanted to live in Phoenix, so I just went there to look for a job. I've been here ten years and still love it."

More education could be attractive. Ryan Turner left a good job as a financial analyst to pursue an advanced degree at Harvard. "I wasn't in a career path I wanted so I decided to explore other opportunities," he explains. Additional education can be a definite benefit in all career fields.

When you decide to change jobs, professionalism is essential. Typically, you will schedule an appointment with your immediate supervisor to discuss the upcoming change. The person may try to persuade you to stay. If this doesn't happen or if you decide you still want to leave even after the persuasion attempt, one matter to discuss is the length of time between your resignation announcement and your last day, what is called **notice.** The usual minimum amount is two weeks; however, if you can stay longer, offer to do so. Either at that time or shortly thereafter, submit a written resignation letter. Being willing to help train your replacement is a positive action. Employers expect people to leave jobs, and a good supervisor will not take your resignation personally. Being professional and gracious will instill a positive

A career change means researching and making contacts again.

impression that will be beneficial in the present and perhaps the future, too.

No job is totally secure. An employer may **downsize,** which means laying off workers. Other names have been given to this practice, such as organizational readjustment or "right-sizing." However phrased, the effects are the same—people lose their jobs. Mergers between companies also lead to reduction in employees.

You may be one of those affected, and you have a right to know why. Just as you can be involved in an accident simply because you are in a particular place at a certain time, you can be seriously affected by downsizing or a merger for reasons that have nothing to do with your own actions. Depending upon the employer, you may be given **severance pay,** an amount of money as compensation, and you could be aided in a job search.

Even if you are given no compensation or help, controlling your frustration and maintaining a professional attitude and behavior are in your best interest. It can help to realize that because downsizing is so common, unemployment doesn't have the stigma of the past. Coping with stress, covered in Chapter 8, will be beneficial to anyone going through a career transition.

A more difficult situation is being fired, sometimes called **termination.** Different reasons could account for this; however, it usually means that an employee hasn't done a satisfactory job. "Whenever I fired anyone, it meant that the person was either incapable of performing the tasks or not willing to make the effort. People were not terminated after a first instance; warnings were always given," said David Hanna, a retired regional office manager.

"Incompetence and absenteeism are two major reasons for termination."

DAVID R. HANNA, Assistant Vice President (retired), New York Life Insurance Company, Cleveland, Ohio

Certainly there are other reasons a person is fired that may not be that individual's fault. In such cases, termination can come as a total surprise. A challenge is to remain calm and under control, as you only hurt yourself more by being hostile. After the initial shock, you can accept the firing and leave without even knowing the reason. A better choice and certainly your right is to find out all you can. Then you can either ask for another chance with an assurance that you will improve, or, if you feel you have been unjustly treated, you can take legal action. A professional association or trade union probably has resources, or you can hire your own attorney. The use of open communication is again recommended. Notice the difference in the following two responses.

> *CLOSED: Nobody could work for you. You've been unfair with me and everyone else since the beginning. You never have liked me. You can take this job, and . . .*

> *OPEN: I understand why you took this action although I would have appreciated more feedback about the problem. As for me, I've learned from the experience and am determined to do much better in my next job.*

The open style may be more difficult, especially in an intense emotional situation, yet it's much more effective. Put yourself in the place of the employer. Would you provide a positive recommendation for the person who used the open communication style? Most employers would at least be as positive as possible. How about the one who was closed? Not a chance!

Leaving even the worst situation in a positive way can make a definite difference. As in all of life's crises, the more you can learn, the better. Being fired can be necessary motivation. "I remember being fired from my second job because I was late so often. I learned the hard way the importance of punctuality and never let it stand in my way again," said the president of a large construction company. He is the classic example of someone who weaved a new pattern into the fabric of life when it began to unravel.

Beginning a new career or job is akin to starting over although you do so with more maturity and experience. Change can be frightening, and the old, familiar life seems so safe: "I really hate what I'm doing, but this isn't a good time to make a change. I'll do it next year" or "I'm too old to start over. I can just 'hang on' until retirement." Yet, in a survey of its members, the American Association of Retired Persons found that only one in five said their quest for a new career ended unhappily (Lewis, 1996). Consider the impact of career satisfaction and nudge yourself out of that comfort zone toward fulfillment of self.

Owning Your Own Business

You may always have had aspirations of owning a business, or the desire may evolve later. Business ownership is not easy and, in some ways, not as desirable as one might think. "I want to own my own shop so that nobody can tell me what to do," said a young automotive technology student. He was surprised when a business owner told him that he would have even more people telling him what to do. Customers or clients typically take priority over the owner's time and personal desires. This section will cover only the basics of entrepreneurship. Further research, then weighing the pros and cons are wise investments.

What's required? Unless you plan to have a one-person business, you must possess the leadership qualities described earlier in this chapter. In addition, you will either have to have a "head for business" or be able to hire someone who does. So many creative, innovative visionaries fail because the boring bookwork doesn't get done well.

Offering a needed product or service of high quality is stressed by Louis and Jerre Garcia, retired successful retail business owners. According to them, a customer can always find a cheaper price, so quality, service, and interpersonal skills are essential. Betty Knapp, a top real estate agent and relocation specialist for Coldwell Banker Burnet Realty in Minneapolis, says, "To excel, make the present client believe he or she is the focus of your full attention and be sure to provide the finest service."

"A successful business owner recognizes a regular customer. Using the person's name and knowing what he or she wants truly makes a difference."

LOUIS GARCIA, retired business owner, Sun City West, Arizona

Persistence is also necessary. Typically, a new business owner has to face many pitfalls and endure frustrating and depressing situations. Being determined and tenacious can bring you through adverse times such as facing the reality that owning your own business usually means that you put in more time and effort than your employees, and they get paid before you do. You may have more flexibility, yet successful entrepreneurs work far more than the standard number of hours. Even aside from actual work on the job is a common occurrence of "living your work," which means you don't walk away from it when the workday ends. Ryan, a young man who had an opportunity to take over his parents' business, showed keen awareness when he declined the offer and said, "I don't want to own something that owns me."

Another surprise to many would-be business owners is the amount of paperwork required by the government along with what is needed to keep proper records. Then there is the shock of realizing that making a profit isn't easy. Too often, people forget about **overhead,** all the expenses involved in running a business. Employees might not realize that employers pay out much more for them than just wages, including workers' compensation insurance, unemployment insurance, and liability insurance, as well as half of the employee's Social Security and Medicare payments. Additionally, business owners pay their own Social Security. The costs can seem unending. "A major mistake of many new owners is committing too much money too soon. Some will spend far too much to rent or buy an office or building or buy fancy new equipment. Even extensive advertising can 'eat away' at profit," says Bob Dinkel, a business owner since 1980. Conferring with an accountant and an attorney before starting a business is an excellent idea.

"Even though I loved owning my own business, I realized from the beginning that there would be demands, either from customers or myself, for me to take care of business outside of regular business hours. You don't just leave work and go home."

BOB DINKEL, former owner, Accent Fence Company, Lincoln, Nebraska

If you decide you really want to become a business owner, a major decision is whether to buy an existing business or start your own. Many factors enter into this choice. "It's important to be sensible and analytical and not allow emotion to override your logic when it comes to making decisions," according to Jeanne Baer, owner of a consulting business she started herself. "You also want to know what your passion is and incorporate that into your business. It's essential to do what you love."

Free help is available to business owners from SCORE, Service Corps of Retired Executives (see Online Resources at end of this chapter). The group provides advice and help in drawing up business plans and in learning how to run a profitable enterprise.

In spite of the challenges, having your own business provides many benefits such as given on the following page.

- Potential for reaping a substantial profit
- The pride and joy of being responsible for a successful venture, which leads to an increase in self-esteem
- Feelings of power and influence
- Rewards that come from making a contribution
- Flexibility to do as much as you want and, in some instances, when you want to do it

Rapport between a business owner and office manager increases the likelihood of success.

Whether you decide to buy an existing business or begin your own, you are likely to encounter skepticism. According to Ted Milner, who started his own employment agency, others will attempt to destroy your dream. "Courage is the most important ingredient. My advice is to go for it 100 percent!" Going for it 100 percent is excellent advice after you have explored carefully all aspects of business ownership and decided that "doing your own thing" is worth the necessary sacrifices.

Ending Your Career

The end of a career seems so far away for most people that few begin to plan actively for retirement until it is almost upon them. Yet, the best advice is to begin years before you think your career will end. For example, a 22-year-old who saves $50 a week can have almost $1 million by age 65. Waiting a year to begin investing reduces this amount almost $77,000 (Chandler, 2001).

Generally, those who do not plan find themselves financially handicapped. If people do plan, they usually rely on their own knowledge and instincts. About 63 percent of adults have never discussed retirement needs with a professional financial advisor (Lach, 2000). About 17 percent of workers in their 40s say they haven't begun saving for retirement (Clifford, 2000). Women, who commonly become wholly responsible for their own financial welfare, are especially at risk. More than 80 percent of retired women are not eligible for pension benefits, and only 50 percent of working women have retirement plans. It is no wonder that nearly 75 percent of the elderly poor are women (*Women in Business*, 2000). It is hoped that young women are not making the same mistake of not providing for their own retirement. Regardless of your sex, the best course of action is to save and invest on your own in addition to any employer retirement plan.

People also fail to plan for a rewarding retirement. Not having a positive reason to get out of bed in the morning is almost certain to lead to feelings of worthlessness and depression. A recommendation is to examine the reasons you chose your career field. Can you find satisfaction for similar reasons during retirement? Paul had led an active professional life—serving people, as a college chaplain then as a minister of visitation. After retirement, he volunteered to continue to work in social service agencies and at a hospital. "The only difference is I don't get paid, but I didn't get that much money even when I was working," he said with a twinkle in his eye.

A retirement advantage is having more discretionary time to pursue hobbies and other interests. According to David Hanna, "The best part is an obvious one—not having to go to work each day. The freedom from career responsibilities and the flexibility in making your own schedule offer a laid-back lifestyle that is extremely enjoyable." Retirement that lacks meaning and purpose isn't as pleasant. "I love gardening and reading, and I enjoy taking trips, but after a while, I decided I missed making a difference. Now I'm tutoring young children, and it has filled the void," reported a 70-year-old woman. Other possibilities lie in organizations that could benefit from your help. Whether you are a member or serve as a volunteer for a nonprofit group, you can continue to make a positive difference in the world throughout your life.

If you were to retire tomorrow, what would you do?

Assessing the benefits and drawbacks of retirement is recommended as such knowledge can help one decide when and if to retire. "Not being in the mainstream and feeling somewhat isolated from the career world have been somewhat bothersome," reports Dave Hanna. Obviously, if your financial situation is such that you would suffer from loss of income, retirement will be much less enjoyable. Retirement, like all the stages of a career, requires planning and adjustment. After a successful career you deserve the finest retirement. Remaining actively and purposefully involved in the world can make this time of life as successful and rewarding as the preceding stages.

KEY POINTS

- A critical part of a career is negotiating your compensation package. Analyzing benefits and researching salary ranges are parts of the preparation. Making sure you are getting what you are worth will make a major difference in your long-term income. Acceptance of an offer should include details in writing.
- Rejecting a job offer is to be done in a professional way.
- Beginning a new job will be challenging. Knowing what to expect and what will be expected of you makes this easier.
- Early in your career it may be difficult to maintain a balance between your professional and personal life. Learning how to do this will benefit you throughout your career.
- Keeping accurate and detailed records related to your career will save you time and alleviate stress.
- Continuing to network is highly recommended.
- Most jobs include a formal evaluation or performance review. Avoiding negative responses to any criticism and responding positively will further your career. You have an advantage if you are prepared to discuss salary increases. You may initiate the subject either during the evaluation or at another time.
- One of the best ways to enhance your career is to continue to learn and update your skills.
- Advancement throughout your career requires action on your part along with wise promotion decisions.
- Leadership skills are essential for upward mobility. Using an appropriate role model and developing characteristics of an effective leader make advancement possible.
- Changing careers and jobs isn't unusual. Either because of a "push" or a "pull," you may find yourself in transition. Even if you don't want a change, you may be let go because of downsizing, mergers, or termination. Accepting this and moving on are important.
- If you want to buy or start your own business, a positive course of action is to examine exactly what this involves and weigh advantages and disadvantages. Resources are available to help new business owners.
- At some time you will probably end your career by retiring. Planning for this in advance makes the transition much more positive. Part of this involves understanding the drawbacks and the benefits and then doing all you can to ensure a positive retirement experience.

ONLINE RESOURCES

American Association of Retired Persons (AARP): www.aarp.org

Leadership Test (nominal fee):
www.queendom.com/tests/career/leadership_r_access.html

Networking: www.networking.monster.com

Service Corps of Retired Executives (SCORE) (free business counseling): www.score.org, 1-800-634-0245

Small Business Administration:
www.sba.gov/starting_business/index.html

U. S. Department of Labor (benefits): www.bls.gov/ncs/ebs

KEY STEPS

KNOWING WHAT YOU WANT

Before accepting a position, answer the following.

- From your research and what you know about yourself, what is the minimum starting salary you will accept?

  ____

  ____

- From the list of possible benefits, identify at least five that you consider most important and write them below.

  ____

  ____

  ____

  ____

  ____

- How many hours of work are you willing to put in per week?

  ____

  ____

- List any other factor that you consider necessary before you would accept a job. *Be sure that you find out whether a position meets these requirements before you accept it.*

  ____

  ____

  ____

  ____

  ____

POSITIVELY RESPONDING TO CRITICISM

Learning to handle criticism will help you in performance reviews as well as in everyday experiences. Review the positive responses given earlier in this chapter then complete the following.

Your employer has said to you, "Lately you don't seem to want to work here."

Following the suggestions, write the two-step response you would use if you understand the reason for the criticism.

1. ____

____

____

____

2. ____

____

____

____

Write the recommended two-step response you would use if you do not understand the reason for the criticism.

1. ____

____

____

____

2. ____

____

____

____

PROGRESSING IN YOUR CAREER

Below write a number of ways you can continue to learn and keep updated after you accept a position. What you write can be useful during an interview as this is one of the typical questions.

____

____

____

____

____

____

____

____

If you would like to own a business, challenge yourself by conducting an informational interview with a business owner or contact a local SCORE group and find out what is involved. Below, write any concerns you have or personal drawbacks that might be obstacles. Then think how you will handle these.

____

____

____

____

____

____

____

____

LEADERSHIP ASSESSMENT

Assess your leadership capabilities by honestly answering the following questions with yes, no, or unknown.

______ 1. Am I reasonably intelligent?

______ 2. Have I or will I achieve an adequate education?

______ 3. Do I show good judgment?

______ 4. Do I understand emotions and handle mine well?

_____ 5. Do I demonstrate initiative?

_____ 6. Am I usually objective in dealing with situations?

_____ 7. Do I have a balance between my personal and professional lives?

_____ 8. Am I enthusiastic?

_____ 9. Do I think optimistically?

_____ 10. Am I energetic?

_____ 11. Do I "stick with" things? Do I have perseverance?

_____ 12. Am I self-confident?

_____ 13. Do I anticipate problems before they happen?

_____ 14. Am I continually seeking to improve myself?

_____ 15. Do I manage my time well?

_____ 16. Can I work well with others?

_____ 17. Am I an understanding person?

_____ 18. Do I approach conflict resolution as win-win?

_____ 19. Can I give clear directions?

_____ 20. Do I use the open style of verbalizing?

_____ 21. Am I an excellent listener?

_____ 22. Am I a good planner?

_____ 23. Am I well organized?

_____ 24. Am I a visionary? Do I have vision?

_____ 25. Can I delegate?

_____ 26. Do others look to me for leadership?

_____ 27. Do I openly praise others?

_____ 28. Can I build teamwork?

_____ 29. Do I promote positive relationships?

_____ 30. Can I deliver criticism in a positive way?

Count the number of *yes* answers as they indicate leadership. If you marked number 30 as *unknown* or *no*, complete the activity below.

Practice delivering criticism. Using the suggestions given in this chapter, pretend you are a supervisor and you are talking with an employee who has been repeatedly late to work. On a separate sheet of paper or on the back of this page, write exactly what you would say. Include three steps.

Positive relationships don't just happen.

Building Relationships at Work

During a career you have choices in the quantity and quality of your relationships. Most of us haven't received formal training in relationships; instead, we have just been expected to know what to do. Yet, positive relationships don't just happen! Because interpersonal relations can be taught, you may be able to improve your skills as you design your career. If so, seize the opportunity to enhance your success potential.

Promoting Positive Relations

Employees are more valued if they add to a productive, positive work environment. The ability to relate well with others pays off. "People, including others outside your immediate area, will help you achieve your goals if you get along well with them," says Mitch Hall, Senior Project Manager, Domino's Pizza, Inc. Relationships with support staff, such as secretaries and administrative assistants, are instrumental. Actually, anyone with whom you work can contribute to your success, and you will experience more happiness and satisfaction at work if you enjoy the interactions.

"Highest on the list of employable qualities are interpersonal skills–the ability to interact with and relate to all kinds of people is absolutely essential."

MARCIA PHELPS, Ph.D., Director of Career Development Services, University of West Florida, Pensacola, Florida

What do you think will create a positive work environment?

Because satisfying, positive relationships don't just happen, you are responsible for the quality of the experiences you have with others in the workplace. As you read about each of the following desirable behaviors, apply them to yourself and strive to either develop or improve in each area.

POSITIVE COMMUNICATION

At the heart of all interactions and relationships is communication. Throughout your career, your communication skills will either "make you or break you." The essential skill in the workforce for the twenty-first century is the ability to communicate appropriately (Sabo, 2000).

Communication is a necessary element in productivity, teamwork, development of relationships, and, most important, in others' perception of you. Review the communication skills presented in Chapter 2 and continue to evaluate and improve both how well you listen and how you express yourself.

REALISTIC EXPECTATIONS

Expecting a relationship to be 100 percent harmonious and believing that people will always act as you want are unrealistic ideas. Nobody is perfect, and we are all humanly limited. Having unrealistic ideas about a co-worker, supervisor, or customer leads to frustration and disappointment. In fact, congenial relationships are more likely when people are clear about expectations. Consider this scenario.

When Scott started his job, he wasn't properly oriented. The second day, he left a great deal of work for the administrative assistant to do by the next day. The next morning he was given a cool reception and later told by his supervisor that he was expecting too much. Who was to blame?

Ideally, his orientation would have included realistic expectations. Otherwise, he needed to ask questions and request guidelines. In many companies, who does what, how much, and other such pieces of information are handled casually or not at all.

Employers may be unrealistic. If you feel overworked and overwhelmed, you can take steps to improve the situation. One is to be honest about your work habits and productivity. Could you make some changes to improve the situation? After that, be observant and talk with your co-workers. Do they share your feelings? At this point it would be easy to let this dissolve into a "mutual griping society," yet your best course of action is to remain positive. If you decide that the expectations are unrealistic, a final step is to make an appointment with your supervisor. Later in the chapter you will learn ways to resolve issues.

Have you ever worked for someone who had unrealistic expectations? If so, what were they and what did you do?

POSITIVENESS AND FRIENDLINESS

In the workplace your ability to maintain a positive attitude will make a vital difference. If you have ever been surrounded by people who give off an aura of "gloom and doom," you probably realize how difficult it is to remain positive. On the other hand, if you are cheerful and look on the bright side of life, you will undoubtedly infect others. This doesn't mean that you must wear a constant smile and never utter a less-than-positive word. Seeing the pleasant in the middle of the unpleasant is greatly appreciated. "No matter what kind of a day she is having, you can almost always count on Patti for a smile and a kind word. She is like a ray of sunshine on a cloudy day" is how a staff person at our college has been described. One of a person's most empowering assets is a positive attitude.

Friendliness is a positive behavior. While individuals are friendly in their own unique ways, greeting others with a smile is expected in the workplace. Especially affirming is to use the person's name. Sincerity is important. Nancy told of a co-worker who greeted her and everyone else with the exact same words each time their paths crossed. "Hello and how are you today?" began to sound hollow after a while. Another friendly behavior is to express interest in other people by asking questions about their vacation plans, hobbies, and family. As long as you don't go beyond sensible inquiries, most people will appreciate your interest. Generally, if people inquire about your holiday, they would like to tell about theirs. Be sure to ask!

Can you be too friendly in the workplace? Think of some conditions or situations when this might be so.

You may find yourself working for an employer with definite policies about **fraternizing,** a term used to mean socializing with others from your workplace. Generally, co-workers are not restricted from social activities with each other outside of work. However, you may be discouraged from dating or becoming seriously involved with a co-worker, and there may be rules regarding socializing with supervisors. Obviously, you will want to become aware of any such policies. Beyond that, maintaining a healthy balance in degree of involvement is beneficial.

A positive attitude and friendliness create a congenial work environment.

A balance of time is also worthy of attention. Be sure that you are not spending too much time being friendly as opposed to getting your work done. You may not realize how much productivity is lost while you and co-workers visit about your weekends. Succeeding in a career and maintaining friendly relationships are both feasible as long as you know where the fine line of time and energy lies.

SENSITIVITY AND UNDERSTANDING

Having an awareness or sense of the perceptions of others and being able to discern the world from their perspectives is **sensitivity.** When employees and supervisors are aware of each other's responsibilities, capabilities, and even limitations, sensitivity is likely. Co-workers who take the time to get to know one another and then are sensitive create a more positive working environment.

As they do so, they help themselves. Emotional empathy and a tendency to join with others are related to career and financial success (Mehrabian, 2000).

Of particular help in understanding others is to use your knowledge of personality preferences. Individuals with an intuition preference who usually like to do several things at a time can become impatient with the strong sensors who need to focus their attention and who like to complete one task before beginning another. Those with a judging preference want matters settled sooner than the perceivers do and are usually more traditionally organized. Feelers and thinkers who don't understand each other will "rub each other the wrong way." Sensitivity and understanding enable us to accept that people have their own preferred modes of thinking and behaving.

Even more enlightening is to understand temperament type, which is made up of two preferences (Keirsey & Bates, 1984). If your preference for taking in information (second letter of your type) is sensing (S), link it with your fourth preference, either judging (J) or perceiving (P). If your second letter is intuitive (N), join it with the third one, either thinking (T) or feeling (F). In understanding temperament type and other combinations in the workplace, two useful books are *Type Talk at Work* (Kroeger, Thuesen, & Rutledge, 2002) and *Work Types* (Kummerow, Barger, & Kirby, 1997). Increase your understanding of yourself and others by being aware of the difference among the four temperament types.

SJ (sensing–judging) is orderly, dependable, realistic; expects others to be realistic; can be critical of mistakes more easily than he or she will praise what is expected; strives to belong and contribute; prizes harmony and service.

SP (sensing–perceiving) is flexible and open-minded; willing to take risks; highly negotiable; hungers for freedom and action; best at verbal planning and short-range projects; can be perceived as indecisive.

NF (intuitive–feeling) is empathic and highly responsive to interpersonal transactions; keeps in close contact with others; sees possibilities; searches for meaning and authenticity; gives and needs verbal and nonverbal praise and affirmation.

NT (intuitive–thinking) is responsive to new ideas; hungers for competency and knowledge; is not always aware of others' feelings; likes to start projects but may not follow through; focuses on possibilities and nonpersonal analysis.

Find the strengths and weaknesses in each temperament type. Think of situations in which this knowledge would be useful.

In crisis situations sensitivity can make a positive difference. When Raoul's son was ill, his supervisor showed concern and understanding when he made out the monthly schedule of assigned projects. "You can catch up later," he told Raoul.

Individuals with different personality preferences often misunderstand each other.

SUPPORTIVENESS

Sensitivity sets the stage for helpful actions that show understanding and caring—**supportiveness.** Raoul received several comments and notes from co-workers, and a few took over some of his duties.

Opportunities abound to show support in the workplace. Even little actions can mean a lot. After learning of a co-worker's diagnosis of cancer, Sally suggested that they get together soon to talk. Because Sally had recovered from the same disease, she could be especially supportive. Eduardo sent a cheerful balloon to the hospital room of his supervisor's daughter. Patti, who had received some training in family counseling, spent some lunch hours with Alicia, who was going through a divorce. Just showing in some way that you care and are thinking about a person in crisis can do wonders.

In addition to being supportive to those with whom you work, the same behaviors toward customers, clients, or patients may be appropriate. The following

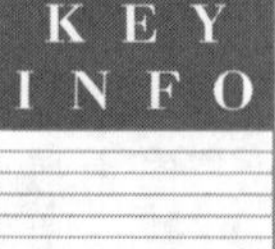

Priceless Supportive Qualities

A positive attitude while providing help is invaluable. Wolfgang Kuss, a positive and supportive person, had a most unusual occupation—making artificial eyes. I called him an eye designer. His talent went beyond that, however, because he put his clients at ease. He was empathic, yet light hearted. His positiveness was contagious.

experiences with health-care employees underscore the major impact they have on patients.

- The nurse at the University of Illinois Medical Center in Chicago gave the patient a reassuring smile and said, "Don't worry. We see many patients with these tumors, and we know exactly what we're doing!"
- The world-renowned specialist muttered to himself and to the medical students who were observing an eye scan, "Melanoma, melanoma—doesn't look like it, but I don't know what else it could be. Hmmm." The patient heard these comments about a virulent type of cancer.
- The young radiologic technician at Mayo Clinic chatted in a friendly fashion. "Where are you from? Do you like living there?" Before the scans, she calmly explained what would happen.
- The young resident said a brief hello to the patient then read what appeared to be medical records. For 10 long minutes he didn't look up or say anything except an occasional "Hmmm" as he read and cracked his knuckles.

What were the supportive and nonsupportive behaviors in each of these actual situations?

If your job involves people in stressful circumstances, be aware that what you say and don't say and how you behave will make the situation better or worse. To those in need, positive, supportive interactions are powerful influences. In building the best possible relationships, you will be sensitive to and aware of opportunities to be supportive to everyone with whom you connect throughout your career.

What have you ever done at work or in school to show supportiveness?

COOPERATION AND COLLABORATION

Acting or working willingly and agreeably with another person is **cooperation,** an essential element of success that is evident in your attitude and actions. Being cooperative could mean that you won't be able to do something exactly the way you want or that your way will not necessarily prevail. Yet, the rewards of cooperation generally outweigh temporary frustrations.

In the process known as **collaboration,** all participants contribute ideas or efforts to solve a problem or produce an end result. It's necessary to be receptive and nonthreatening. The open communication style of verbalizing and active, receptive listening can make the difference between a constructive or a destructive climate. Also important is the use of body language. Picture the following meeting.

Trish felt uncomfortable when Bill began to talk. "You all know that nothing will ever come of our work here unless we are all in total agreement," he said as he pointed his finger directly at the other group members. Trish had good reason to think that "total agreement" meant agreeing with Bill's ideas.

What communication errors did Bill make? Do you agree with Trish's assessment?

Negotiation skills are well worth developing because in almost every group situation, **conflict**—which means disagreement—is inevitable. Actually, having a difference of opinion is positive as long as it's handled well. A major obstacle is the tendency to think that being right is essential. Once you realize that conflict is not a matter of who's right or wrong and is simply a difference in thinking, the stage is set for artful negotiation. A suggested format for resolution of an issue or topic follows.

1. *Define and describe the issue or problem and the common goal.* Clarity is essential. All members are to agree on the specific issue to be resolved and the goal to be achieved. Putting these into writing is a good idea.
2. *Brainstorm to generate all possible solutions.* The key to brainstorming success is: All ideas, no matter how ridiculous, are accepted, and no judgmental comments are allowed.
3. *Evaluate each possible idea or solution.* Any member has the right to eliminate an idea if it is completely unacceptable. Then for other reasons the possibilities are narrowed to about two or three.
4. *Decide on the best solution at the time.* A vote, either verbal or written, selects one solution.
5. *Agree to test the agreed-upon solution and meet again to evaluate.* This step is especially valuable. When a solution is treated as tentative, consensus is easier to gain. A date for evaluation is established at this time. At the agreed-upon time, if the solution isn't working acceptably, the process begins again.

Teamwork is more than a "buzz word"; the workplace demands it.

During the evaluative stage, a positive communicator will use certain questions and phrases that express openness and encourage everyone's participation.

- "I understand your reasoning, and I'd like to hear how you would go about it."
- "Good idea. How would you put it into effect?"
- "I liked your first idea; however, I have a few reservations about . . . "
- "Another possibility that ties in with your idea is . . . "
- "I agree. Have you also considered . . . "
- "I think that's an excellent suggestion, and I'd like to add to it."
- "I'd like your input."

Knowledge of personality preferences and temperaments can be put to good use in resolution efforts. Notice what each of the following temperament types contributes when a group tries to find ways to increase productivity.

NF: *I have several ideas to share. I think it's important that we try to avoid downsizing as that would seriously impact on people's personal lives.*

NT: *Looking at that idea logically, I doubt if it will work. However, I have another possibility.*

SJ: *That sounds practical to me. I'm ready to decide.*

SP: *I'm in no hurry to decide and certainly willing to compromise. I would like to make sure that all ideas have been thoroughly discussed.*

Differences in personality can lead to some problems in collaborative efforts; yet, the encouragement of diversity will typically yield the best results. Using the negotiation steps, open communication, and the strengths of different personalities helps ensure that shared goals are achieved, and everybody wins.

CONSIDERATION AND HELPFULNESS

Being thoughtful and showing courtesy are appreciated behaviors. A considerate person does not assume that a co-worker or supervisor is available at all times. Instead, use a technique called **approachability checking.** Whether you are in the same personal space or contacting the person by telephone, asking if this is a good time to talk is highly recommended. A simple, "Do you have a few minutes right now?" is polite and sets the stage for a positive exchange. Incidentally, don't ask for a few minutes if you really want a half hour.

Related to asking about approachability is to be available. Said a supervisor, "When I walk up to an assistant's desk and it's obvious that he or she is involved in a personal phone call, the worst thing the person can do is continue to talk;

yet, it happens all too often." Be sure that you have your priorities in order and are available to others at work.

You will have numerous occasions to be helpful. Sometimes it may be only a matter of letting someone with a smaller job use a copy machine ahead of you. Other times you may fill in for another employee or assist with his or her duties. Keeping a proper perspective is imperative as being overly helpful can lead to feeling overwhelmed. Leigh was a secretary in a large firm. She frequently took on extra work and tasks assigned to others. One day she exploded to her immediate supervisor and was amazed to realize how resentful she felt about the additional load she had so cheerfully assumed.

If you're considerate, you will also avoid irritating behaviors. In a small office area that housed several desks, Jeff had his radio tuned to a loud rock station. His choice of music was not shared by everyone. Ashley spent several minutes at a time making personal phone calls. To make matters worse, she rarely answered the telephone, letting it ring until someone else answered it. Spending your employer's time on personal matters can be a definite detriment to your career.

What in the workplace would or does irritate you?

What is irritating to one person may not be to another. An informal survey yielded some interesting answers to the question of annoyances identified in the Key Info "Irritants in the Workplace." With career experience in both banking and education, Richard Ross, a college dean, described the attitude of "I don't ever make mistakes" as especially bothersome. "Everyone makes mistakes," he said. Relating positively to others means that you are keenly aware of what would typically be offensive or annoying and then try to avoid those behaviors.

Consideration is extremely important when you relate to customers or clients. Being a positive representative of an employer isn't always easy and requires patience, determination, and an understanding of human behavior. For example, most people do not like to wait for long periods of time so the best employees do all they can to serve customers efficiently. At times, waiting is unavoidable; in these cases, a considerate employee can explain the situation, then be aware of who was there first or, if necessary, ask. Apologies for delays are also in order.

The impression you make on another can be damaged by modern technological devices. For example, do you recall telephoning a business then being put "on hold" even if you weren't asked if you wanted to be? Even if a caller gives permission, you can create a positive impression by keeping the time short or checking back with the person at short intervals.

KEY INFO

Irritants in the Workplace

People who:

- gossip
- are late
- leave early
- don't look at me when I speak
- don't return my greeting
- talk too much or too loudly
- don't talk
- lie
- won't take responsibility
- blame others
- use too much profanity
- are overly opinionated
- think they know it all
- wear too much cologne
- complain too much
- don't respond to messages
- take much longer breaks than others
- ask too many personal questions
- believe that they work harder than others

Effective telephone skills are essential if you want to avoid offending those who call. The following deserve attention.

- Sound friendly and professional. Tone of voice will create a definite impression.
- Speak slowly and distinctly enough to be understood. This is especially necessary when you are leaving a message. Have you ever had to rewind a message several times because the person seemed to be going 80 miles per hour when giving a return phone number?
- Use approachability checking to find out if the person has time to talk to you.
- Avoid irritating noises such as clicking your tongue.
- If you have another call, keep that conversation short in order to get back to the initial caller.
- If the telephone rings when you're waiting on a customer, don't completely forget about the person you were helping.

Other customer relations tips include greeting people with a friendly smile, listening attentively to their requests or complaints, handling complaints in an

Effective, positive telephone skills are essential in the work world.

accommodating and cheerful manner, and treating the customer or client as if your roles were reversed. Create an open, positive impression with your body language, especially facial expressions. Remember how it feels to be on the other end of the telephone line or on the other side of a desk or counter. Being rude or condescending wouldn't be appreciated by you; neither are these behaviors pleasing to anyone else.

Customer relations can be challenging, yet the rewards are well worth the effort. Even if you are not monetarily rewarded, you can give yourself a well-deserved "pat on the back" for being considerate and for probably preserving your job. Because customer relations can dramatically increase profits (Challenger, 1999), employees who turn customers away or even create negative impressions are usually fired. Customers and clients don't care if the employee is an honors college graduate from a prestigious university. If they are not treated with understanding and respect, consumers will take their business elsewhere (Gibbs, 1995). You can prove to be an invaluable employee if you excel in customer relations.

> *"Courteous behavior on the part of each employee is crucial in maintaining positive customer relations."*
>
> **BOB DINKEL,** former owner, Accent Fence Company, Lincoln, Nebraska

Consideration means that you won't engage in **gossiping,** defined as idle talk about others. When the gossip is based on rumor or innuendo that is potentially hurtful or damaging to somebody, it is especially troublesome. Conceivably, idle talk can be harmless; generally, it is not. When asked to advise people just starting their career, Lori Hall, Vice President of Health Initiatives, American Heart Association, said, "Be friendly to everyone and avoid gossiping like the plague. It's a waste of time, you'll never get ahead that way, and it could come back to 'haunt' you." People who gossip are typically regarded by others as petty and even unethical. Essentially, you are hampering your chances for success.

Good questions to ask yourself are what good comes of it and why do I want to gossip? You might put yourself in the place of the subject of the gossip. How would you feel? Even with the best intentions, gossip may be hard to avoid because the practice is common. You do, however, have choices. If particular people or groups are prone to gossip, you can avoid them, or you can be like Cindy who said assertively to three co-workers:

> Whether it's true or not, I feel uncomfortable discussing her personal life, and I'd like for us to talk about something else.

If this honest disclosure of feelings brings about a negative reaction from someone, that person is probably not worth your time.

TEAMWORK

In most jobs, teamwork is expected, and your contribution is vital to the total effort. Lazy workers are looked down upon by co-workers and supervisors, and an inefficient team member sets up obstacles to task completion. While you are at work, your responsibility is to the job at hand. Tammy worked in a law office as a clerk and word processing specialist. When the attorneys were gone, she used her time to read magazines and even polish her fingernails. "The work can wait" was her attitude. She was surprised when another employee told her how offensive her behavior was. Be sure not to cheat your employer and, in the long run, yourself by just getting by.

A common occurrence in most businesses is for employees to believe that their work is more demanding and stressful than anyone else's. Picture this scenario: Kent, Roberto, and Anh are on their break in the cafeteria having a conversation.

> KENT: *I'm so busy I can't stand it. All the quarterly reports I have to do are really getting to me.*
> ROBERTO: *Just be glad you don't have to fill all the orders that are coming in right now. I probably won't even have time to take a break later.*
> ANH: *You think you guys have it rough. If I have to field one more irate phone call, I think I'll find an easier job.*

As they're busily trying to "one-up" each other with a worse story, another employee walks by the cafeteria and thinks, "I don't see how those three have time to take a break. They evidently don't have nearly as much work to do as I do!" Acknowledging others' workloads would be a refreshing change from this scene. Less griping, refraining from a "poor me" attitude, more receptive listening, and recognition of the contributions of others will create a much more positive work environment.

PRAISE

Appropriate affirmations can create a warm atmosphere and be rewarding to all involved. **Positive strokes** are verbal and nonverbal behaviors given in reference to another that feel good to the receiver. The workplace provides countless opportunities to give positive strokes. Some ideas follow.

- Compliment someone on personality, efforts, and, as more commonly done, appearance.
- Congratulate people for accomplishments and awards.
- Thank all those who help you.
- Simply tell someone you enjoy working with him or her.

Because of fear of misinterpretation, employees may hesitate to give their supervisors a positive stroke. Remember that they, too, are human beings, and if you are sincere, the stroke will most likely be appreciated.

Praise is verbal affirmation and, if given sincerely, generally brings about a favorable reaction. Even if the recipient doesn't respond, that person probably enjoyed the feeling. Praise is a powerful, inexpensive motivator. The most positive work environments are those in which sincere praise abounds. Supervisors can enhance relationships with their employees by providing praise and recognition. In addition, leaders at work improve morale by showing respect to everyone, being honest, soliciting input, and being encouraging. Reassurance and encouragement are motivational tonics and are bound to improve working relationships.

APPRECIATION OF DIVERSITY

Rather than fear what is new and different, a successful career person is open to what is novel. Today's work world is a mosaic of diverse ethnicities, races, religions, sexual orientations, and ages. Racial and ethnic minorities will constitute nearly one-half of all Americans in the near future (Sabo, 2000). The mixture provides opportunities to learn and expand your horizons. Hopefully, you agree with nearly two-thirds of college students who believe it is important to work for an employer or company that values diversity (Scheinholtz, 2000).

Two individuals tell of the benefits of daily interactions with members of minority groups.

SARAH: I had no opportunity to know any African Americans in my small rural-based community. I'm so glad this job has given me the experience of working with Bob, who is really great. It's been fun and enlightening.

MATT: Ever since the terrorist attacks on September 11, 2001, I harbored resentment toward anyone who came from the Middle East. However, after working with Tariq, I've realized that all groups have wonderful people. I don't stereotype any longer.

Even if your impression of a person is positive, it's better to resist a tendency to stereotype. One person or even a small number does not represent an entire group. In fact, you will probably find more diversity within an ethnic or a racial category than between two different groups.

In recent years most employers have promoted **multiculturalism,** an appreciation of differences, for a variety of reasons including evidence that diversity positively influences morale (Jehn, Northcraft, & Neale, 1999). Even if your employer does not value diversity, try seeking out and learning as much as you can about a particular person, including that individual's cultural uniquenesses. Except for some educational institutions, the workplace offers more possibilities for diverse interactions than you will find anywhere. "I didn't realize how much fun people over the age of 50 can be until I worked with a couple of them," reported Greg. "I enjoy being with them as much as my own age group."

In order to succeed, today's employees and employers need to understand and appreciate cultural diversity as was pointed out in Chapter 2. Conversely, lack of tolerance is a major handicap. According to Mark Munger, a captain in a fire department, "A psychological profile and targeted questions during the interview quite successfully identify any applicant who is biased in any way. That person's chances of being hired are 'slim to none.' If a person does get hired as a firefighter and then demonstrates prejudice, he or she is subject to serious discipline."

"The fire department is extremely intolerant of bigotry and intolerance."

MARK MUNGER, Captain, Lincoln Fire Department, Lincoln, Nebraska

Appreciating diversity in your co-workers contributes to a more successful and satisfying career. Variations of human beings interacting together are as appealing as multicolored gardens of different sizes and shapes of flowers. The splendor of diversity provides opportunities for expansion of self.

Managing Conflict Effectively

Despite your best attempts to maintain positive relationships, disagreement will inevitably occur. Earlier in this chapter negotiation skills were emphasized. This section focuses on interpersonal conflict outside of a formal group setting.

CHOICES IN CONFLICT SITUATIONS

A beginning point in effective conflict management is to recognize alternative courses of action. Instead of being a reactor, you can be the actor and decide how to behave. Human beings create or construct their own reality by their actions and interactions. Because a situation evolves entirely as a result of the behaviors of the individuals who are involved, you, as a participant, have the power to determine the course of the interaction.

One possibility is to ignore an irritation. Most work environments have at least one annoying person, and even those who aren't disagreeable will occasionally rub you the wrong way. You can simply disregard the behavior. Because you are not at the mercy of another person's behavior, another choice is to act positively regardless of that individual's actions. "I'm glad you called my attention to that," was Pat's reply to an antagonistic comment about an error she had made in a report. Even though the person had no business being critical, Pat chose to defuse a potentially volatile situation. She even topped it off with a smile!

At other times, avoiding or defusing isn't advisable, and resolving the conflict may be in your best interests. In most businesses, there is a "chain of command" and either stated or unstated norms for handling disagreements. Regardless, you must eliminate certain obstacles in order to manage conflict effectively.

OBSTACLES TO ELIMINATE

A major barrier is unwillingness to take responsibility in a conflict situation. "The devil made me do it" syndrome makes resolution extremely difficult, if not impossible. Who or what else besides the devil gets blamed when things are difficult? The list is seemingly endless: other people, the employer, the weather, and even the time of the month! Comments typical of lack of responsibility are "It's not my fault," "He is just impossible," "Nobody can get along with her," "If only . . . ," "I can't help it," and "There's nothing I can do about it." Ironically, when people perceive themselves as responsible or at fault and recognize their own errors, conflict is easier to resolve. Isn't it less difficult to change yourself than it is to change another person? Shouldering your share of responsibility for the problem and the solution-finding process is empowering.

Intentions can become another obstacle. Human beings feel good when they are right. Some even act as if being right is essential, so their intention in any conflict situation is to convince another person to accept their point of view. When both parties are working hard to win, resolution is impossible. Another intention is self-protection, which can be taken to extremes. Self-disclosure can be a useful tool for resolving issues. If a primary goal is to shield the self, a person is likely to reveal little. In addition, he or she may appear quite defensive.

Related to intentions are **conflict styles,** the ways people handle disagreement. Two styles are likely to block a satisfactory resolution. A familiar one is the competitive style, in which a person uses aggression to defeat what that individual perceives as an opponent or adversary. The intent is to win or get one's way. The other is an avoidant style, in which a person refrains from conflict. This person may be upset yet will avoid any confrontation. Avoiders tend to **gunnysack**—suppress legitimate grievances and irritants or "stuff" them into an imaginary gunnysack. This can go on for a long time until the gunnysacker has a bagful of concerns. People who do this can damage their own health, and as the resentment builds up, relationships inevitably suffer. The gunnysack image is intended to illustrate what can happen when the sack gets too full. The bag bursts, and often the avoider becomes aggressive. To empty your gunnysack, use the exercise in Key Steps at the end of the chapter.

Perhaps you have heard of passive-aggressives, who combine the two. For some time the passive-aggressive person utilizes the avoidant style, and all seems fine. Then, and often over the smallest thing, the style changes to a hurtful antagonistic one. Or the person uses covert and manipulative behaviors to get even. Obviously, these styles prevent positive management of conflict.

CHARACTERISTICS OF EFFECTIVE CONFLICT MANAGERS

Conflict is more easily resolved if the people involved possess certain characteristics. If you want to become more capable in the area of conflict management, the following qualities will help.

Self-esteem. With high self-esteem, you have an advantage. Individuals with lower levels of self-esteem are easily threatened. In times of disagreement, they may come off as tough and abrasive in an attempt to defend the self. Others who feel inadequate may refrain from being involved in resolution of conflict even though they have legitimate concerns and points of view. People who feel good about themselves don't see conflict as a personal war, and with self-worth not at risk, they expend their energies in resolving the problem.

Assertiveness. A hallmark of positive conflict management is assertive behavior that is revealed in body language and in the way ideas are expressed. The open style of verbalization is assertive language. Review assertiveness in Chapters 1 and 2.

Optimism. The optimists of the world enter a conflict situation the way they do other realms of their lives—with the belief that this issue can be resolved. An optimist with an open mind is committed to an attitude of wanting everybody to win. "Negaholics," on the other hand, dampen the spirits of those involved. Optimists are usually adept at coming up with alternatives, and in a conflict situation, the ability to see numerous options is valuable. When things are seemingly "bogged down," the person with an optimistic attitude can bolster spirits and restore a sense of enthusiasm.

Internal locus of control. When people are responsible for their own behavior, conflict is easier to handle. Conflict resolution can be severely sidetracked if participants spend their time finding fault and affixing blame. Individuals who "are in the driver's seat of their own lives" set the stage for conflict resolution because they want to do so. They aren't limited by feelings of "We *have* to settle this," "This *needs to be solved*," or "We *should* discuss the matter." Those forcing thoughts stifle enthusiasm and lead to a rather dour communication climate.

An internal locus of control also means that others do not control your thoughts or behaviors. You can choose to be civil even though another is being rude, and because you aren't reacting, you have the power to lead the resolution process. Being in charge of yourself is also necessary in order to manage emotions. Instead of thinking, "She made me so mad when she left her work for me to finish," you can choose whether you want to be angry or not. If you use thought-changing and other relaxing techniques, you can remain calm even when it might be easier to erupt. On the other hand, emotional management means that you can convey feelings during conflict so you can let the other person know of your disappointment or frustration in appropriate ways. Most people have difficulty finding the proper balance of emotionality during conflict, so don't be dismayed if you don't manage your feelings as well as you would like. Remember that you can call a time-out if your emotions are getting the best of you.

Flexibility. "My mind is made up, and that's it," Darcy said with a nod of her head and a self-satisfied look. This happened during the first five minutes of what developed into a serious confrontation. Her lack of flexibility was frustrating to the other two participants. Instead of priding yourself on having your mind set, realize that flexibility is sorely needed in positive conflict management. Being able to see the other's perspective can help you quickly change a deadlock into resolution. Changing your mind is a sign of thinking power and strength, not a sign of weakness. If you want to become skilled at conflict resolution, practice flexing your brain frequently!

Positive communication skills. Obviously, the open style of verbalizing is highly preferable to the closed one. Equally important is receptive listening followed by a response that indicates understanding whether you agree or not.

Understanding. Correctly comprehending the other's point of view is invaluable and is much more possible when you understand personality differences. A quick review of personality preferences in Chapter 1 and temperament types, discussed earlier in this chapter, can help you see how individuals can think, feel, and act so differently. Different personality types define conflict and handle it differently; disagreeable situations tend to magnify differences and bring out the worst. To read more about different types at work, see Recommended Reading, Chapter 7, at the end of this book.

Empathy, which is a deep level of understanding, can enable you to accept behavior that would ordinarily bother you. "I remember what it was like when I was going through a divorce," said Beth, "so I'm able to understand and empathize with him even when his mood seems irritable." Understanding everyone's perspective sets the stage for successful conflict resolution.

Sense of humor. During a disagreement a positive sense of humor can defuse the situation, as long as any humor is not at the expense of someone else. Ideally, the humor is related to yourself. When Bob Kerrey of Nebraska was initially running for the Senate, a loud critical voice from the audience said, "I don't know why I should vote for you. During one whole year when you were governor, I don't remember anything you did except entertain that actress, Debra Winger." Kerrey smiled and replied, "I know what you mean. Sometimes I don't remember much else about that year either!" The crowd broke into laughter, including the critic, and what could have been an adversarial situation didn't materialize.

CONFLICT MANAGEMENT SKILLS

A **collaborative style** is one in which individuals seek mutually satisfying solutions by being assertive and cooperative. A key word in turning disagreement into resolution is "yes." As much as possible, use this magic word as a powerful tool in disarming the other side. "Yes, you have a point there," "Yes, I agree with you," and "Yes, that's right" create a positive communication climate necessary to resolve conflict.

An essential ingredient in the resolution process is a common shared meaning. If you were asked, "True or false? It's better to withdraw from a discussion rather than fight," your answer would depend upon how you define certain words, especially *fight*. Those who conceptualize fighting as hurtful, threatening behaviors would probably respond with true. Others who see fighting as a potentially fair way of handling conflict would answer false. Countless examples of different meanings are possible. Jason was told that he wasn't being productive, and he thought he was. He and the other person had dissimilar ideas of productivity. At any time during a discussion, checking whether or not meanings are shared or different is highly recommended.

A technique called *fair fighting* can produce positive results. Incidentally, **fighting** is simply defined as a way of resolving disagreement. Unfair fighting, the type with which most of us are familiar, is definitely to be avoided. **Fair fighting** consists of behaviors that aim to resolve conflict in an amicable way.

Setting the stage involves selecting the best time, place, and conditions for resolving the issue. Most important is to wait until you have calmed down before you have a discussion. Even the finest management skills can be forgotten in the wake of anger. Even though most of us prefer to settle disagreements quickly, a waiting period is usually preferable. Especially beneficial is to agree on one issue to discuss as well as a common outcome.

The following are criteria of fair fighting.

- *Getting past winning–losing.* Getting rid of the win–lose notion is necessary. If only one person wins, the relationship loses. The focus is on resolving the issue; with a good resolution, everyone wins.
- *Being involved.* Have you ever had a discussion that was more of a monologue than a dialogue? When you fight fairly, all individuals are involved in the exchange. Verbalizing and listening are shared behaviors.
- *Communicating.* Open communication is to be used. "I" statements, not "you" statements, coupled with active, receptive listening and a high level of disclosure of key elements of the issue, are essential. A review of the dimensions of awareness, described in Chapter 2, would be helpful. An important one to share is each person's desired outcome. Also, making use of ways to give and receive criticism from Chapter 6 can create a much more positive communication environment.
- *Avoiding injury.* Be sure to direct criticism to behaviors, avoid personal attacks, and maintain consideration for the feelings of others.
- *Being direct.* Remaining focused in the present and on the subject at hand is difficult, yet vital to a fair fight. If a new topic is presented, the issue gets sidetracked. You can agree to discuss other topics at a later time and get back to the matter at hand.

- *Being specific.* Clarity, not vagueness, is essential. The first clarification involves the issue. What exactly is to be discussed? After the conversation begins, people may interpret words and behaviors differently. In fact, many workplace problems are caused by differences between what one person intended to mean and another's interpretation. Achieving shared meanings is everyone's responsibility.
- *Acting responsibly.* All parties are to take a share of the responsibility for the disagreement itself and the process required to resolve it.
- *Sharing feelings.* Depending upon the nature of the relationship and the situation, you may want to share emotions. What may appear to be anger could actually be hurt or disappointment. When people honestly reveal what they are feeling, confusion disappears, and a positive connection can occur. Yet, feelings can interfere with discussions, so managing emotions is necessary.
- *Showing humor.* As strange as it seems, if in some way positive humor creeps into the discussion, the mood of both parties will probably lighten. Any use of sarcasm or nasty humor is to be avoided.

A "Spoonful of Sugar"

The use of sincere affirmations during a conflict discussion can make a major difference. Kelly was frustrated with an immediate supervisor and found herself saying things she knew she would regret later. The supervisor said, "I consider you to be a good thinker, and I'm sure we can get this resolved." Kelly found herself becoming calmer as she realized that the supervisor would listen to her ideas. Even when you disagree, acknowledging another's strengths is usually quite beneficial.

What about an issue between you and a supervisor? The same criteria can certainly be applied. You don't want to come off as a complainer who doesn't offer any alternatives. If perceived mistreatment has come from the supervisor, you can address this specifically using open communication. It is advisable to document the discussion and, depending upon the situation, make sure that the main points and the final resolution are agreed upon in writing. Company policies may address the exact procedures to be followed. Fair fighting isn't easy and requires more time and effort than just erupting, but each time you resolve issues fairly, your degree of career success increases.

Dealing with Difficult People

Who is a difficult person? "No matter what I do or say, nothing makes any difference because I work for the most difficult person in the world," "She's just impossible," "Nobody could get along with him" are descriptions of difficult people. The difficult person may be an irritable co-worker, a passive-aggressive supervisor, or a hostile client.

You might put this into a different perspective by asking, "Am I ever a difficult person?" Truthfully, we all can be difficult at times. However, a difficult person makes a habit of it and, as such, creates major challenges in work relationships.

TYPES OF DIFFICULT PEOPLE

Difficult behavior falls into seven categories (Bramson, 1988).

- *Hostile-aggressives:* People who try to bully and overwhelm others.
- *Complainers:* Individuals who gripe incessantly but do not act to improve their situation.
- *Silent and unresponsive:* People who respond as little as possible so aren't helpful.
- *Super-agreeables:* People who seem to be reasonable but who either don't produce or act differently when not in your presence.
- *Negativists:* Pessimists whose favorite reaction is, "No, that won't work."
- *Know-it-all experts:* People who seem to think that they know much more than you do on every subject.
- *Indecisives:* Individuals who don't seem to be able to make up their minds and stall all decisions, as well as perfectionists who don't complete tasks.

Can you add any difficult types to the list?

Incidentally, if you see yourself in any of the categories, do what you can to change those behaviors.

EFFECTIVE BEHAVIORS

Being aware of difficult behaviors is a good first step. The next step is to learn indispensable coping skills that allow you to handle your career in spite of a difficult person. If possible, avoiding the difficult person is probably the best solution. This may not be realistic; however, you can try to decrease contact time. As much as he tried, Chad found it extremely difficult to get along with Todd, who operated the copy center in a large investment firm. "As often as I can, I have someone else take and pick up my work from the copy center," he said. "It's just not worth the stress."

Understanding the difficult person's perspective is useful. Is there a reason for the annoying behaviors? Most people aren't naturally nasty, and if you can figure out the underlying causes, your reactions will likely be less negative. Empathy can be especially helpful.

Try to resist attributing a person's behavior to a permanent flaw of character. We usually realize that our own temperamental ways, annoying behaviors, or angry outbursts are situational; yet, someone else is "just that way." After Gary tells a crude joke that demeans women, you might think, "Gary is sexist and rude." Yet, he may consider the joke just humorous or be reacting to a feeling of anxiety regarding assertive women. You can use "I" statements and verbalize your objection to the comment or behavior and keep the door open for positive change. Usually, reasons for difficult behavior are more complicated than we might think, yet over time can be remedied.

Putting into practice what you know about personality preferences helps. For example, I used to become quite frustrated with a staff member who absolutely would not leave the matter at hand. "Don't bother me right now. I'm busy with this," was a common reply to a request. Initially, this seemed a sign of rudeness and inflexibility. Then, I realized that he had a strong sensing preference and that being interrupted and then sidetracked would be especially bothersome to him. I learned to wait patiently until he completed what he was doing. It's not uncommon to be uncomfortable with a preference opposite from ours even though it could be useful behavior for us.

Both cognitive and behavioral techniques can alleviate the stress of a difficult person. Remember that other people do not control you and aren't able to make you feel, think, or do anything. Try using cognitive restructuring. "Just because she was short-tempered (and usually is), that doesn't mean it's going to ruin my day" changes the reality. You can make a behavioral change as well. Interestingly, whenever one person in a relationship changes, the interaction will also change. For example, kindness in the face of animosity is a powerful behavior. **Reciprocity**—the tendency to "pick up on" and reflect each other's feelings—can change a relationship. Think of a person for whom you felt no particular liking or disliking. If this individual showed a genuine liking for you, it was probably hard to not reciprocate or feel similarly toward her or him. With a difficult person, you can try to indicate regard even if you are forced to fake it for a while. The results may be amazing.

When you are confronted with a difficult person, positive communication skills, especially the open style of verbalizing and receptive listening, are powerful tools. Difficult people usually want to express their opinions and grievances, and you can alter a stressful interaction just by listening. Check how you deal with difficulty and conflict with the exercise at the end of the chapter.

Coping with a difficult boss. If the difficult person is your supervisor or boss, you have an even greater challenge. Some individuals value control more than people. One employee said, "All of us have just learned to conceal things from her. Attitudes and behaviors that are controlling destroy communication and trust." Unfortunately, a difficult supervisor can be so threatening that an employee just decides to quit. Instead, you may want to try to change the situation. Above all else, it's not advisable to just gripe to other employees, as this can be hazardous to your career well-being. Instead, try the following.

- Decide what the boss or supervisor does or does not do that is annoying or frustrating.
- Evaluate your actions, reactions, and interactions with the person. Could a change in your behavior be helpful?
- Determine your specific wants and goals and think about how to communicate those.
- Use a costs versus benefits analysis to decide exactly whether and what to discuss with a supervisor or boss.
- If appropriate, involve others in a discussion with the person.
- Carefully follow the suggestions in the fair fighting section in this chapter. The way you communicate will make a definite difference.
- In the event that bringing this to the person's attention results in reprimand or termination, be prepared to move on.

Have you ever had a difficult boss? What made the person difficult? How did you handle it?

Regardless of the behavior of anyone else, you can utilize positive relationship skills. Doing so will greatly increase the chances of turning a difficult person into a pleasant one. In the process you will have enhanced a relationship and the potential for your career success.

Forgiving and Moving On

One of the most disturbing situations in the work environment is to have a confrontation with someone that seems to never end. Unfortunately, some people find it hard to let go, and they carry a grudge. Teresa was hurt and upset when she felt as if she had been criticized by Steve, another supervisor. Even though he attempted to explain his position, Teresa refused to listen. Two years later she was still snubbing Steve and making remarks about him to other employees. Who was really being hurt?

Grudge bearers damage themselves as much as they do others. If you are such a person, consider the negative consequences. Harboring grudges, resentments, and other bitter feelings requires energy and ends up diminishing your own self-esteem. The inability to forgive can lead to increased blood pressure, loss of sleep, and other health problems. The person who forgives is released from anger and freed from any psychological hold the injurer may have had.

Thinking of forgiveness as simply letting go of the past may make it more acceptable. To "forgive and forget" isn't necessary; you can forgive without forgetting. Erasing a wrongdoing from memory is unrealistic and usually impossible. Forgiving doesn't mean that an injury is condoned or pardoned. If you have truly been ill treated, you can still put it behind you. What can help is to realize that people can agree to disagree and then to separate the issue from the person. Too often, people like Teresa seem to think if someone doesn't see it the way they do, that person is unlikable. To continue with a petty, "let's get even" attitude is immature and will be a major career obstacle.

Those who can forgive are strong people. They usually have high self-esteem and are able to forgive imperfections in themselves, as well as in others. When you err, do you forgive yourself? If you have forgiven yourself, then you can also extend forgiveness to others. You may not resume the same type of relationship you once had, yet you can be civil and get along in the workplace. To do less is a disservice to your employer as well as to yourself.

Do you have a grudge? Is there someone you haven't forgiven? Challenge yourself to do so and move on with your life.

As you design your career, realize that relationships will play a major role. Whether interactions and relationships are positive is largely your choice. The activity "Improving Work Relationships" at the end of this chapter asks you to describe your interactive behaviors. To a great extent, the caliber of your work relationships will determine both your career satisfaction and your degree of success.

KEY POINTS

- Career development is keenly influenced by interactions and relationships.
- Certain attitudes and behaviors are important in promoting the most positive relations with employers, supervisors, and co-workers as well as clients, customers, or patients. These include:
  - Positive communication
  - Realistic expectations
  - Avoidance of irritating behaviors
  - Positiveness

- Friendliness
- Sensitivity and understanding
- Consideration and helpfulness
- Supportiveness
- Teamwork
- Cooperation and collaboration
- Appreciation of diversity
- Praise

- The ability to manage conflict effectively will be a major asset throughout your career life.
- In order to resolve conflict, it helps to recognize your choices and to eliminate obstacles such as lack of responsibility, an intention to win, and use of the competitive and avoidant conflict styles.
- Specific personal characteristics are useful in conflict resolution.
- Conflict management skills can be learned. Open communication and other fair fighting techniques pave the way to satisfying work relations.
- Dealing with difficult people, including a difficult boss, is challenging; yet, people have choices and can learn to cope.
- Resentments and ill feelings in the workplace are harmful. Those who can forgive and move on beyond disputes possess an invaluable asset.

ONLINE RESOURCES

Conflict Skills Test (nominal fee): www.queendom.com/tests/relationships/conflict_management_access.html
Diversity: www.diversityweb.org
Voices of Civil Rights: voicesofcivilrights.org

KEY STEPS

UNLOADING YOUR GUNNYSACK

Using "I" statements, describe three resentments you either have or have had, then express your feeling and want with "I" statements.

	RESENTMENT (I resent it when you)	**FEELING** (When this happens, I feel)	**WANT** (I want you to)
1.	____________	____________	____________
2.	____________	____________	____________
3.	____________	____________	____________

DEALING WITH DIFFICULTY AND CONFLICT

- Identify at least three behaviors that do or would irritate you in the workplace.

  ____

  ____

  ____

  ____

  ____

  ____

- In the past, what have you done that has been or could have been irritating to someone at work or in your personal life?

  ____

  ____

  ____

  ____

  ____

  ____

- Complete the following sentences:

  To me, a person is being difficult when he or she

  ____

  ____

  I usually deal with this by

  ____

  ____

  An effective way to deal with it might be to

  ____

  ____

  I probably am "difficult" to others when I

  ____

  ____

IMPROVING WORK RELATIONSHIPS

If you are employed, use your current work situation. If you are not employed, either use past employment or a personal situation to answer the following and describe demonstrations of the behaviors. Then begin or continue to behave positively in each of these areas.

How and in what situation did I demonstrate open communication?

____

____

____

How and when were my expectations realistic?

____

____

____

In what way and when did I demonstrate positiveness and friendliness?

____

____

____

When was I sensitive and understanding?

____

____

____

How have I been supportive?

____

____

____

How and when was I cooperative?

____

____

____

When and how have I been considerate and helpful?

In what situation was I a part of a team and showed that I could work effectively with others?

When and how did I recognize someone else's contributions?

When did I last praise someone? What did I say and do?

How have I shown an appreciation of diversity?

When and how did I manage conflict effectively?

How did I deal with a difficult person?

When did I last forgive?

LEARNING MORE ABOUT DIVERSITY

Go online to the Web site Voices of Civil Rights (www.voicesofcivilrights.org). Write a brief review of what it has to offer and include ways in which this can be used to inform people about diversity.

THINKING ABOUT TEMPERAMENT TYPES

Go back to page 275 and review the four different temperament types. Consider the following scenario then follow the directions below.

An interview and selection team is trying to decide between two top candidates. Amanda is very friendly, personable, and creative yet seems to be a definite free spirit and loosely organised. Stephanie is quieter, somewhat serious, professional, and seems to be well-organised and reliable.

Record below the likely reactions and opinions (both positive and negative) of each temperament type on the team to each of the two candidates. Write the name of the candidate you think would be favored by each.

Individual who is SJ:

____

____

____

____

Would want to hire _______________________________

Individual who is SP:

____

____

____

____

Would want to hire _______________________________

Individual who is NF:

____

____

____

____

Would want to hire _______________________________

Individual who is NT:

____

____

____

____

Would want to hire _______________________________

A challenge is an opportunity in disguise.

Handling Career Challenges

8

Challenges are inevitable in the world of work. This chapter identifies predictable tribulations—and some you might not expect—and, most important, suggests ways to handle them.

Discrimination

Being treated unfairly is frustrating and challenging. **Discrimination** is making a distinction against someone on the basis of the group, class, or category to which that individual belongs. When such a distinction is made in the workplace, an injustice has occurred.

SOURCES OF DISCRIMINATION

Although discrimination is illegal, it still exists, and you may experience it when you apply for a job. In 2002, charge filings alleging employment discrimination by the Equal Employment Opportunity Commission increased by 4.5 percent over the previous year. The following shows the greatest increases in discrimination (Ehrlich & Grinberg, 2003):

religious discrimination—up 21 percent

age discrimination—up 14.5 percent

national origin discrimination—up 13 percent

From the mid-1990s to 2002, color bias filings increased over 200 percent, according to the EEOC. Obviously, discrimination that results in court cases still occurs in the United States. Other types may not be as apparent. A study showed that job applicants with African American–sounding names were far less likely to advance in the process than were similarly qualified white candidates (Perina, 2003).

Even an incorrect perception can be an obstacle. Marcus explained, "I'm a heterosexual male with some effeminate mannerisms. Even though I can't prove it, I'm certain that's why I wasn't in a final pool of applicants." He was probably correct; 73 percent of survey respondents thought that gays and lesbians were most likely to experience discrimination (DuLong, 2002). Moreover, they are the least protected. According to the National Gay and Lesbian Taskforce, cited on MyLawyer.com in 2003, approximately 62 percent of people have no legislative protection based on sexual orientation.

On the job, you may be a victim of discrimination. Privileges and promotions can be unfairly awarded. A female employee told of an incident: "The manager told me I was doing a great job but that a younger man who had a wife and five children needed my job more than I did. He said I was to be laid off. After I threatened to bring charges, he transferred me to another department." Past discriminatory practices have contributed to a generally segregated hierarchy of power. In 2000, women occupied only 12.5 percent of corporate-officer positions at the largest companies (Gutner, 2002). In terms of compensation, the 20 highest-paid male executives averaged $138.5 million, whereas the 20 best-paid female executives averaged considerably less at $11.2 million (Lavelle, 2001). Examples of prejudice and discrimination came to light in a survey. Forty-five percent of minority executives said that they've been targets of a racial or cultural joke, and 59 percent had observed a double standard in delegation of assignments (Mehta, Chen, Garcia, & Vella-Zarb, 2000). Conditions have improved, yet much remains to be done to ensure equality for all.

Have you ever been a victim of discrimination? What did you do?

HANDLING DISCRIMINATION

What can be done? Because being perceived as defensive lessens the chance to be hired, you are best served by adopting an optimistic attitude and assuming that an employer is not going to discriminate. You can accept your uniqueness and use it to your advantage.

A potential deterrent can be explained or camouflaged. A young woman who stammered decided to mention this at the beginning of the interview. "Interestingly, because I revealed it initially, I had less difficulty during the discussion," she said. Another candidate wore a long-sleeved blouse so that a tattoo was invisible during a job interview. "I'm certainly not ashamed of it, yet as a practical measure, I realize that not everyone approves of tattoos."

You may not be able or want to cover up a uniqueness. If so, you can still present yourself positively. Susan Dunn spoke candidly about limitations resulting from cerebral palsy. "I haven't suffered from overt discrimination; yet, I'm confined in applying for positions because of dependence on public transportation. I accept this and go from there." Her attitude and determination to overcome the challenges make others forget about her disability, and she doesn't allow circumstances to interfere with her career.

If you don't land a position, assess the situation rationally. Unsuccessful applicants may soothe disappointments by rationalizing or blaming. "I didn't get that job because I'm a woman (or a man)," "It's because they're giving all the jobs to minorities," or "They just won't hire minorities" are obvious scapegoating thoughts that become further obstacles.

If you honestly believe that you have been a victim of discrimination in the hiring process, you can contact the Equal Employment Opportunity Commission office and learn your options. The laws are both preventive and punitive. The 1964 Civil Rights Act and its later amendments make it unlawful for an employer to refuse to hire, discharge, or discriminate against an individual based on race, color, religion, sex, or national origin. The EEOC, which was created to enforce the act, investigates complaints, seeks conciliation, and files discrimination suits. "Discrimination based on outmoded stereotypes continues to exist. Ignoring it won't make it 'go away,'" says Ruthe Parker, Design Engineer, Interface Data Systems, Phoenix, Arizona.

The Americans with Disabilities Act (ADA) makes it illegal for employers with more than 15 workers to discriminate against people with physical or mental impairments if they are qualified to perform the essential functions of a position. Reasonable accommodations are to be made unless the change would result in an undue hardship on the business or a direct health/safety threat to any employee. For example, a person adept in using sign language assisted in a job interview for Jill, who is deaf. A person who is disabled can request accommodations that are necessary to perform a job. Knowing your rights is essential, and if you have a little-known disability or one that isn't readily apparent, you may need to be assertive to see that your rights are upheld.

In addition to these protective legal acts, another preventive program is affirmative action. In the early 1960s the administration of President John F. Kennedy introduced affirmative action to provide broader opportunities for qualified minorities (Macionis, 2004). The policies opened doors that had been closed to racial and ethnic minorities as well as women. Affirmative action programs vary yet have one common theme: to encourage employment of diverse groups of people while eliminating past discriminatory practices. "Our goal is to have a workforce that represents the population. Affirmative action removes barriers and gives all people a chance to fairly compete. All applicants must be qualified to be considered," states Pat Kant, Personnel Coordinator for the City of Lincoln, Nebraska.

A controversy over affirmative action stems from a perception of reverse discrimination. Becoming well educated in this area is important. For example, many people do not know that quota systems are not necessarily a part of affirmative action programs. Because some programs will use screening criteria to overcome discrimination against people of color or women, a white man could be affected. Though unfortunate, it is beneficial to keep in mind that he is being hurt in only one area of life and only as an exception to his group, whereas racial and ethnic minorities and women usually suffer because their entire groups have been and still are subordinated (Feagin & Feagin, 1999).

Accurate information can make a difference. A few years ago the word had spread among students in a fire protection technology program that the city fire department was helping minorities by boosting their entrance-test scores. After checking, they learned that the rumor was false. Deputy Chief Dean Staberg contends that all candidates who are hired must possess very high qualifications and test scores. "A minority status is not enough to get a firefighting position." Ideally, in the future this society and others will no longer require a system for righting past wrongs or formal programs that bring about a diverse workplace. Then we will all benefit. "I have been stigmatized because of perceptions that I got my job on the basis of my minority status, and this is difficult to handle because I know I was highly qualified," said a Native American. According to Jose J. Soto, J.D., an expert on affirmative action, "At least 90 percent of affirmative action is at the front end of the hiring process—in targeting people who have been excluded and in encouraging and recruiting applicants from all groups. Any preferential treatment is minimal and is not what the programs are about. Having a diverse workplace is valued, and this is made possible through affirmative action."

"Affirmative action does not guarantee that any one type of person, a minority, or a female, will get a particular job. It does guarantee, however, that everyone will have an equal opportunity to compete for available jobs."

JOSE J. SOTO, J.D., Vice President for Affirmative Action/Equity/Diversity, Southeast Community College, Lincoln, Nebraska

Give reasons for and against affirmative action. Seek to get accurate information about this timely issue.

How can you go about handling discrimination after being hired? Most companies have written policies regarding discrimination that include a description of the procedures to follow if you feel you have been wrongfully treated. You can also talk to a supervisor or owner about the matter. The company may have an equal opportunity specialist or someone in the human resources area to provide advice. Another possibility is an employees' association. If you aren't satisfied with the help you receive in house, the Equal Employment Opportunity Commission is a valuable resource (see Online Resources at the end of this chapter). Legal action is a possibility; however, exploring all options carefully before making a decision is in your best interest.

Equity issues will continue to exist for some time. Erasing past injustices takes time and effort. Laws are in place to prevent, protect, and redress injustices. Changing attitudes and behaviors typically takes longer. During your career life you can contribute to the worthy goal of equality by challenging discrimination.

KEY INFO

A Case of Gender Discrimination

"I did it for my granddaughter," is how Kathy Craig of San Jose, California, explains her gender bias suit against a major electronics company that was settled out of court in 2003. When hired, she had been assured of advancement to a high level position. Each time an opportunity arose, a white male was hired, usually from outside the company. What she had heard, "They don't put women in those jobs," was confirmed several times.

Sexual Harassment

Often thought of as a form of discrimination, **sexual harassment** was given a formal legal definition by the Equal Employment Opportunity Commission in 1980. Harassment behaviors are unwelcome sexual advances, requests for sexual favors, and other verbal or physical conduct of a sexual nature. Sexual harassment is present when submission or rejection of such behaviors is made a term or condition of employment; is used in employment decisions; or creates an intimidating, hostile, or offensive working environment. The conduct may be verbal or physical and may also include the circulation of sexually explicit photographs or literature.

The main motive in most incidents of sexual harassment is power, not romance, and while women are often the victims, in recent years the number of cases of harassed men has steadily increased. About 15 percent of men believe they have been harassed, whereas experts predict that 50 to 75 percent of women will experience sexual harassment on the job (Wallis, 2000). Two out of five gay people report harassment at work (DuLong, 2002).

No type of harassment has a place in the workplace. To avoid being a harasser, assume that off-color jokes, sexual innuendos, and advances are not welcome, realize that a "no" means just that, and honestly assess how you would feel if you or someone you cared for became a victim. Because faulty communication can lead to a perception of harassment, you can take responsibility for sending and receiving messages that have a clear meaning. Also important to realize is that although most sexual harassment charges are made against men by women, most men are not harassers (Bravo & Cassedy, 1999).

As with other forms of discrimination, a business is likely to have written policies about sexual harassment. If not, you can educate yourself and be assertive if confronted with sexually explicit or implicit behavior. The Affirmative

DILBERT reprinted by permission of United Feature Syndicate, Inc.

Action/Equity Office at Southeast Community College recommends the following actions.

- *Object!* Let the harasser know that the behavior is offensive and unwelcome and that it must stop. No response is usually interpreted as approval. If you do not wish to confront the person, be sure to communicate with a supervisor or staff person.
- *Document!* Keep a record of incidents including date, time, specific behaviors, your reactions, and outcome.
- *Talk!* Let a third party know of the harassment.
- *Report!* If the behavior continues, you are better off reporting it to an appropriate authority.

The work world of today is much different from that in the past. Most employers are intolerant of sexual harassment and have provided safeguards and resources to eliminate unethical behaviors.

Family Issues

How do people manage both career and family? In the past, the question wasn't relevant because traditional family roles called for only one wage earner. The other person, usually the woman, took care of the family and the house. Those days for most people are gone.

What has changed is the significant increase of women in the workforce and altered attitudes. Today, both women and men want a balance between career and family. In fact, a national survey revealed that men in their 20s are more willing than women to give up pay, power, and prestige for more time with their families (Rayman, Carré, Cintron, & Quinn, 2000). Since the tragic events of September 11, 2001, more than 75 percent of survey respondents said that spending time with family matters more to them than before (Yin, 2001). Failure to achieve balance leads to higher stress levels, increased family problems, and lower life satisfaction for employees along with negative impacts on the employer because of absenteeism and reduced productivity (Hobson, Delunas, & Kesic, 2001). Fortunately, almost all employers today realize that balancing work and family is a major issue.

Rather than accept an either–or principle of work or family, as was typical of women in the past, it's better to learn what is possible. As Melanie stated, "I used to think that when I had a child, I would 'put my career on hold,' and I was willing to sacrifice. Now I've decided that there are several alternatives and that it doesn't have to be one or the other." Many dual-career parents are able to develop what is called a shared or egalitarian marriage, in which roles are flexible and household and child-care responsibilities are fairly shared. After they had their third child, Mitch and Lori Hall refined their shared marriage and both parents opted to decrease their work schedules. Mitch reports, "People always search for the perfect way to balance work and family, but there is no perfect way. There are always trade-offs. We both decided to work four days a week and use day care some of the time because it's a good experience for the children. For me, the job is a little lower profile, but I can make it to soccer practice this way. We're thankful our employers have been so flexible."

What are some ways parents can deal with work and family issues? What can employers do to help?

Having a baby requires a commitment of time from both parents. Maternity leave has been common for many years, while paternity leave is relatively new. In the past, whether to grant a leave and what type of leave employees received were completely up to the particular company. Only recently did the United States join other industrialized countries and adopt a national family-leave policy. The Family and Medical Leave Act, which took effect in 1993, stipulates that in companies with 50 or more employees, a person can take up to three months of unpaid leave for births, adoptions, and family emergencies. Even with its limitations, the law is a milestone in recognizing the value of family.

Employers may also make provisions that include:

- Permanent part-time employment with benefits
- Job sharing in which two workers split a single full-time job
- Telecommuting whereby an employee can complete tasks at home, especially with a computer
- Flextime that allows employees to choose within limits when they arrive at and leave from work
- Compressed time in which 10 or more hours are included in a workday so that the person works fewer days a week

Flextime is the most common practice as it was offered by 64 percent of companies in a survey of work alternatives (Cain, 2003).

Many families face a dual challenge of high costs and limited accessibility to quality care. A promising trend is for employers to provide a child-care benefit either financially or physically. Ideally, a child-care facility is available at or near the place of employment. This relieves parental anxiety and allows parent–child interaction during the day. Approximately 8,000 workplaces now have on-site centers, a dramatic increase from a decade ago (Leonard, 2000); however, because this is a small percentage of the total number of workplaces, much remains to be accomplished. If you have children, look for employers who are understanding and flexible. The Working Mother Internet site (www.workingmother.com) can provide more information.

Education and a change in thinking broaden possibilities. Often, a female will say she must stay home with a child. Males typically don't feel they have to stay home, although they might prefer to do so. If staying home is a person's free choice and it is affordable, being a full-time parent may be the best course of action—for either sex. However, career interruptions do handicap people; in actuality, such suspensions of employment partly account for the gender gap in earnings because women, far more than men, "put their careers on the back burner."

The good news is that your career development doesn't have to be sidetracked if you become a parent, and your child will not necessarily suffer if you continue to work. Research shows that high-quality child care is a factor in improving parent–child relationships, cognitive performance, language abilities, and readiness for school, as well as reducing problem behaviors. Most important in a child's development is the quality of the parent–child relationship (Peth-Pierce, 1998). The key is to provide the most positive experience for a child while you are at work. If you have been apprehensive about combining parenthood with a career, listen to what Rosa said: "By working and parenting, I'm delivering a powerful message to my children that life can be as full and satisfying as we are willing to make it. None of us is suffering; in fact, our lives are enriched." If family and child care are priorities for you, find an employer who shares these values and who is willing to provide what you need.

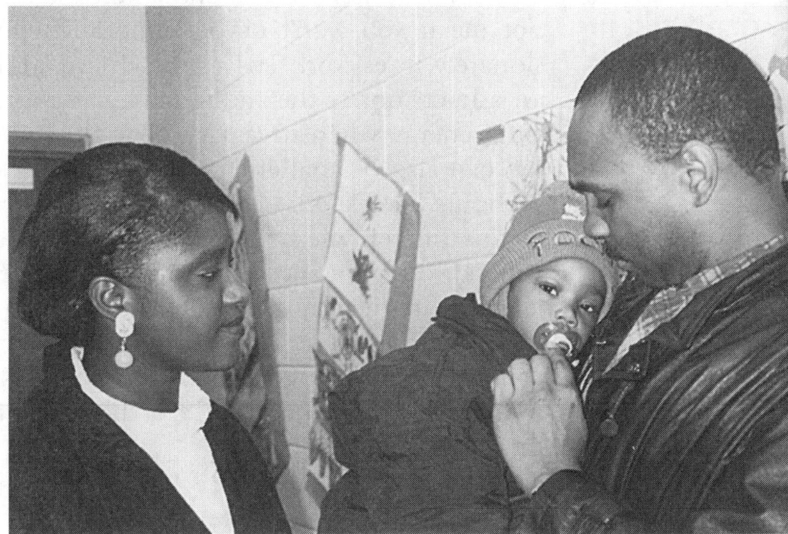

Quality day care is beneficial to children and allows both parents to pursue careers.

A related, contrasting challenge is **addiction to work** (Conroy, 1995). Referred to as "workaholism" in the early 1970s, it is a compulsive, single-minded dedication to a job to the exclusion of almost everything else. A Gallup Poll found that 44 percent of Americans call themselves "workaholics" (*U. S. News & World Report*, 2000). Obviously, addiction to work is not compatible with a happy family life. Even if an addict wants to contribute to family life, that person is often too exhausted physically and mentally to do so.

What is especially difficult about this type of addiction is that society smiles on hard work, and employers are likely to promote the addictive behaviors. The drive to excel is instilled in most human beings during childhood. Excellence is rewarded, and addictive work behaviors are reinforced. The American society reinforces the concept of "work, work, work" with its limited number of annual vacation days. The average in the United States is 16 days, whereas Australians and Europeans receive four to six weeks' paid leave (Lopez, 2000). Addicts may believe they are just doing what is necessary and then find themselves dissatisfied unless they are doing more. They begin to feel panicky or depressed when they aren't working.

Prevention is the best way to escape from becoming a work addict. That does not mean you won't devote time and effort to your career. A person who passionately loves work, strives to achieve, and works toward goals is not necessarily an addict; nor is the individual who works overtime periodically or puts forth extra energy when necessary. "The flexible time scheduling that I love about my job can also be challenging during the peak sales times when I may work 60 to 70 hours a week," says Laura Mann, a sales representative for Prentice Hall. As long as you differentiate between what is necessary at times and an addiction to work, you can design a successful career. Balance is the key. Overdoing your work and jeopardizing health or personal relationships is at-risk behavior. If your own conscious efforts to restore balance to your life don't make a difference, seek counseling. Amazingly, when your personal and professional lives are in harmony with each other, the quality of both is higher. Sacrificing one for the other is unnecessary.

Time Management

Too much to do in too little time is a common challenge for almost everyone who pursues a career. To add to the dilemma, you may find yourself in a job where support resources are lacking. When you feel overwhelmed, it's difficult to enjoy even the best of jobs. To compound the problem for some people, chronic procrastination will magnify the pressures. Creating an environment and structuring your activities so you can work most effectively and efficiently is one of life's greatest challenges.

"I didn't (or don't) have time" has probably been said by everyone at one time or another. When I remind students that they really did have time to complete a paper or study for an exam, I can get indignant protests. There just wasn't any time, some say. How much time do we literally have? The answer is that each of us has 24 hours in every day, which is 8,760 hours each year. In reality, we do have time; we just may not have time left over. "We always have time if we but use it aright [*sic*]," said the German poet and dramatist Johann Wolfgang Goethe, who died in 1832. This is still true today.

When we persist in thinking that we don't have time, it really does seem to be nonexistent. Kelly insisted that she wanted to exercise regularly, but she just didn't have time. After a suggestion from a friend, she decided to awaken 20 minutes earlier and use that time to exercise. She found time that had actually always been there. Another fallacy in thought is, "I'll do that when I have more time." The reality is that we will never have more time available than we have right now.

Do you ever say, "I don't have time"? If so, challenge the thought!

FINDING TIME

How does one find time to manage? Begin by keeping track of exactly how you are currently spending your time. After accounting for a full 24-hour period, Angela said, "I was amazed at how much time I spent on the telephone!" Enlighten yourself with "How Do You Spend Your Time?" at the end of the chapter.

You will probably find small segments of time that you could use differently. At work can you spend a few less minutes at lunch or on break? Can you consolidate trips from one part of the building to another? Is it possible to shorten your telephone conversations? At home can you give up a television program? How much time are you actually using for pleasure? Even though enjoyment is necessary, you may be indulging yourself more than you realize. Cutting out just 30 minutes of spent time a day gains you about 183 hours a year!

Even consciously increasing your rate of speed can save precious time. At work, Nikita often walked to different parts of a large building. "I doubled my walking speed, saved several minutes each trip, and, in the process, probably did something good for my health." In other activities, without realizing it, you may be taking longer than necessary. To save time, become aware of this and then decide that you can easily increase your speed.

Think of routines in your workday. How could time be cut?

Another way to "find" precious minutes is to make use of the time you spend waiting. Catch up on your reading, write notes and letters, or even meditate to relieve stress. The key is to be prepared for such occasions. Says Staci, "I never go anywhere without something to do in case I have to wait." Remember that small increments of time add up and can be significant ways to find time!

ELIMINATING TIME WASTERS

Do you spend time looking for misplaced items such as papers? Because these searches can add up to hours of time, it pays to be careful about where you place things. Taking precious time to organize a desk and file cabinet and then making sure to put items away can increase the amount of time you have later.

The next idea is so simple that it might not occur to you. Look for things to *stop doing*. People who are trying to manage their time better often look for ways to become more efficient at what they do—even if they are doing things that don't need to be done. Make conscious choices about how to spend your time *and how not to spend it* (Jasper, 1999). Pay special attention to the technology in your life. Wireless phones, computers, and the like can help you save time—or squander it. For example, are you spending a lot of time online or configuring your computer or palm organizer? If so, take some time to evaluate whether this is really a wise investment of your most precious commodity.

Your own personality may be a reason why you lose time. Each of the preferences identified on the Myers–Briggs Type Indicator® has its own potential drawback.

E (extraversion). Because they draw energy from human interactions, those with a strong extraverted preference may spend far too much time connecting with others. Just walking from one area to another may take twice as long because the person stops to chat along the way. Also, the individual may be easily distracted by the activities of others.

I (introversion). Living in an inner world and relishing introspective activities may result in time passing with no observable accomplishments. If a task involves interacting with large numbers of people, a person with a strong introverted preference is likely to procrastinate.

S (sensing). The strong sensor can become immersed in details and figures and let a great deal of time go by. Because strong sensors usually prefer to do one thing at a time, they may plod along and take longer to complete a series of tasks.

N (intuition). Having a mind full of endless possibilities, a vivid imagination, and vision is an asset; however, mulling over endless ideas can become overly time consuming.

T (thinking). Deep analysis is not usually done quickly. Strong thinkers weigh facts objectively and then apply reason to their decisions. These behaviors take time.

F (feeling). Because they want to take into consideration personal feelings and values and make everyone happy, people with strong feeling preferences may have a hard time making a decision. Time goes by while a "feeler" agonizes over any choice that might upset another person. Also, individuals with definite feeling preferences have a hard time saying no to the requests of others.

J (judgment). Planning and closure are fundamental, and while people with a strong judging preference are usually well organized and skilled in scheduling, they may spend more time than necessary figuring out how to accomplish a task and not enough time actually doing it.

P (perception). "Going with the flow" has its advantages, yet a strong perceiver is typically a procrastinator. For these people, planning is a challenge, and they usually do not schedule well. When a deadline is on the horizon, perceivers can find themselves in trouble. Strong perceivers also tend to be unorganized and usually have difficulty locating things. Being aware of potential pitfalls that stem from personality preferences allows you to use your weaker preference when that's in your best interest. Each preference also has its strong points when it comes to time management.

Thinking of your own personality preferences, what time wasters can you identify in yourself?

Another aspect of personality, perfectionism, can be a handicap. Listen to the woes of Kiley.

> It takes me a long time to get started on a project because I want everything around me to be neat and in place. Then I worry about each word I write or layout design I'm working on. On top of that, I'm concerned about my appearance so it takes me a long time to get ready for work. On the job, time goes by, and I feel as if I've accomplished nothing.

Perfectionists are expert time wasters and are bound to be frustrated, because no matter how hard they try and how much time they spend, perfection is impossible.

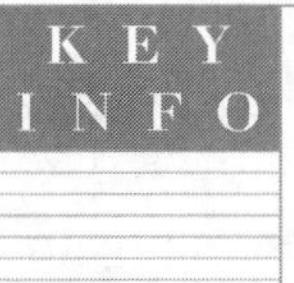

Saying "No"

In order to effectively manage your time, saying "no" is often necessary. For many, doing this is challenging; yet, if you continue to accept more work than is fair and reasonable, you will not have time for your own goals and activities.

DEFEATING PROCRASTINATION

The habit of procrastinating, or **chronic procrastination,** is a formidable enemy of constructive time management. Putting tasks off once in a while for positive reasons is no cause for alarm and can even be in your best interest. However, if procrastination keeps you from getting what you want and increases stress, any effort to rid yourself of it is time well spent. If you honestly want to complete a task, putting it off postpones the pleasure that comes from achievement and creates undue stress during the interim. Procrastination eventually saps motivation. Lack of accomplishment leads to feeling "What's the use?" Over the long term, procrastinators are likely to suffer more and perform worse than other people (Tice & Baumeister, 1997).

Reasons for procrastinating. When you identify your reasons for chronic procrastination, you can find other ways to satisfy your needs or decide whether the reason is worth the costs.

- *Is the task unpleasant or seemingly overwhelming?* Certainly if you don't want to do something or feel defeated before you begin, you are likely to postpone any action. What can be done? Break an activity into smaller segments to make it simpler and more manageable. Also, evaluate unpleasant tasks. For example, reorganizing a file drawer isn't usually a delightful task. Ask: (1) How important is this? (2) How bad will it be if I don't do it? (3) What are the rewards? You can then decide if it's worth your effort.
- *Is procrastination used as an excuse for a poor performance?* "Well, I know if I had started on that project earlier, I could have done a great job" or "I could have made thousands of dollars more in sales if I had spent more time" could be true statements, or they might be wishful thinking. Rather than play the "if only" game, start earlier and spend the time needed to be successful.
- *Is procrastination a safeguard against lower self-esteem?* If you have a tendency to evaluate your self-worth on the basis of a single project or completion of a task and are fearful of your capabilities, you may delay rather than risk failure. Perfectionism poses a problem because those who think an imperfect performance will diminish self-esteem will probably opt to do nothing. "I didn't get it done" may be a cover-up for "I was afraid it wouldn't be good enough." Rather than measure yourself by a "narrow yardstick," restructure your thinking into realistic standards of achievement and realize that self-esteem is not dependent upon one particular performance.
- *Is procrastination a way to gain sympathy?* Amanda played the "poor me" game to explain why things didn't get done. "I want to be a good mother, but too many other things always come up. As a single mother, all the responsibilities

are on my shoulders, and having to work every day doesn't leave any time for pleasure or just time to myself." Finally, after hearing numerous pleas for sympathy, a friend told her she was tired of all the tales of woe. Amanda then maturely took a look at herself and decided to make some changes.

Check your behavior in this regard. If you have a pattern of procrastination, do something about it *now!*

EFFECTIVELY MANAGING TIME

Experts in the time management field offer the following strategies. Select the ones that work for you.

Make use of self-knowledge. Are you more energetic in the morning, afternoon, evening, or late at night? Unless you are getting adequate rest, this answer may not be obvious. "I'm just not a morning person. Of course my going to bed at 1:00 or 2:00 A.M. may explain that!" said Jennifer laughingly. With enough rest, you can feel more energetic at all hours. Most people are more productive at certain times of day, and tackling the most difficult tasks during this time makes sense.

If you have several tasks, which one do you undertake first? If you are energized by doing the easiest ones, that's the best choice. Or you might opt to begin with the least pleasant or most difficult ones in order to get them out of the way. For example, in writing this chapter I chose to work first on the subjects that would require more research. With each completed difficult portion, I knew I was getting closer to the easier part. Whatever motivates you the most is the best choice for you.

What physical environment works best? You may require a quiet atmosphere with few distractions or be more productive in the middle of noise and activity. What skills can you utilize to increase your productivity? For example, can you save time by typing a memo rather than handwriting it? What tasks are time consuming for you? If you are slow at some tasks and speedier at others, you may be able to do some trading. For example, whenever there is a collating-of-papers job, I either ask or get someone else to do it while I, in turn, am willing to perform a task in return. Knowledge of self means understanding facets of your personality and modifying your behavior if a different mode is likely to be more time effective.

Use planning and scheduling to your advantage. You may be well organized and an excellent planner. If so, you may skim this part! If you are lacking in this area, read on.

- *Decide whether to develop a schedule that is macro (bigger picture and longer span of time) or micro (more focused over a shorter time frame).* You can also create a schedule for both. For example, you may want to look at what you want to accomplish during a month (macro) or decide to focus on one day at a time (micro). Often, people opt to maintain a weekly schedule.

- *Categorize what you want to do.* The most helpful way to organize tasks is by priority. You may have a category of "must do" activities, such as meeting with your supervisor or paying a bill. Other activities could be classified as either moderately important or unnecessary, but nice. Other ways to categorize are by types of activities, goals, or subjects. For example, I have an ongoing list of tasks under such headings as family, textbook, college work, paperwork of life (insurance, taxes, and the like), and household.

- *Be realistic and flexible.* Planning to accomplish too much only results in frustration and stress. Keep a reasonable perspective on task completion. If you find that you have done what you planned and have time left over, you can always do more. No matter how well you plan and schedule, unexpected events, interruptions, and distractions will occur. Be flexible, and even schedule a percentage of your available time for such occurrences. Then if they don't happen, you will have that wonderful extra time.

- *Plan efficiently.* If you take time to plan, you can often save both energy and time. Either the night before or early in the day, spend time looking ahead. Find ways to conserve time. Can one meeting with two people take the place of two meetings with each one individually? Todd decided to contact his staff of 15 more efficiently by using voice mail before business hours instead of waiting and calling each person. "When we converse on the phone, it takes at least twice as much time as leaving a message does. While talking personally is a good idea, there are times when it's better to be more expedient." Thinking ahead and planning will help make you a more effective time manager.

- *Allow for inefficient periods.* In the quest to become an expert time manager, you can become overzealous and then be bitterly disappointed when you fall behind or suffer from unproductive periods. You help yourself by accepting the fact that you will likely stumble at times. Whether it's related to your mood or your biological clock, or stems from no apparent cause, the attitude that this, too, will pass and tomorrow will be a better day can get you through the most inefficient times.

- *Schedule enjoyment and pleasure.* Whatever category system you use, make sure you have time for fun. People often make lists to ensure that important tasks get done. However, how many include pleasurable activities? We often say we will enjoy ourselves when our lists are completed. My husband saved me from this when he stated a truism: "Sharon, your list will never be completed, so adding pleasurable activities to the list is a 'must.' " Besides a chunk of time for pleasure, carve out smaller segments for just relaxing or what can be called "down time." Such time is usually invigorating and increases productivity levels.

■ *Reward yourself.* We typically forget to give ourselves a pat on the back for completing tasks. Instead we lament what didn't get done. Emphasizing our lack of accomplishment creates the illusion that our time management efforts didn't work. Consequently, people tend to resort to former patterns of inefficient behavior. You can solve this dilemma by focusing on and giving yourself credit for all you did accomplish.

When are you most energetic and efficient?

People who are effective time managers can keep their job stress to a minimum. In order to both succeed and enjoy the process, learning and using time management methods that work for you are essential during all stages of your career.

Burnout

Nate, a computer analyst, groaned as the alarm clock sounded. He had slept poorly and had awakened with a throbbing in his head that he was sure would worsen as the day progressed. He was still recovering from a cold that had plagued him for weeks. He barely talked to his wife before she left for work, and he became increasingly depressed as he drove through the city to his office. He thought about the new program he was to develop and how he had postponed working on it. "I just can't concentrate," he said aloud. "I don't seem to have the ability I once had." Later at work, he responded abruptly to a co-worker's question and snapped at one of the secretaries. "What's wrong with me?" he asked himself.

Nate is the victim of **burnout**—a state of mental, emotional, social, and physical exhaustion characterized by a lack of interest and enthusiasm for one's job. Burnout occurs when work loses its meaning, and the costs seem to outweigh the rewards. Another name for burnout that clearly describes its effect is **work exhaustion.** Perceived workload and insufficient staff and resources are major factors (Moore, 2000), resulting in an imbalance between effort put into a job and the outcomes or rewards. Julio related a common tale: "I put in long hours and work as hard as I can, and it never seems to be enough. I don't get recognition except with a paycheck, and I'm not experiencing personal satisfaction right now either." Other contributors are inadequate communication, unrealistic expectations, conflicts, and lack of support.

SYMPTOMS AND EFFECTS OF BURNOUT

Signs of burnout include sleep loss, chronic exhaustion, hair loss, feeling hopeless and overwhelmed, poor concentration, irritability, unprovoked anger, resentment, and changes in appetite (Clarke & Edmond, 2003).

An employee with burnout may be chronically late or miss work frequently, withdraw from others, and accomplish little. *Sluggish* is a good word to describe burnout victims. The victim typically doesn't understand what is happening, and this leads to extreme frustration with oneself, others, and the workplace itself. Isolation is a common reaction. Because burnout is dreadful, knowing how to prevent or remedy it is crucial.

Have you ever suffered from burnout? Did you know what it was?

OVERCOMING BURNOUT

You can prevent burnout by employing stress management techniques that are covered later in this chapter. Sometimes, burnout occurs despite one's best efforts to deal with stressors. Then it's best to recognize that you have symptoms of burnout, know that you can reverse your condition, and take steps to counteract it. Use the questionnaire at the end of this chapter to diagnose burnout. By the way, student burnout is also possible!

Seeing burnout as surmountable may be difficult while you are experiencing it. During a burnout period, lowering your expectations is advisable, because the reality is that you won't accomplish as much as you usually do. If poor time management is involved, take steps to improve in this regard. Use positive self-talk, cognitive restructuring, and self-reward for achievement. What you think influences how you feel and act. Realistically, burnout isn't a permanent condition. Think instead, "Just because I'm not enthusiastic about my career right now doesn't mean this is the way it will always be."

An understanding co-worker can help you cope with burnout.

Social support from co-workers and supervisors can be quite beneficial in lessening job-related tension. Being frank with those around you is necessary because your behavior could easily be misinterpreted. In order to receive support, you are wise to explain burnout and ask for help. As in all aspects of your career, communication skills are your greatest ally. If you can verbalize assertively, responsibly, and clearly about what you are experiencing, others will be likely to support and assist you. As with most problems, it helps to realize that you are not alone in your thoughts and feelings. Because burnout is so common, you will probably discover that others also are experiencing or have experienced it. Ultimately, control over burnout is up to you!

The Value of a *Mental Health Day*

Staying away from work for a day or so, when appropriate, can prevent or overcome burnout. An employer may offer personal leave for such purposes. If so, consider it a wise career investment.

Stress

Stress underlies all challenges at work and is responsible for intensifying any hardships. Hans Selye (1974), the "father of stress research," defines **stress** as the nonspecific response of the body to any demand made upon it. When you perceive any demand to adjust, you experience stress. Stress has been studied for years, and one fact is clear: Stress cannot be avoided. **Stressors,** the conditions that cause stress, are numerous and never-ending. Instead of life being a bowl of cherries, one could say that life is a bowl of stressors!

Stress from your personal life almost always affects work performance. Likewise, stress at work can "spill over" into non-work environments. Knowing that both one's personal and professional lives are fraught with stress, interviewers often ask, "How well do you handle stress and pressure?" and "How do you cope with stress?" This section will explore effects, sources, and, most important, coping strategies.

EFFECTS OF STRESS

Stress that is either not handled or mishandled is related to numerous physical and psychological problems. For years it has been obvious that stress may be the greatest single contributor to illness in the industrialized world (Eliot & Breo, 1991). Approximately 60 to 90 percent of visits to doctors are for conditions related to stress (Benson, 2001). Even though stress doesn't cause a disease, it appears to be involved in cardiovascular disease and cancer (Senior, 2001) along with high blood pressure, pain, insomnia, allergies, and infertility (Benson, 2001). Researchers have found that people with high stress levels are twice as likely to get colds compared with those with lower stress levels (Zimmer, 2000). How can stress be involved in such diverse physical conditions? The common thread seems to be the immune response that can be lowered by chronic stress (Senior, 2001).

The other three areas of self can also suffer. Mismanaged stress contributes to relationship or social problems, emotional distress, and severe mental challenges. Stress leads to irritability, and a "stressed-out" person easily becomes a difficult person. Stress is related to mental concentration (Vernarec & Phillips, 2001), depression (Evans, 2000), and anger in the workplace (Calabrese, 2000). Family life suffers as well. Violence and other abusive behaviors are more likely when high levels of stress are present.

KEY INFO

Unhealthy Stress Clues

Frequent headaches	Uneasiness
Stomach distress	Tension
Minor aches and pains	Irritability
Muscle tension	Lack of concentration
Fatigue (for no apparent reason)	Apathy

HEALTHY STRESS

Even with its potentially high costs, stress is not always negative. A certain amount of stress can be motivating and healthful. Equate stress to the strings on a violin. If they are stretched tightly, the tone of the violin is sharp; too loose and the sound is flat and lifeless. Either way beautiful music is an impossibility. The key is to adjust the strings to a desirable degree of tightness. Similarly, individuals can benefit from knowing how much and what type of stress is good for them. Each person is different. For example, you may be one who feels quite relaxed sitting in a boat all day fishing. Another person would be bored and actually experience stress engaging in the same activity. Stress that is good for you is called **eustress.** One's attitude about an experience is what determines whether a person experiences eustress or not (Selye, 1978). All human beings need some stress in order to flourish. "Stress is the spice of life. Who would enjoy a life of no runs, no hits, no errors?" wrote Hans Selye (1974) in one of the first books about stress. Learning about stress, what is an optimal level for you, and how to handle it in a positive way, will help you maintain a healthy self and career success.

SOURCES OF STRESS

Most of us have long lists of stressors. Some deny that they have stress; this means they are either unaware of what stress actually is or they try to ignore its existence.

What are the stressors in your life?

Stress has a myriad of sources that researchers have uncovered. One of the earliest studies (Holmes & Rahe, 1967) identified major changes and their ranking. The top stressful events then were (1) death of spouse, (2) divorce, (3) marital separation, (4) jail term, and (5) death of close family member. When students are asked how they might avoid the top three, they quickly see that not getting married would seem to do it! Among the top 20 of the life event stressors specifically related to career were:

- Being fired at work (#8)
- Retirement (#10)
- Business readjustment (#15)
- Change to a different line of work (#18)

Others were outstanding personal achievement, trouble with one's boss, and change in work hours or conditions.

The life-change study was published in 1967. Can you think of other career-related stressors today?

A current work stressor is the high demand placed on most employees. Even though individuals have always been expected to perform well, the parameters were generally well understood, and a manageable eight-hour day was the norm. According to Doc Chaves, Marketing Communications Manager, Li-Cor, Inc., "Today we're all trying to do more with less, which puts more work on everyone." And from Jody Horwitz, Vice President of Human Resources, the WB Television Network, Los Angeles: "In our multi-task-oriented and fast-paced environment, a person is often asked to go beyond traditional, narrowly defined job duties and cross over into many different areas. One individual can have a tremendously broad range of responsibility."

How does one cope with the inordinate amount of pressure that is characteristic of most positions? Obviously, the time-management suggestions presented earlier and the stress-coping tips covered later are highly recommended. Here are two more ideas, from interviews with employers and business owners.

> If you feel overwhelmed, first do an honest self-assessment and try to relieve the load. Then check with peers. Are they, too, feeling too much pressure? If several of you are experiencing high stress levels, a good idea is to discuss this with your supervisor.
>
> —*Doc Chavez, Li-Cor, Inc.*

> Take a hard look at what you want out of life, keeping in mind that it's important to take care of your physical and mental health. Individuals must set some limits and realize that too much pressure damages quality. Communicate your concerns to someone who can change the situation.
>
> —*Jeanne Baer, Creative Training Solutions*

In the early stages of any job, overwhelming feelings of confusion and frustration are to be expected. After a reasonable time, however, what is expected of you and what is realistic will need to be in equilibrium if you are going to experience career success. Know what is realistic, and avoid trying to go beyond it.

A potent stressor in today's work world comes from concerns about or the actuality of being let go as companies readjust themselves. Today's employee has no guarantee of absolute stability. Unlike yesteryear when individuals believed that unless they faltered, their jobs were secure, downsizing can affect anyone at any stage of career. "I knew it was happening to others. After giving 22 years to this company, I just never thought it would be me," said Roberto, "It's a shock, and I felt lost and hurt for a while." Because this type of termination is relatively common, help is now available through various groups.

Rather than live in fear of being let go, do all you can to perform your job as well as possible, update yourself continuously, and have some contingency plans. Most people find that it's not the end of the world to lose a job and, once the initial shock is over, they are in a position to profit from the experience.

An interesting aspect of life changes is that both negative and positive events are stressful. The common ingredient is the prompting of some type of coping or adaptive behavior. When too many events happen in succession, the strain may produce unhealthy effects. As you probably know, college life itself has one stressor after another. After studying college students, researchers concluded that negative life events predicted depressive symptoms. The good news was that a higher level of positive life events seemingly reduced the effects of depression (Dixon & Reid, 2000). During your career life, you are bound to have rewarding experiences as well as some setbacks. Knowing that either type will increase your stress level can help you cope effectively.

What about the hassles of everyday life? These minor irritants are ongoing stressors, often left unattended because they occur so often and are seemingly routine. Jan was annoyed by a tiny squeak every day as she drove to work. She kept telling herself that someday she would get it fixed. That someday never seemed to come, until she realized that her irritation at work and at home might be related to the annoyance she experienced each day. Just one day at work can be filled with such stressors. The little annoyances and frustrations that continually plague us may add up to more stress than life's major events cause (Lazarus, 1981). In this regard, too, college students were studied (Ross, Niebling, & Heckert, 1999), and an interesting list of hassles emerged. In order of frequency, they were: (1) change in sleeping habits, (2) vacations/breaks, (3) change in eating habits, (4) new responsibilities, and (5) increased class workload. Financial difficulties and change in social activities were not far behind.

What everyday hassles bother you? What are you doing about them? If you are doing nothing, the accumulation of stress may be harmful.

Stressors are either external or internal. **External stressors** are those that come from outside yourself. Other people, events beyond your control, and the environment deliver daily doses of stress. Can you name some? **Internal stressors** are those we create. Irrational thoughts, unrealistic expectations, inability to express emotions, and unnecessary worry fall into this category. When thinking about stress at work, it's helpful to divide the stressors into these two categories. Generally, you have little or no control over the external ones and almost total control over the self-created ones. When you feel the tension mounting, ask yourself:

- Is this external or internal? Can I do anything about it?
- Are my thoughts rational? Am I thinking logically?
- How realistic are my expectations about myself, about others, and about my work?
- Am I constructively expressing what I feel? Do I have positive outlets for frustration and anger? Am I dealing adequately with my emotions?
- Am I a "worrywart"? Do I fret and worry needlessly?

If you tend to create more stress for yourself, focus on the areas that are especially troublesome and change your behaviors. **Worry,** one of the internal stressors, is a feeling of unease or tension. Worry is usually needless. A study from years ago showed that college students worried during much of each day. Academic success was the most common reason; social relationships, health, finances, and career were also mentioned (Vasey & Borkovec, 1992). Do you think this is true today? People have a hard time differentiating between worries and concerns. The difference lies in your ability to do something about potential problems. Concern leads to action, while worry arises from feelings of powerlessness. People who worry usually do not act; they simply fret and multiply the stress they already have.

Interestingly, 90 percent of what we worry about never happens (Buscaglia, 1994). Concern about people and events is normal, and some situations are tense.

Ways to Decrease Worry (Hallowell, 2000)

- Change "what if" to "so what if." For example, instead of, "What if I don't get this job?" to "So what if I don't get this job?" This isn't intended to promote a don't-care attitude but to allow you to put things in proper perspective.
- Set aside 30 minutes to really worry, and refuse to do so at other times.
- Keep a worry journal and put the thoughts on paper. Usually, you will then reduce the amount of time you dwell on the issue.
- Definitely act on your worry if possible.
- Use the thought-stopping technique. Say to yourself firmly, "Stop thinking this way!"

The key is to not allow worry to take over. Worriers manufacture and magnify stress in their lives. If worrying is one of your traits, make a concerted effort to eliminate as much of it as possible. Remember that worry will not prevent problems; instead, it robs the present of potential joy.

You can control other internal stressors by not overloading yourself, not having unrealistic goals, avoiding negative self-talk, taking care of your physical health, and living an interesting, fulfilling life. An awareness of the sources can let you analyze your stressors, and possibly decrease their numbers and impact.

TAKING CHARGE OF STRESS

Perhaps, you are one of the fortunate people who already has what is called **psychological hardiness** (Kobasa, 1979). A classic study of middle- and upper-level executives who had experienced high degrees of stressful life events found differences between those who became ill and those who did not. Those who stayed well shared the following personality characteristics of hardiness:

- A strong commitment to self and various areas of life
- A sense of meaningfulness or purpose
- The attitude that change is challenging and invigorating
- An internal locus of control ("I control my life.")

An empathic supervisor is open to concerns about stress.

Having an internal locus of control is extremely beneficial for many reasons, including sound physical health. David Felten, M.D., Ph.D., has identified lack of control in any situation as a factor in a diminished immune system (Moyers, 1995). If the descriptors of hardiness don't sound like you, consider what you can do to become hardier!

When faced with a stressor, you can choose to deal with the problem or issue, negotiate or compromise to resolve conflict, or stay away from stressful people and situations. Regardless of whether a stressor is apparent, it's a good idea to employ a regular stress-management routine that protects you from the effects of daily stressors. Several practical stress-reducing suggestions and elaborations follow. The challenge is to put them into regular practice.

- Whenever possible, reduce or wisely schedule major life events. For example, don't begin college, start a job, move, get married, quit college, and get divorced in the same year!
- Prioritize hassles in your life. Take action to eliminate or reduce the most annoying ones. If a messy desk is bothering you, take the time to clean it. Carry extra keys in case you lock one inside the car or house.
- Challenge worrisome or anxiety-provoking thoughts. Don't be afraid to seek information. When faced with physical pain or other symptoms, don't ignore them if you have the slightest worry. Ask questions so that you feel in control. Act when you feel concerned rather than succumb to worrying.
- Change stress-producing thoughts. Your assumptions can manufacture much unnecessary stress. Try asking yourself, "What's the worst thing that can happen here?" Many times the worst isn't so awful. Or, if you think that saying no isn't a nice thing to do, change your thinking to, "Nice has nothing to do with this."
- Develop a decision-making process and use your thinking preference. Don't be hasty, yet remember that staying "on the fence" and delaying a decision too long is stressful.

- If you feel frustrated or worried, ask yourself what you can do about it, then either act or let go of the feeling. Be realistic about what is possible.
- Say no and stick with it if you truly don't want to do something. Pent-up resentment is stressful.
- Learn to manage your time constructively and schedule well enough so you aren't rushing through life. Make time for relaxing, pleasurable activities. If you are a person who is always in a hurry or a workaholic, attempt to change. Add variety to your daily routine. Slow down and "smell the roses."
- Escape periodically. Physical and mental changes of scene offer temporary respite.
- Express your feelings and begin to communicate and share more with others. Find a reliable support system.
- Write in a journal or diary. Studies confirm the value of expressing stressful thoughts to others or getting them down on paper (Stone, Smyth, Kaell, & Hurewitz, 2000). Have a good relieving cry. Find someone to hug and a pet to love.
- Develop a healthy degree of self-efficacy and an internal locus of control.
- Schedule pleasurable activities and engage in them often. Laugh and enjoy life. Have a relaxing massage. Engage in an enjoyable hobby or diversion. Don't take most things too seriously.
- Breathe deeply and frequently. Proper breathing comes from the diaphragm, the thin muscle that separates the lung and abdominal cavities (Williams & Harris, 1998). It is a full, deep expansion of the lungs followed by complete expiration with a slow and quiet rhythm. Proper breathing nourishes the central nervous system, creates a harmonious pattern for other bodily rhythm, and regulates moods and emotions (Weil, 1998). Breathing deeply is not only relaxing; it also enhances health by increasing the amount of oxygen in the blood (Williams & Harris, 1998). See the deep breathing instructions at the end of this chapter.
- Keep your body well rested, nourished with nutritious food and water, and in the best possible health.
- Raise your self-esteem level. Low self-esteem affects reactions to stress.
- Exercise regularly. Select something you enjoy and stick with it, or try something new.
- Use a deep-relaxation technique and learn biofeedback.
- Keep your sense of humor—or develop one. If you try, you can find something humorous in most situations.

Along with deep breathing, the last three are among my favorite methods. Exercise is a popular antidote for stress. Research supports the role of physical activity in relieving long-term chronic stress and as a quick way to calm yourself in a stressful situation (*Consumer Reports*, 2000). Another benefit is a more pleasing appearance. When asked to identify the everyday hassles in life, middle-aged people listed weight as their main concern (Lazarus, 1981). Doesn't it seem likely that exercise would do much to alleviate this problem, thus reducing stress? Even if you don't engage in a full-scale aerobic exercise program, try walking, an activity that has earned much praise for its stress-reducing benefits. Enthusiastic walkers talk as much about the relaxation benefits as they do the physical benefits. Nothing keeps most people from becoming more physically active except their own thoughts. You have the power to change yours. Take those extra 10 minutes over a lunch period and *WALK*. A medical examination before you begin any strenuous program is suggested. If reduction in stress and other listed benefits are not motivation enough, consider that you can feel better, have more energy, and save money on medical bills. The time spent exercising could be the wisest investment you'll ever make. By the way, if you're thinking, "I don't have time to walk or to exercise," you definitely need to do it!

"Give me an hour of your time because what I want to show you could make all the difference in the world," said Andrea Sime, a biofeedback and stress management specialist and a friend. She suggested this after learning that I was facing surgery for removal of what would, in all probability, be a cancerous eye tumor. I gave her the hour, and I am tremendously grateful to her for introducing me to biofeedback and deep-relaxation techniques and teaching me that I can change my physiological reactions to stress.

Progressive relaxation is one method of **deep relaxation,** a profoundly restful condition in which one feels physically relaxed, somewhat detached from the immediate environment, and usually to some extent even from body sensations. Deep relaxation allows the body to become balanced, or homeostatic, and, thus, work as it is intended to. Meditation is a physical act of remaining quiet, breathing deeply, and focusing on your breath, a word, or a phrase. The actions quiet "mental chatter" and reduce stress (Barbor, 2001). The following benefits have been demonstrated in research. Participants in ongoing meditation programs had a 40 to 45 percent reduction in medical symptoms and psychological distress and a 4 to 8 percent alleviation of stress (Salzberg & Kabat-Zinn, 1997). Meditation and other relaxation techniques led to significantly higher GPAs for college students (Hall, 1999).

Additionally, methods that produce similar results are yoga, self-hypnosis, guided imagery, and autogenic training. Using a relaxation technique for only about 15 to 20 minutes on a regular basis can produce astonishing results. Most people report feeling more energetic, exuberant, optimistic, cheerful, and congenial. The effects of stress on the body are remarkably diminished.

A sense of humor acts as a buffer against stress and seems to strengthen the immune system (Witkin, 1999). Related to a sense of humor is laughter. While stress and anger can lead to high blood pressure, laughter can lower it. Studies show that laughter lowers the stress response, increases oxygen in the blood, exercises the lungs, and stimulates the immune system (Gard, 1998). Can you think of a more enjoyable way to reduce the effects of stress? In almost every stressful situation, you can find a measure of humor if you try. Perceiving events in a more humorous light and then laughing about yourself in the situation can significantly alleviate the harmful effects of stress.

When was the last time you had a good laugh?

Stress will be present in your life. What you do with it is up to you. Several earlier recommendations in this book—having a positive attitude, taking responsibility for self, developing an internal locus of control, expressing emotions constructively, building self-esteem and self-efficacy, and changing irrational, negative thoughts—will lead to stress reduction. Additionally, learning all you can about stress and practicing the active coping techniques that have been outlined will have a major impact on your career success. "Coping with Stress" at the end of the chapter can raise your awareness and give you important deep breathing instructions.

You can learn more about handling career challenges by reading books such as those listed in Recommended Reading, Chapter 8, at the end of this book. No matter what challenge you face during your career, you can either take action or find coping strategies. Having the courage to face a challenge and, when necessary, seek help are characteristics of a well-adjusted person.

KEY POINTS

- Discrimination in the workplace still exists. Recognizing its sources and learning how to handle any actual instances provide protection from its negative effects.
- A challenge for many is sexual harassment. Because of public awareness, guidelines are in place to help any victim.
- Balancing work and family continues to be a problem. Employers need to be encouraged to do all that is possible to help employees balance professional and family lives.
- Rather than have a personal life, some people are addicted to work. Finding more balance in life is important.

- Time management is a matter of understanding the reality of time, finding time, identifying time wasters, and defeating chronic procrastination. Understanding the costs and causes of procrastination helps to overcome the habit.
- Making use of self-knowledge, moving faster, and planning and scheduling efficiently are key elements of controlling your time and accomplishing your goals.
- Burnout is a state of emotional, mental, social, and physical exhaustion that many people face at some time in their careers. You can overcome it by recognizing the symptoms, identifying possible causes and effects, and employing effective techniques to combat it.
- Stress is present in everyone's life. Even though a certain amount and type of stress, known as eustress, is beneficial, a major challenge for most people is too much stress.
- Because too much stress takes its toll on physical and mental health, everyone can benefit from knowing how to cope with it. Several strategies are effective and are well worth putting into practice on a regular basis.

ONLINE RESOURCES

Department of Labor: www.dol.gov (link to Research Library)

Equal Employment Opportunity Commission: www.eeoc.gov

National Council on Family Relations: www.ncfr.org (link to Tips for Families)

The Working Mother: www.workingmother.com

KEY STEPS

HOW DO YOU SPEND YOUR TIME?

For one week, keep a detailed record of how you spend your time using this page and the next. Then, see if you can find at least an hour of time that you could put to better use.

	MONDAY	TUESDAY	WEDNESDAY	THURSDAY	FRIDAY	SATURDAY	SUNDAY
1:00 A.M.							
2:00 A.M.							
3:00 A.M.							
4:00 A.M.							
5:00 A.M.							
6:00 A.M.							
7:00 A.M.							
8:00 A.M.							
9:00 A.M.							
10:00 A.M.							
11:00 A.M.							

	MONDAY	TUESDAY	WEDNESDAY	THURSDAY	FRIDAY	SATURDAY	SUNDAY
12:00 P.M.							
1:00 P.M.							
2:00 P.M.							
3:00 P.M.							
4:00 P.M.							
5:00 P.M.							
6:00 P.M.							
7:00 P.M.							
8:00 P.M.							
9:00 P.M.							
10:00 P.M.							
11:00 P.M.							
12:00 A.M.							

ARE YOU BURNED OUT?

Answer Yes or No to these questions to determine burnout now and in the future.

_______ 1. Do I dread going to work more times than not?

_______ 2. Am I more rigid than usual in my thinking?

_______ 3. Am I thinking unrealistically about my job?

_______ 4. Is it hard to make decisions that were once rather simple?

_______ 5. Is my attitude less positive than normal?

_______ 6. Do I doubt my work abilities and often feel defeated?

_______ 7. Do I feel pessimistic about my career?

_______ 8. Do I feel as if I am not in control of my life?

_______ 9. Am I more often depressed? helpless? hopeless? frustrated? annoyed?

_______ 10. Am I more irritable than I usually am?

_______ 11. Have I displayed more hostility than I usually do?

_______ 12. Is my sense of humor less evident?

_______ 13. Am I choosing to be alone more at work than usual?

_______ 14. Do I feel less energetic?

_______ 15. Am I tired more often than normal?

_______ 16. Recently, have I had any of the following?

headache	muscle tension and aches	gastric problems
backache	insomnia	complexion problems
colds	change in eating habits	nausea

_______ 17. Have I been late to work more frequently?

_______ 18. Have I missed more work than usual?

_______ 19. Is my productivity at work lower than normal?

_______ 20. Do I feel less zest for life than I used to?

Even though these symptoms can be associated with other ailments, the more yes answers you give, the more that burnout is indicated.

COPING WITH STRESS

Use the following to deal with stress. Coping is of utmost importance.

- Identify sources of stress in your life from the following areas:

  A major life change:

  ___

  A common hassle or everyday irritant:

  ___

  Internal or self-imposed sources:

  ___

- What can you do about any of these?

  ___

  ___

  ___

- Try deep breathing several times during the day.

Breathe in slowly and deeply through your nose, hold briefly, then exhale through your mouth. To check if you are breathing deeply enough, place your outstretched fingers (middle fingers lightly touching each other) over your diaphragm. Inhale. Did your middle fingers separate slightly? If not, you are not breathing deeply. Deeply inhaled air will move the diaphragm down slightly, thus pushing the abdomen out, and your fingers will spread slightly. A few of these deep breaths can relieve stress and anxiety in most situations, including before an interview. If you want to use a relaxation technique, get into a comfortable position and use several deep breaths to lower your body's state of arousal.

Take charge of your stress by putting into practice one of the stress-reducing suggestions in Chapter 8.

The one I've selected is:

___

When I will start is:

___

Recommended Reading

Chapter 1

Bloomfield, H. H., with Felder, L. (1996). *Making peace with yourself.* New York: Ballantine Books.

Carducci, B. J. (1999). *Shyness: A bold new approach.* New York: HarperCollins.

Carter-Scott, C. (1999). *Negaholics: How to overcome negativity and turn your life around.* New York: Villard.

Covey, S. R. (1999). *The 7 habits of highly effective people.* New York: Simon & Schuster.

Goleman, D. (1995). *Emotional intelligence.* New York: Bantam Books.

Goleman, D. (1998). *Working with emotional intelligence.* New York: Bantam Books.

Hanna, S. L. (2003). *Person to person: Positive relationships don't just happen.* Upper Saddle River, NJ: Prentice Hall.

Holland, J. L. (1997). *Making vocational choices.* Odessa, FL: PAR.

Jeffers, S. (1996). *Feel the fear and do it anyway.* New York: Fawcett Columbine.

McKay, M., & Fanning, P. (2000). *Self-esteem.* New York: HarperBusiness.

O'Neill, S. L., & Chapman, E. N. (2002). *Your attitude is showing.* Upper Saddle River, NJ: Prentice Hall.

Seligman, M. E. P. (1995). *What you can change and what you can't: The complete guide to self-improvement.* New York: Ballantine.

Seligman, M. E. P. (1998). *Learned optimism: How to change your mind and your life.* New York: Ballantine.

Related to Myers–Briggs Type Indicator®

Dunning, D. (2001). *What's your type of career? Unlock the secrets of your personality to find your perfect career path.* Palo Alto, CA: Davies Black.

Keirsey, D., & Bates, M. (1984). *Please understand me.* Del Mar, CA: Prometheus Nemesis.

Kroeger, O., Thuesen, J. M., & Rutledge, H. (2002). *Type talk at work: How the 16 personality types determine your success on the job.* New York: Delacorte.

Kummerow, J. M., Barger, N. J., & Kirby, L. K. (1997). *Work types.* New York: Time Warner.

Myers, I. B. (1995). *Gifts differing: Understanding personality types.* Palo Alto, CA: CPP.

Tieger, P. D., & Barron-Tieger, B. (1999). *The art of speedreading people.* Boston: Little, Brown.

Tieger, P. D., & Barron-Tieger, B. (2001). *Do what you are.* Boston: Little, Brown.

Chapter 2

Alberti, R., & Emmons, M. (1995). *Your perfect right: A guide to assertive living.* San Luis Obispo, CA: Impact.

Butler, P. E. (1992). *Self-assertion for women.* New York: HarperCollins.

Chaney, L. H., & Martin, J. S. (2000). *Intercultural business communication.* Upper Saddle River, NJ: Prentice Hall.

Condrill, J., & Bough, B. (1998). *101 ways to improve your communication skills instantly.* Alexandria, VA: GoalMinds.

Goleman, D. (1998). *Working with emotional intelligence.* New York: Bantam Books.

Hanna, S. L. (2003). *Person to person: Positive relationships don't just happen.* Upper Saddle River, NJ: Prentice Hall.

Krizan, A. C., Merrier, P., Jones, C. L., & Harcourt, J. (2002). *Business communication.* Cincinnati, OH: ITP.

Orbe, M. P., & Harris, T. M. (2001). *Interracial communication.* Belmont, CA: Wadsworth.

Pachter, B., with Magee, S. (2000). *The power of positive confrontation.* New York: Marlowe.

Smith, M. (1989). *When I say no, I feel guilty.* New York: Bantam.

Chapter 3

Ackley, K. M. (2000). *100 top Internet job sites.* Manassas Park, VA: Impact.

Bolles, R. N. (2001). *Job-hunting on the Internet.* Berkeley CA: Ten Speed Press.

Bolles, R. N. (2003). *What color is your parachute?* Berkeley CA: Ten Speed Press.

Burnett, R. E. (2002). *Careers for number crunchers and other quantitative types.* Lincolnwood, IL: VGM Career Horizons.

Dunning, D. (2001). *What's your type of career? Unlock the secrets of your personality to find your perfect career path.* Palo Alto, CA: Davies Black.

Eberts, M., & Gisler, M. (1998). *Careers for talkative types & others with the gift of gab.* Lincolnwood, IL: VGM Career Horizons.

Edwards, P., & Edwards, S. (1996). *Finding your perfect work.* New York: Putnam.

Farr, J. M., & Ludden, L. L. (2001). *Best jobs for the 21st century.* Indianapolis, IN: JIST Works.

Figler, H. E. (1999). *The complete job-search handbook: Everything you need to know to get the job you want.* New York: Henry Holt.

Gabler, L. R. (2000). *Career exploration on the Internet: A student's guide to more than 500 web sites.* Chicago: Ferguson.

Gisler, M., & Eberts, M. (2001). *Careers for hard hats & other constructive types.* Chicago: VGM Career Books.

Graber, S. (2000). *The everything online job search book.* Holbrook, MA: Adams Media.

Hanna, S. L. (2003). *Person to person: Positive relationships don't just happen.* Upper Saddle River, NJ: Prentice Hall.

Jackson, T. (1993). *Guerilla tactics in the job market.* Toronto: Bantam Books.

Kay, A. (1999). *Greener pastures: How to find a job in another place.* New York: St. Martins Griffin.

Kocher, E., & Segal, N. (1999). *International jobs.* Reading, MA: Perseus.

Krannich, R. L. (2000). *Change your job, change your life.* Manassas Park, VA: Impact.

Krantz, L. (2002). *Jobs rated almanac.* Ft. Lee, NJ: Barricade.

Michelozzi, B. N. (1999). *Coming alive from nine to five: The career search handbook.* Mountain View, CA: Mayfield.

Straub, C. (1998). *Jobsearch.net.* Menlo Park, CA: Crisp.

Tieger, P. D., & Barron-Tieger, B. (2001). *Do what you are.* Boston: Little Brown.

Directories and Reference Books

The Almanac of International Jobs and Careers

Directory of American Firms Operating in Foreign Countries

Dun and Bradstreet Million Dollar Directory

Dun's Employment Opportunities Directory

Encyclopedia of Associations

Encyclopedia of Business Information Sources

Job Seeker's Guide to Private and Public Companies

Mac Rae's Blue Book

Moody's Complete Corporate Index

Occupational Outlook Handbook

Standard and Poor's Register of Corporations, Directors, and Executives

Thomas' Register of American Manufacturers

Chapter 4

Beatty, R. H. (2003). *The perfect cover letter.* Hoboken, NJ: John Wiley & Sons.

Beatty, R. H. (2003). *The resume kit.* New York: Wiley.

Bolles, R. N. (2001). *Job-hunting on the Internet.* Berkeley, CA: Ten Speed Press.

Graber, S. (2003). *The everything online search book.* Holbrook, MA: Adams Media.

Nemnich, M. B., & Jandt, F. E. (2001). *Cyberspace resume kit: How to build and launch an online resume.* Indianapolis, IN: JIST Works.

Smith, R. (2002). *Electronic resumes and online networking.* Franklin Lakes. NJ: Career Press.

Straub, C. (1998). *Jobsearch.net.* Menlo Park, CA: Crisp.

Washington, T. (2003). *Resume power.* Bellevue, WA: Mount Vernon Press.

Whitcomb, S. B., & Kendall, P. (2002). *eResumes: Everything you need to know about using electronic resumes to tap into today's job market.* New York: McGraw-Hill.

Chapter 5

Adams, B. (2001). *The everything job interview book.* Holbrook, MA: Adams Media.

Eyre, V. V. (2000). *Great interview.* New York: Learning Express.

Fry, R. W. (2000). *101 great answers to the toughest interview questions.* Franklin Lakes, NJ: Career Press.

Washington, T. (2000). *Interview power.* Bellevue, WA: Mount Vernon Press.

Yate, M. (2000). *Knock 'em dead.* Holbrook, MA: Adams Media.

Chapter 6

Andrusia, D., & Haskins, R. (2000). *Brand yourself: How to create an identify for a brilliant career.* New York: Ballantine.

Bolles, R. N. (2003). *What color is your parachute?* Berkeley, CA: Ten Speed Press.

Covey, S. R. (1999). *The 7 habits of highly effective people.* New York: Simon & Schuster.

Heldmann, M. L. (1990). *When words hurt: How to keep criticism from undermining your self-esteem.* New York: Ballantine.

Krannich, R. L. (2002). *Change your job, change your life.* Manassas Park, VA: Impact.

Chapter 7

Alessandra, T., & Hunsaker, P. (1993). *Communicating at work.* New York: Simon & Schuster.

Bolton, R., & Bolton, D. G. (1996). *People styles at work: Making bad relationships good and good relationships better.* New York: AMACOM.

Hanna, S. L. (2003). *Person to person: Positive relationships don't just happen.* Upper Saddle River, NJ: Prentice Hall.

Keating, C. J. (1984). *Dealing with difficult people.* Ramsey, NJ: Paulist Press.

Kroeger, O., Thuesen, J. M., & Rutledge, H. (2002). *Type talk at work: How the 16 personality types determine your career success.* New York: Dell.

Kummerow, J. M., Barger, N. J., & Kirby, L. K. (1997). *Work types.* New York: Time Warner.

Scott, G. G. (1990). *Resolving conflict with others and within yourself.* Oakland, CA: New Harbinger.

Tieger, P. D., & Barron-Tieger, B. (1999). *The art of speedreading people.* Boston: Little, Brown.

Ury, W. (1993). *Getting past no: Negotiating your way from confrontation to cooperation.* New York: Bantam.

Chapter 8

Benson, H. (2001). *The relaxation response.* New York: Avon.

Bravo, E., & Cassedy, E. (1999). *The 9 to 5 guide to combating sexual harassment.* Milwaukee: 9 to 5 Working Women Educational Fund.

Burka, J. B., & Yuen, L. M. (2000). *Procrastination: Why you do it, what to do about it.* Reading, MA: Addison-Wesley.

Hallowell, E. M. (2000). *Worry: Controlling it and using it wisely.* New York: Pantheon.

Jasper, J. (1999). *Take back your time: How to regain control of work, information, and technology.* New York: St. Martin's Press.

Lakein, A. (1989). *How to get control of your time and your life.* New York: New American Library.

Morgenstern, J. (2000). *Time management from the inside out.* New York: Henry Holt.

NiCarthy, G., Gottlieb, N., & Coffman, S. (1993). *You don't have to take it! A woman's guide to confronting emotional abuse at work.* Seattle, WA: Seal Press.

References

Adams, B. (2001). *The everything job interview book*. Holbrook, MA: Adams Media.

Aschwanden, C. (2000, April 11). Study bolsters link between smoking and breast cancer. *Science Now*, 3. Retrieved August 7, 2000, from EBSCOhost database.

Babcock, L., & Laschever, S. (2003). *Women don't ask: Negotiation and the gender divide*. Princeton, NJ: Princeton University Press.

Barbor, C. (2001). The science of meditation. *Psychology Today*, 34(3), 54–58.

Bates, S. (1999). Your emotional skills can make or break you. *Nation's Business*, 87(4), 17. Retrieved July 26, 2000, from InfoTrac database.

Benson, H. (2001). Mind-body pioneer. *Psychology Today*, 34(3), 56–59.

Bloomfield, H. H., with Felder, L. (1996). *Making peace with yourself*. New York: Ballantine Books.

Bolles, R. N. (2001). *Job-hunting on the Internet*. Berkeley, CA: Ten Speed Press.

Bolles, R. N. (2003). *What color is your parachute?* Berkeley, CA: Ten Speed Press.

Booher, D. (1999). Communicate with confidence and make your body language say the right thing. *Women in Business*, 51(6), 36–39.

Bramson, R. M. (1988). *Coping with difficult people*. Garden City, NY: Anchor Press/Doubleday.

Branden, N. (1983). *Honoring the self*. Los Angeles: Tarcher.

Bravo, E., & Cassedy, E. (1999). *The 9 to 5 guide to combating sexual harassment*. Milwaukee: 9 to 5 Working Women Educational Fund.

Brinkerhoff, J. R. (1994, March 15). The biggest obstacles to making things happen. *Bottom Line Personnel*, 9–10.

Buscaglia, L. (1994). *Born for love: Reflections on loving*. Thorofare, NJ: Slack, Inc.

Butler, P. E. (1992). *Self-assertion for women*. New York: HarperCollins.

Cain, J. D. (2003, March). Balancing acts. *Essence*, 33(11). Retrieved June 20, 2003, from EBSCOhost database.

Calabrese, K. R. (2000, November). Interpersonal conflict and sarcasm in the workplace. *Genetic, Social and General Psychology Monographs*, 126(4), 459–495.

Caldwell, D. F., & Burger, J. M. (1998). Personality characteristics of job applicants and success in screening interviews. *Personnel Psychology*, 51(1), 119–137.

Canadian Manager. (1999, Summer). Meeting the people challenge, 20–24.

Carl, H. (1980, December). Nonverbal communication during the employment interview. *ABCA Bulletin*, 14–18.

Carrig, M. (1999). Interpersonal skills are key in office of the future. *TMA Journal*, 19(4), 53.

Caudron, S. (2000). And the point is. *Workforce*, 79(4), 20–21.

Centers for Disease Control. (2002). Annual smoking—attributable mortality, years of potential life lost, and economic costs—United States, 1995–1999. Retrieved June 16, 2003, from http://www.cdc.gov.

Challenger, C. (1999). CRM provides significant competitive advantages, Andersen Study finds. *Chemical Market Reporter*, 256(25). Retrieved August 14, 2000, from WilsonWeb database.

Chandler, M. (2001, August 11). Gen Xers saving habits vary. *Lincoln Journal Star*, p. 4A.

Chaney, L. H., & Martin, J. S. (2000). *Intercultural business communication*. Upper Saddle River, NJ: Prentice Hall.

Clarke, C. V., & Edmond, A. A., Jr. (2003, February). Guarding against the stress of success. *Black Enterprise*, 33(7). Retrieved June 20, 2003, from EBSCOhost database.

Clifford, L. (2000, August 14). Getting over the hump before you're over the hill. *Fortune*, 145–150.

Cole, J. (1997). Spotting communication problems. *American Management Association*, 42(5), 8.

Conroy, R. (1995, May). Addiction to work proves harmful. *The Menninger Letter*, 5, 7.

Consumer Reports. (2000). All the right moves for stress relief. 65(2), 38–39. Retrieved July 31, 2000, from EBSCOhost database.

Cormack R. W. (1992). The attitude factor. In M. B. Canning (Ed.), *Ready, aim, hire*. Oak Brook, IL: PerSysCo Publishing.

Covey, S. R. (1999). *The 7 habits of highly effective people*. New York: Simon & Schuster.

Daniel, A. G. F. (1998, October 26). Success secret: A high emotional IQ. *Fortune*, 293+. Retrieved July 26, 2000, from InfoTrac database.

Derr, C. B. (1986). *Managing the new careerists: The diverse career success orientations of today's workers*. San Francisco: Jossey-Bass.

Dixon, W. A., & Reid, J. K. (2000). Positive life events as a moderator of stress-related depressive symptoms. *Journal of Counseling & Development*, 78(3), 343–347.

DuLong, J. (2002, October 29). Workplace woes. *Advocate*. Retrieved June 19, 2003, from EBSCOhost database.

Ehrlich, H. J., & Grinberg, D. (2003, February 6). *EEOC reports discrimination charge filings up*. Retrieved June 20, 2003, from http://www.eeoc.gov.

Eisenberg, D. (1999, August 16). We're for hire, just click. *Time*, 46–47.

Eliot, R. S., & Breo, D. L. (1991). *Is it worth dying for?* New York: Bantam Books.

Ellis, M. (2000, October). Self-exploration: Take stock of who you are and make better career decisions. *Black Collegian*, 31(1), 20–22.

Evans, K. (2000). Is stress wrecking your mood? *Health*, 118–129.

Farr, J. M., & Ludden, L. L. (2001). *Best jobs for the 21st century*. Indianapolis, IN: JIST Works.

Feagin, J. R., & Feagin, C. B. (1999). *Racial and ethnic relations.* Upper Saddle River, NJ: Prentice Hall.

Fisher, A. (1999). Readers speak out on illiterate MBAs and more. *Fortune,* 139(4), 242. Retrieved August 21, 2000, from EBSCO-host database.

Fisher, C. S., Jackson, R. M., Stueve, C. A., Gerson, K., Jones, L. M., & Baldassare, M. (1977). *Networks and places: Social relations in the urban setting.* New York: Free Press.

Fry, R. W. (2000). *101 great answers to the toughest interview questions.* Franklin Lakes, NJ: Career Press.

Gallois, C., Callan, V. J., & Palmer, J. M. (1992). The influence of applicant communication style and interviewer characteristics on hiring decisions. *Journal of Applied Social Psychology,* 22(13), 1041–1060.

Gard, C. J. (1998). Humor helps. *Current Health 2, 24*(8), 22–23. Retrieved July 31, 2000, from EBSCOhost database.

Gardner, H. (1993). *Frames of mind: The theory of multiple intelligences.* New York: Basic Books.

Gardner, H. (1999). *Intelligence reframed.* New York: Basic Books.

Gibbs, N. (1995, October 2). The EQ factor. *Time,* 61–68.

Glasser, W. (1984). *Control theory: A new explanation of how we control our lives.* New York: Harper & Row.

Goffman, E. (1959). *Presentation of self in everyday life.* New York: Anchor Books.

Goleman, D. (1995). *Emotional intelligence.* New York: Bantam Books.

Goleman, D. (1998). *Working with emotional intelligence.* New York: Bantam Books.

Gottfredson, G. D., & Holland, J. L. (1996). *Dictionary of Holland Occupational Codes.* Lutz, FL: Psychological Assessment Resources.

Gutner, T. (2002, September 2). The rose-colored ceiling. *Business Week.* Retrieved June 19, 2003, from EBSCOhost database.

Hall, E. T. (1969). *The hidden dimension.* New York: Anchor Press/Doubleday.

Hall, P. D. (1999). The effect of meditation on the academic performance of African American college students. *Meditation,* 29(3), 408–416.

Hallowell, E. M. (1999). The human moment at work. *Harvard Business Review,* 77(1), 58–65.

Hallowell, E. M. (2000). *Worry: Controlling it and using it wisely.* New York: Pantheon.

Hanna, S. L. (2003). *Person to person: Positive relationships don't just happen.* Upper Saddle River, NJ: Prentice Hall.

Harju, B. L., & Bolen, L. M. (1998). The effects of optimism on coping and perceived quality of life of college students. *Journal of Social Behavior and Personality,* 13(2), 185–201.

Hill, L. A. (1994). Managing your career (Note 9-494-082). Boston: Harvard Business School Publishing.

Hispanic Times Magazine (2002, September). Beating the odds. Retrieved June 18, 2003, from EBSCOhost database.

Hobson, C. J., Delunas, L., & Kesic, D. (2001). Compelling evidence of the need for corporate work/life balance initiatives: Results from a national survey of stressful life-events. *Journal of Employment Counseling,* 38(1), 38–44.

Holland, J. L. (1997). *Making vocational choices.* Odessa, FL: Psychological Assessment Resources.

Holmes, T. H., & Rahe, R. H. (1967). The social readjustment rating scale. *Journal of Psychosomatic Research, 11,* 213–218.

Jackson, T. (1993). *Guerilla tactics in the job market.* Toronto: Bantam Books.

Jackson, T., & Jackson, E. (1996). *The new perfect resume.* New York: Broadway Books.

Jasper, J. (1999). *Take back your time: How to regain control of work, information, and technology.* New York: St. Martin's Press.

Jeffries, W. C. (1991). *True to type.* Norfolk, VA: Hampton Roads Publishing.

Jehn, K. A., Northcraft, G. B., & Neale, M. A. (1999). Why differences make a difference: A field study of diversity, conflict, and performance in workgroups. *Administrative Science Quarterly, 44*(4), 741–763.

Jung, C. G. (1923). *Psychological types.* New York: Harcourt Brace.

Jung, C. G. (1968). *Analytical psychology: Its theory and practice.* New York: Vintage Books.

Keating, C. J. (1984). *Dealing with difficult people.* Ramsey, NJ: Paulist Press.

Keirsey, D., & Bates, M. (1984). *Please understand me: Character and temperament type.* Del Mar, CA: Prometheus Nemesis.

Kemper, C. L. (1999). Emotional intelligence and the heart take their rightful place beside IQ and the brain. *International Association of Business Communicators, 16*(9), 15.

Knouse, S. B., Tanner, J. T., & Harris, E. W. (1999). The relation of college internships, college performance, and subsequent job opportunity. *Journal of Employment Counseling, 36*(1), 35–43.

Kobasa, S. C. (1979). Stressful life events, personality, and health: An inquiry into hardiness. *Journal of Personality and Social Psychology, 37*(1), 1–11.

Koretz, G. (2000, November 13). Yes, workers are grumpier. *Business Week,* 42.

Krannich, R. L. (2000). *Change your job, change your life.* Manassas Park, VA: Impact Publishing.

Krantz, L. (2002). *Jobs rated almanac.* Fort Lee, NJ: Barricade Books.

Krizan, A. C., Merrier, P., Larson Jones, C., & Harcourt, J. (2002). *Business communication.* Cincinnati, OH: International Thomson Publishing.

Kroeger, O., Thuesen, J. M., & Rutledge, H. (2002). *Type talk at work.* New York: Dell Publishing.

Kummerow, J. M., Barger, N. J., & Kirby, L. K. (1997). *Work types.* New York: Time Warner Books.

Lach, J. (2000). Asset analysis. *American Demographics, 22*(6), 15–17.

Lam, S. S. K., & Schaubroeck, J. (2000). The role of locus of control in reactions to being promoted and to being passed over: A quasi experiment. *Academy of Management Journal, 43*(1), 79.

Latas, M. (1993). *Job search secrets.* St. Louis, MO: Job Search Publishers.

Lavelle, L. (2001, April 23). For female CEOs, it's stingy at the top. *Business Week,* 70–71.

Lazarus, R. S. (1981, June). Little hassles can be hazardous to your health. *Psychology Today,* 58–62.

Leonard, B. (2000). HR update: Employers explore on-site day care options. *HR Magazine, 45*(5), 29–33.

Lewis, R. (1996, June). Career changers find road to success marked by perils. *AARP Bulletin*, 8–11.

Lopez, S. (2000). What you need is more vacation. *Time, 155*(24), 8.

Macionis, J. J. (2004). *Society: The basics.* Upper Saddle River, NJ: Prentice Hall.

Mackay, H. (1993). *Sharkproof.* New York: HarperBusiness.

Madry, B. (1988, September-October). *Getting jobs,* 2(3). Bronx, NY: MPC Educational Publishers.

Masikiewicz, M. (1999). You've got what it takes. *Career World, 28*(3), 18–21.

Maslow, A. (1968). *Toward a psychology of being.* New York: D. Van Nostrand.

Mayer, J. D., Caruso, D. R., & Salovey, P. (1999). Emotional intelligence meets traditional standards for an intelligence. *Intelligence, 27*(4), 267+ . Retrieved July 26, 2000, from InfoTrac database.

McKay, M., & Fanning, P. (2000). *Self-esteem.* Oakland, CA: New Harbinger.

Mehrabian, A. (1968, September). Communication without words. *Psychology Today,* 53–55.

Mehrabian, A. (1981). *Silent messages.* Belmont, CA: Wadsworth.

Mehrabian, A. (2000). Beyond IQ: Broad-based measurement of individual success potential or 'emotional intelligence.' *Genetic, Social and General Psychology Monographs, 126*(2), 133–239.

Mehta, S. N., Chen, C. Y., Garcia, F., & Vella-Zarb, K. (2000, July 10). What minority employees really want. *Fortune,* 180–185.

Miller, S., Wackman, D. B., Nunnally, E. W., & Miller, P. A. (1992). *Connecting with self and others.* Littleton, CO: Interpersonal Communication Program.

Moore, J. E. (2000). One road to turnover: An examination of work exhaustion in technology professionals. *MIS Quarterly, 24*(1), 141–168.

Moyers, B. (1995). *Healing and the mind.* New York: Main Street Books.

Myers, D. (1997). *The pursuit of happiness.* Dresden, TN: Avon Books.

Myers, D. G., & Diener, E. (1995). Who is happy? *Psychological Science,* 10–19.

Myers, I. B. (1993). *Introduction to type.* Palo Alto, CA: Consulting Psychologists Press.

Myers, I. B. (1995). *Gifts differing.* Palo Alto, CA: Consulting Psychologists Press.

Nelson-Gottschalk, A. (1998). A new era in sexual harassment. *Diversity Training Group.* Retrieved July 20, 2000, www.diversitydtg.com.

Nemnich, M. B., & Jandt, F. E. (2001). *Cyberspace resume kit: How to build and launch an online resume.* Indianapolis, IN: JIST Works.

Newsweek. (2000, September 18). The kids in the corner office, 74L, 74N, 74P.

Occupational outlook handbook. (2002–2003). Indianapolis, IN: JIST Work, Inc.

O'Neil, S. L., & Chapman, E. N. (2002). *Your attitude is showing.* Upper Saddle River, NJ: Prentice Hall.

Pachter, B., with Magee, S. (2000). *The power of positive confrontation: The skills you need to know to handle conflicts at work, home, and in life.* New York: Marlowe & Company.

Perina, K. (2003, April). Race card or resume: Job discrimination. *Psychology Today, 12.*

Peth-Pierce, R. (1998). The NICHD study of early child care. Washington, DC: National Institute of Child Health and Human Development.

Phillips-Miller, D. L., Campbell, J. J., & Morrison, C. R. (2000). Work and family: Satisfaction, stress, and spousal support. *Journal of Employment Counseling, 37*(1), 16–31.

Rayman, P., Carré, F., Cintron, L., & Quinn, S. (2000). *Life's work: Generational attitudes toward work and life integration.* Cambridge, MA: Radcliffe Public Policy Center.

Reed-Woodard, M. A., & Clarke, R. D. (2000). Put some feeling into it. *Black Enterprise,* 30(10), 68.

Ross, S. E., Niebling, B. C., & Heckert, T. M. (1999). Sources of stress among college students. *College Student Journal, 33*(2), 312–317. Retrieved July 31, 2000, from EBSCOhost database.

Roth, P. L., & Bobko, P. (2000). College grade point average as a personnel selection device: Ethnic group differences and potential adverse impact. *Journal of Applied Psychology, 85*(3), 399–406.

Sabo, S. R. (2000). Diversity at work. *Techniques: Connecting Education & Careers,* 75(2), 26–28.

Sales & Marketing Management. (1999, September). What keeps employees happy, *151*(9), 92. Retrieved May 15, 2000, from EBSCOhost database.

Salzberg, S., & Kabat-Zinn, J. (1997). Mindfulness as medicine. In D. Goleman (Ed.), *Healing emotions* (pp. 107–144). Boston: Shambhala.

Savageau, D., & D'Agostino, R. (2000). Places rated almanac. Foster City, CA: IDC Books.

Scheinholtz, D. (2000, August 16). What do college students want? Ernst & Young survey reveals priorities. Retrieved August 18, 2000, from www.diversity.com.

Seligman, M. E. P. (1998). *Learned optimism: How to change your mind and your life.* New York: Pocket Books.

Selye, H. (1974). *Stress without distress.* Philadelphia: Lippincott.

Selye, H. (1978, March). On the real benefits of eustress (as interviewed by Laurence Charry). *Psychology Today,* 60–63.

Senior, K. (2001). Should stress carry a health warning? *Lancet,* 357(9250), 126.

Shakoor, A. T. (2000a). Career success in the new millennium. *Black Collegian,* 30(2), 60.

Shakoor, A. T. (2000b). On-campus interviewing: The dress rehearsal for success. *Black Collegian, 31*(1). Retrieved June 18, 2003, from EBSCOhost database.

Smigla, J. E., & Pastoria, G. (2000). Emotional intelligence: Some have it, others can learn. *CPA Journal,* 70(6), 60–61.

Smith, R. (2002). *Electronic resumes & online networking.* Franklin Lakes, NJ: Career Press.

Sousa-Poza, A. A. (2000). Well-being at work: A cross-national analysis: The levels and determinants of job satisfaction. *Journal of Socio-Economics,* 29(6), 517–538.

Stone, A., Smyth, J. M., Kaell, A., & Hurewitz, A. (2000). Structured writing about stressful events: Exploring potential psychological mediators of positive health effects. *Health Psychology,* 19(6), 619–624.

Switzer, G. (1996, June 2). Plan now for your golden years in retirement. *Lincoln Journal Star,* p. 2.

Thomas, P., McMasters, R., Roberts, M. R., & Dombkowski, D. A. (1999). Resume characteristics as predictors of an invitation to interview. *Journal of Business and Psychology,* 13(3), 339–356.

Tice, D. M., & Baumeister, R. F. (1997). What are the effects of procrastination? *Psychological Science, 8*(6), 454–458.

Tieger, P. D., & Barron-Tieger, B. (1998). *The art of speedreading people.* Boston: Little, Brown and Company.

Tieger, P. D., & Barron-Tieger, B. (2001). *Do what you are.* Boston: Little, Brown and Company.

U.S. News & World Report. (2000, June 26). No time to slow down, 14. Retrieved July 21, 2000, from EBSCOhost (Academic Search Elite), www.ebsco.com.

Vasey, M. W., & Borkovec, T. D. (1992). A catastrophizing assessment of worrisome thoughts. *Cognitive Therapy and Research, 16*(5), 505–520.

Vernarec, E., & Phillips, K. (2001). How to cope with job stress. *RN,* 64(3), 44–49.

Villar, E., Juan, J., Corominas, E., & Capell, D. (2000). What kind of networking strategy advice should career counsellors offer university graduates searching for a job? *British Journal of Guidance & Counselling,* 28(3). Retrieved June 18, 2003, from EBSCOhost database.

Wallis, T. J. (2000). Sexual harassment on the job. *Career World,* 28(5), 16–19.

Washington, T. (2003). *Resume power.* Bellevue, WA: Mount Vernon Press.

Weil, A. (1998). *Health and healing.* Boston: Houghton Mifflin.

Wessel, H. (2003, September 2). "Paid time off" is fast replacing sick days. *Lincoln Journal Star,* p. 4A.

Whitcomb, S. B., & Kendall, P. (2002). *eResumes: Everything you need to know about using electronic resumes to tap into today's job market.* New York: McGraw-Hill.

Whitehead, M. (1998, June 10). Employee happiness levels impact on the bottom line. *People Management, 4*(24), 14.

Williams, J. M., & Harris, D. V. (1998). Relaxation and energizing techniques for regulation of arousal. In J. M. Williams (Ed.), *Applied sport psychology: Personal growth to peak performance* (pp. 219–236). Mountain View, CA: Mayfield.

Wiscombe, J. (2002, April). Rewards get results. *Workforce, 81*(4). Retrieved June 19, 2003, from EBSCOhost database.

Witkin, S. L. (1999). Taking humor seriously. *Social Work, 44*(2), 101–104.

Women in Business. (2000, July-August). Money wise: Saving for retirement vital for women. 52(4), 42.

Yin, S. (2001, December). Shifting careers. *American Demographics,* 23(12). Retrieved June 19, 2003, from EBSCOhost database.

Zimmer, J. (2000). Worried sick? *Essence, 31*(2), 78–79.

Index